I'm 35, My Eggs Are Rotting... How's Your Sperm?

Terri Apple

D1320044

Terri Apple
All rights reserved.
ISBN-13 978-0615678900
ISBN-10 0615678904

Formal Dedication

Dedicated to every single person still seeking their
soulmate…
Where the hell are you, stuck in traffic?

INFORMAL THANK-YOU

Rochelle, a nod for your encouragement, otherwise the
book would still be sitting in my computer collecting
bugs. My best friend, Rhonda, for taking time out from
Words With Friends to do a fabulous edit! Thank-you to
everyone who has supported the book throughout the
years; Sharian and Martin Spencer, my gratitude and
thanks for your support, Dad. Thanks for being my
'funny', Craig for the non-stop love and brotherly advice,
Izabella you got me though Hollywood more than you
know and Mom for the never ending stories, laughs and
positive outlook.

A special thanks to my eggs. Which, last time I checked,
were still depleting faster than I could ever say, "I do".

HALF-EMPTY DISCLAIMER

Contents may be hazardous to your ego. I did not make up the information in this book. It has been channeled through me from several hundred dinners, lunches, workouts, coffee breaks as well as being single for 47 years.

Yes, I know the book is titled "I'm 35," but I wrote it at 34 when I actually thought I was going to marry "what's his name," but didn't. So, now I'm 47, still single, quite fine with it and found the book still relevant.

Apparently, so do several hundred thousand other people. Here's my, from one chick to another, non-professional, good-for-nothing advice.

Face it, enjoy it and relax. If you find the material offensive, by all means, run out and marry the first person you see. Otherwise, read on. Maybe you'll learn something helpful. Not guaranteed, but you're sure to laugh and say, "this is so true".

By the way, it's not for women only. I have a 50-year-old brother who finds the book quite funny (except for the parts that made him cry).

Try not to take it, or me, too seriously.

It's just the truth, wrapped in with a little BS and a lot of humor. Remember…you were screwed up in your 20's. Now you're sexy, strong, confident and still screwed up, but maybe a little wiser?

Or maybe just a little older.

SOME RANDOM REVIEWS (I MAY OR MAY HAVE NOT RECEIVED)

"Hilarious book! If only it weren't true, it would even be funnier..."

Chicago Tribune

"Terri sounds like a cynical 35 year-old whose eggs have rotted."
(I take partial responsibility-I took four of those years...)

A NAMELESS EX-BOYFRIEND
(Okay, his name was Dave)

Almost Sad! Kind of depressing, but very funny!"

HER MOTHER

This book is the "Anti-rules", "Anti Getting To I Do". It's more of "Did I miss the boat?" kind of book; which is fun and cynical at the same time.

THE DAILY MAIL (Any City)

Thankfully, Terri is NOT 35 anymore, or this book would be really...bitter!

Her friend Ann

TABLE OF CONTENTS

CHAPTER 1

The Embryo

I'm having delusions of grandeur—they started when I was nine. After the first boy kissed me, I thought I would lose my mind (or, at least, my head would spin off). Every boy, after that, has had a lot to measure up to, but that's just me and my own little delusions.

(Yes, I've seen a shrink about it.)

So, maybe your life's filled with fairy tales and puppy dog tails, but if you're anything like me, you're still waiting way past...(feel free to fill in the blank) for your Prince Charming.

Is he coming or isn't he? 'Cause I've got eggs rotting, here. (Diane on the other hand, who's rich, had hers frozen; so, she's got a bit more time).

CHAPTER 1
THE GLASS SLIPPER

Although a glass slipper is a lovely idea and usually carries most of us from childhood into adulthood...It's just not very realistic. From childhood, we believe that there will be **1** perfect person (negating early death, disease, famine and/or cheating) that will find us, put a ring on it and carry us through life; eagerly awaiting every twist and turn with passion, joy and a hunger for more...

Wow, that sounds terrific.

Even, if it is just a fairy-tale. (And not entirely realistic.)

Fairy-tale's were originally created by lonely, sad people (usually beaten and sent to their room without supper) where they spent hours upon hours creating the life they **wish** they had.

Think about it.

Where does reality fit in with fantasy? You know, bad hair days, cramps, being late for work, telling off your boss, agreeing to go to dinner with that guy you didn't even like over the phone?

All of those people you spent auditioning to be your happily forever after have now disappeared, and you find yourself either fantasizing about someone fictional from your past (or fictional idea of who they were) to creating the perfect person in your...not quite here yet...future.

Then the reality of your day-to-day life slips in. Doing the things that are your life; waking up, going to work, meeting friends for a drink, drinking one too many, going home with the wrong... guy/gal/prostitute/idiot/someone you can't quite name. Thinking you're in love with the wrong guy, chasing after the wrong guy, spending 3 months getting over the wrong guy. You've done some form of this a few times in your life.

Okay, perhaps you didn't go home with him (I know, your future husband could be reading this). Perhaps you made him wait a month(s) to get intimate. No matter, it still ended and you are still here.

Here.

Yes, here. Where you are.

Which may or may not be bad. May or may not be crying you to sleep, or having you jump for joy (that you got away from something that you realized you didn't want). Either way, you're still here.

One of the…drum-roll, please…2320644660 single people in the world. I don't even know where to put the commas, but I do know that means you're far from alone.

Even though you say you can't find anyone to date in your city/state/country/planet (unless, of course, you live out in the country somewhere surrounded by cousins).

Not to push cousins upon each other, but inner-breeding was quite popular at one time.

This number doesn't even include life on other planets. (Although from what we've seen in photos, we might have a hard time getting romantic).

With all those single people out there, you should at least be able to find 1 or 7 to sleep with; or at least go to a baseball game. Even if you don't…want/desire/require…reality/what's out there left to pick from…I imagine there are a few people willing to roll-play and have some sort of fantasy play date with you. Yes, that reality; the one that gets in the way of your wonderful fantasy. The fantasy that you've spent your entire life creating.

That's just downright…unfair.

Two things we kind of know for sure…
WOMEN ARE CRAZY
MEN ARE WEIRD

A thought…being yourself may be exactly what's keeping you from being coupled-up in the first place.

CRACKED EMBRYO

It starts quite young, that fantasy. When you're 2, 3, 4 or 5 (somewhere in there) you develop your first crush. You have fallen deeply into a love coma and you cannot stop saying, and/or writing that person's name all over well…everything you own.

You don't know how to masturbate yet. (God help you if you started this young). But, that feeling of lust, passion and love is still there. It doesn't matter if it's unrequited. You still feel how you feel.

You've spent hours upon hours doing what your parents are doing; playing house, cooking, fighting, holding hands, putting Ken on top of Barbie, or Barbie on top of Barbie, or Ken with Ken. You re-enacted how you life is sure to end up with (*his/her name here)* and then something happens. You graduate, summer comes, you move. And then you do it all over again.

And thus, you go through you life doing this.

You fall in love with that guy/girl who's absolutely perfect in every conceivable way, even if you only like them because they're cute. As you age, you may actually have mutual feelings with that crush. You will probably kiss, go to first, second, third and finally you'll get all the way home. Although quite fast at first, home should be an enjoyable experience and should not include ripping stockings just purchased at the mall, as well as dropping you off 5 blocks from your house and telling you to "hang tight, Man."

Even if it does, it's an experience and like all realities, this fairytale has just been popped.
Just like your cherry.

Don't worry. By the time you reach your 20's, you will have cried over so many guys, you won't even remember Stan.

I mean Dan.

I meant Ron.

Oh, whatever, I was drunk and stoned and it was late at night. The point is, that glass slipper you've been trying to find your entire life just may not exist at all. I know, I know, pretty depressing. Sure some people look great on paper, others are great on paper. While others still don't have any papers. (Green card, anyone?).

Once you've hit a certain age, you may decide the fairytale you were hoping for, isn't real at all. Just like that fantasy you built about Ted and his fabulous six-pack (which only existed from the age of 14 to 16).

Once you've decided to focus on reality instead of fantasy, you may actually do yourself a favor. It's called compromise and sometimes includes being less picky.

God, sounds awful.

But...people do it. Just look around at all those couples. Now ask them to see photos of what they looked like before marriage, kids, bills and mortgages. It's just a shortcut to busting your fairy-tale bubble.

Another option is to go to lunch with a friend who thought she married her fairy tale only to realize she's knee deep in muscle relaxants and Marco the pool boy.

She's staying married for that 5-year mark; no, not Mark. (He doesn't have any money, but was fun for a while). She's waiting for the pre-nup to kick in so she can walk away. This is called reality that **is** a fantasy.

If you've spent your life walking on eggshells trying to be someone you're not (just like in high school) to attract the perfect person (That you are not yourself) you're in for a lot of unnecessary pressure. That pressure along with having to be perfect all the time, may create the illusion of happiness/fantasy/happily ever after, yet more likely will at some point combust and go up in smoke.

Trying to make someone want you, marry you, be with you, is a lot like trying to be a doctor without a degree. You can bullshit for a minute, but at the end of the day, how are you going to operate when you don't even know what a tracheotomy is?

(Look it up, this isn't an educational book.)

So, you got your perfect fairytale and now you have to keep your nails nice all the time, your drawers perfect, your vagina tight (should probably be, regardless).

Now all you have to do is...*stay that way*...for life. Man that sounds like a lot of work.

Reality should set in somewhere around the first few months...while that honeymoon faze is starting to wear off and you just might want *out.* Yes, out. It might be easier to get real and find a good partner that fits all those weird quirks you were hiding from that perfect fairytale you so nicely set up. In fact, finding a guy that fits what you really want and need vs. what he can provide for you/smother you with...sounds a lot better than that house in the Hamptons for $75 grand a month.

(Although, having that house in the Hamptons to yourself sounds amazing. And this way, you can invite whomever you want). Although most people like stuff, the point should not be to acquire. What most people are looking for is a connection. You know, just like in the movies. The harder you have to work for something, the more you may appreciate it, but the less you may want it.

At some point, just like in 1st grade, you want that crush to be immediate requited, the connection real and lasting, or at least until 2nd grade.

People want lasting love so they can move on with the rest of their lives. Things like building a family, building trust, having someone always there.

Animals are fine, they just don't give an opinion.

(Yes, sometimes they are better cuddlers).

The nice thing about finding lasting love, is feeling content and happy so that you aren't constantly looking over your shoulder seeking another.

Wanting someone other than the person you're with for the long haul is depressing. It's also time consuming and takes away from the real person you're meant to be with. That's why some people choose to wait it out, jump ship, move around from state to state until they find the person they're meant to be with. Sometimes it's your next-door neighbor (even when he/she's married to another).

Oops, can't help it, happens.

Eventually you meet someone, build some sort of solidarity with 1 person (unless you're Mormon or European; which enables you to have more, quite openly).

The Embryo

Everything, just like the eggs you purchase at the store, has an expiration date. Everybody wants everything fast. If you haven't married by now, or find yourself still single, there becomes a race to dive into an instant relationship and rush to the altar. No one takes the time to get to know one another. And on the other hand, everyone tells everything about themselves, immediately. No longer must we wait 3 months to find out someone is crazy. They'll let you know all about it on the first date. And shame on you for going on, well…a 2nd. Yes, you've already had sex and it was quite good, so why not? It's just sex. And why not go out on another date? Even though they were crazy, they certainly are fun. My list? What list? That stupid thing got me where I am in the first place? Time to just go for it, let loose, take a chance. Oh, right, I always do that. Okay, one more time isn't going to really hurt. Here's a thought. It's probably easier to forgo that dating thing all together and dive right in. Give yourself 30 days to find a partner.

Come on, you meet friends and proclaim, "you're my new best friend". Which lasts a good 1 to 5, until you realize he/she was psychotic and talked behind your back the entire time. We dive right into everything else these days, getting to know someone after you've committed might not be a bad idea. Just talk to people in arranged marriages. Sure, they may not like whom they're with, but they've moved onto worrying about other things now that they're stuck for life. The good news for you is that you're not in an arranged marriage and can get out whenever you want; providing you aren't being forced with... threats/violence/great sex.

AND IF NO OTHER REASON...

Studies not only show that married people live 6 to 8 years longer than single people; but more miserable. This means that those 6 to 8 years, single people (although already passed on) are in heaven playing tennis, enjoying the country club, living in a mansion, drinking Mai Tai's. Married couples are still living in hell...on earth. What's another 6 to 8 with no time off for good behavior?

Wake Up And Smell The Coffee...Cause It's Burning

When we're little girls running around the house (In our bright pink princess dress) calling out to our prince (so nicely played by our brother or father) we never thought for a second that it wouldn't all work out

Mommy and Daddy got married, all their friends are married, I will get married.

I used to play a game with my father that went something like this...

INT. LIVING ROOM - DAYTIME -CIRCA 1970

DAD

What are you going to be when you grow up?

ME

A famous actress and a Veterinarian.

DAD

When will you get married?

ME

24 or 25.

(That seemed old when I was 5.)

DAD

What will your husband do for a living?

ME

He'll be a doctor, a movie star and a fireman.

DAD

How many kids will you have?

ME

5. 2 dogs, 3 cats, a goldfish and a guinea pig named David Cassidy.

DAD

Where will you live?

ME

New York City, Los Angeles and I'll have a farm in Kansas City. You can live there, too.

When we're young, we think we know exactly how it's going to work out. And for some people, it actually does. Then there's everybody else. For some people it stays that way forever (along with tooth decay, college tuition and that year of experimental orgies.) There are lots of perfect moments neatly divided into that thing we call life.

PLENTY OF PENIS 'AROUND THE CORNER

Which is how you, quite possibly, ended up here. Still looking for the right guy. The only problem is, your personality and idea about what you want in another person change more than the seasons. Seasons change 4 times a year; you change your wardrobe that much in one day. How can you expect to choose 1 particular guy to go through your life? In fact, maybe it's not a guy you're looking for at all.

No, I'm not referring to a chick.

(Although, if that does it for you, by all means enjoy the poodle. (That wasn't a dog reference.)

Maybe you're actually looking for several different men to fulfill several different needs, wants and desires. And, why not? Why should you have to choose just 1?

Many people marry because they think they're in love (at the time) and then realize; 'Holy shit, he/she's insane, I must get out of this!' Hopefully this realization happens before an accident occurs that we read about it in the paper.

Usually one can make a decision while high, drunk, pre-menstrual that they may not make when sober. Sometimes, one can make a bad decision (seemingly terrific at the time) while sober. Can't help you there. A shrink may be of some assistance. Just think about the number of people you've dated. There's always another one. And quite possibly, you always *thought A, B, C, D* was the one, only to come to the (perhaps not so rapid) conclusion that you were wrong.

Which leads you to start to think Polygamy isn't such a bad idea, after all. No, not the marrying in front of God part, but the several partners all co-habitating quite nicely, giving you several options throughout your day, week, month…to decide whom to be with at any given time that floats your boat.

This way, you don't have to be expected to always want/love/laugh with or at…your mate and allows you the freedom to have options. Who doesn't like options? We do it with our clothing, food, animals, cars, furniture, make-up, friends…

You name it and we have lots of different things.

So, why should we have to choose just **1** person to go through life with? Yes, there's that love thing, but that's for sissies.

I'm talking passion here. Romance. Excitement! Great sex, laughter…and your own walk-in closet.

Just think about it, before you jump down the aisle, giddy to say I do.

A FEW REASONS WHY HE MAY NOT WANT TO DATE YOU, BUT IS FINE HAVING SEX WITH YOU

1. He doesn't see you as 'wife' material.
2. You go out too much.
3. You don't seem 'deep' enough, educated enough, the right pedigree (ala *The Way We Were)*
4. He doesn't think you have domestic qualities.
5. He thinks you lack social grace, etiquette, and stripping skills.

(#5 is precisely WHY he does want to have sex with you.)

(USELESS TIP: Stripping skills can be learned. You may not want to learn them).

A guy knows the kind of woman he sees himself with, and you just may not be it. This does not mean that you do not turn him on. This does not mean that he doesn't want to take you home and do nasty things for hours (or minutes; which in that case, you should not proceed). When a guy has sex with you (and only for sex) he has no problem blowing you off afterwards. When women have sex, she will want to have sex with him, again…if it's good. The only reason a woman does not want to have sex with the guy again (if she is only in it for sex) is if the guy is too into her. A guy (even if the woman professes true love) will return, time and time again, just because he likes screwing her -

And likes knowing she wants him (even if he doesn't really want her). It really doesn't matter that she is in love with him/wants to get married/have babies or plan for retirement. He is only interested in having sex and that's it. What kind of woman would be this dumb to fall for that? One that doesn't look at the whole picture, sees only what she wants to see and/or hopes things will change. Dumb girl! Waiting for change is like waiting for seasons in California. It isn't going to happen. And when it does? It's so subtle you won't notice it, anyway.

MAYBE WE ARE SCREWED UP...

And then there's just the thought that you may be... too screwed up to date? Don't worry if that's what you're thinking. Look around. There are plenty of screwed up people just like you, and they want love too!

Isn't this fun? Well, you may not find it necessarily fun, but hey, it gives you something to do other than worry about work, life, health and/or that boob job you're contemplating. There's so many screwed up people that if someone you like asks you out and never calls, you should be thankful and remind yourself that there's more of those around the corner.

Okay, maybe there are some amazing people out there, but waiting to fall in love/get married/shack-up/blah–blah blah...chances are they've got some baggage. And you've got baggage. How fun! Lots of baggage for everyone. Time to decide who has the least amount of baggage and give them a try. No fit? Try another? How about him/her/it? List getting shorter? Baggage getting heavier?

Come to think of it, even when you were younger, didn't you pick screwed up people? Maybe everyone is screwed up and its just levels of how screwed up they are? Oh God, what if I never meet anyone, ever again? What if no one accepts/wants/loves me for me? What if I never meet another screwed up individual, ever again?

Relax. Studies show, you will.

Next time you make a choice, perhaps you should pick someone that doesn't lack empathy, has the same core-values (yes, they're there, somewhere). You may realize that you need to focus on different, deeper qualities (to find that love you've been looking for since you fell in love with David Cassidy at 16). You may be able to put your selfish needs aside (even if you don't have kids) because you've been madly in love with your dog/cat/hamster for several years and take very good care of him/her/it.

Don't let anyone tell you that you're selfish. You've done a fine job of sharing your bed with that pet for many years, given them most of the bed to sleep, have deep conversations on a variety of topics. (Yes, you did most of the talking). You've discussed morals, values and ethics and you've created a list of things you're looking for in another(s) individual(s). Oddly enough, the list looks a lot like the one you made at 5. It's okay. Keep dreaming. You should be able to order characteristics (and sex) ala-carte; just like tapas menus.

Why not?

There are plenty of people to go around. How are we expected to find all of it in one human being?

Searching for a partner that brings adventure into your life isn't such a bad thing, is it? Wanting a bigger life than you currently have is so wrong?

You already have your…apartment/house/condo/castle. You already have amazing friends, a great social life and a great career. You're allowed to find someone that enhances that life you already have.

Or, you can just have great sex until you die.

This isn't meant to be a deep book. In fact, it's quite the opposite. It's supposed to be shallow and fun.

What is the answer? No freaking clue.

Maybe what you are doing is just fine and you should chill out. On the other hand, if you're horny, desperate and really looking for a relationship; you are probably doing something wrong. Well, not wrong, actually, just not exactly...right.

YOUR PERFECT LIFE

You have a perfect life just the way it is. (Quit freaking bragging!) I know, 'cause I've been there.

I was dating a really great guy at the time, having great sex, totally connecting on all levels, making quite a bit of money...and able to travel and have fun.

Then reality hit.

Then the recession hit.

(Yes, reality hit first, then recession.)

You think you connect on so many levels until you realize that his/her mystery is really just hiding that restraining order. You think they fulfill all of your wants/needs/desires when you don't want/need/desire anything, until you suddenly want/need/desire...anything. You think you are getting everything you want in someone, until you meet someone else and you realize this person doesn't fill, well, most of those things you thought they did. There are thousands of reasons people get into relationships and just as many reasons as to why they don't last. And, in between it all, you learn to get happy. If you could bottle the formula for happiness and contentment (regardless of where and whom you're with in your life) you could sell it and make a fortune!

Most people go through their life trying to stay positive, upbeat, live in the moment and not torture themselves over past failures, love relationships and bad decisions.

After we learn the lesson of love gone wrong, we then think we've got it all figured out, until the next one comes along and blind sides us. Usually, we never see it coming. Which leads us, at some point to say, "I need to try something else". Else being things I'm not doing. Things I need to try other than what I've done. Something over *there*...something else. Then, after you've tried something else, you may simply decide screw it. I'm here and here is where my perfect life *is*.

Believe it or not, taking what you have at this exact moment (no matter how bad it may feel) and deciding (yes, simply deciding) that from here forward there's no turning back, you have made a choice that this is your perfect life and you are going to live it. It sure beats regurgitating every relationship over and over into your brain, day after day.

The people that are leading the perfect life always let you know it. How? They tell you. "Everything is great", "I'm terrific",

"Life couldn't be better". How do they do this?

They don't focus on the negative (how boring) and seem to truly be happy.

Lucky Bitches! (Or, great cons.)

SOME HOCUS POCUS YOU SHOULD TELL YOURSELF

Once you've decided that you have the perfect life and are truly happy (no matter what your circumstances are) you can move forward and go after the life you want.

You also will probably start to weed out the wrong choices you make. Since happiness is a state of mind, the less junk you fill it with, the more space you'll have for all the great things/ideas/dreams/goals/porno.

This includes deciding that your perfect, happy life doesn't necessarily become fulfilled, just because you have someone to share it with. This has nothing to do with finding someone to have great sex with, until you find that perfect person. Why waste that perfect Vaginal Rejuvenation session?

The non-ending search for someone can be tiresome. Choosing to be happy no matter where you are in your life will give the illusion that you are independent and don't need anyone. Which is what will attract you to every situation you previously always wanted. No, this isn't a game to get you to act like you don't need or want anyone; it's just the truth that you should let go and live your life. Head down the path you were meant to head down. And hopefully, maybe, or who gives a shit; you may or may not meet that someone that fills (no, not empty holes, cause you don't have anymore of those) but fills (you know, those areas that *God* created). Anyway, It's what I've recently been told. And anyway, we might not get outta here alive, so best to start livin'. (I may have stolen the saying from *an actor.)*

STAGES OF LIFE

You lose your first tooth, break an arm, sock a kid in the eye, get your period, get arrested for petty theft, walk in on your parents having sex (at least I think it was my Dad) lose your virginity (somewhere between birth and college) get a degree, meet the love of your life, blow lots of money on a wedding (correction; your parents money) have a kid or 7, make some/blow some money, catch your husband/wife cheating, divorce, enter therapy, acquire an addiction, start dating again/get married again/ turn gay/ become celibate/find God/worship your dog, start a new career, have a mid-life breakdown, go through menopause, suffer some illness, take up tennis and/or bridge, live through it or die.

Cover everything?

What about when it doesn't work out like you planned? 25? Gone. 30? Gone. Now you're 35 (36, 37, 38 tick, tick tick) and you're not married. You don't have kids. Not that you necessarily want kids, considering you still feel like a kid yourself. Come to think of it, you may not even want to get married.

But what are you supposed to do with your time if you don't want to get married or have kids? Where do you go from here? Bar scene? Done. Singles scene? Done. Career burn out? Done. Climbing the social ladder? Done. When do you grow up? When do you mature like all your friends? Will you ever get there? Not that it bothers you most of the time. Sometimes you even revel in your success, ambition and independence.

It all seems great.

Really. I'm fucking great! (You yell to no one in particular). I can do anything I want. Anytime, anywhere and with anyone!

Seems can be a state of mind.

…And then you freak out.

You wonder what you did wrong. You're this age and haven't married and/or had kids. What were you thinking? What were you doing when everyone was pairing off? It can't just be that we went to the wrong parties. My God, you've been to every party there is, just ask everyone who knows you. No, your social life is probably not the problem. Your social life might have gotten in the way of your problem, but maybe there wasn't even a problem to begin with. (Except if you find yourself wanting to be coupled up/married/with child and you're not).

WHAT'S THE PROBLEM?

Fact. There are too many women and not enough men; except in China and Alaska.

Most of them are in prison.

I'm too busy exhausting NYC, Chicago, LA, Kansas City, San Francisco and the South of France.

When you get older, you get stuck in your routine. You find it harder to share and usually want what we call space. We don't want to share our beds, money, bathrooms or toothbrushes, but we do want to borrow your cool, flannel shirt.

WHAT WHITE HORSE?

What happened to our parents old-fashioned "we gazed at each other from across the room and it was love at first sight?" Or, "We wanted to have sex until we were married, so we got married after dating for 3 weeks". (My parents/your parents/some random people.)

And, what about having babies? They used to just pop 'em out in the old days. Now, it seems, no one can get pregnant. Yes, I know, we're told its sushi and cell phones.

WHAT'S THE POINT?

This book is meant to show you that you are only one of several hundred thousand other single fish trying to swim through that giant pond we call life.

Hell, if that's all it does, it should be enough, shouldn't it? Doesn't it make you feel better knowing you aren't the only one going through all this? No? Well, get over it and get on with your life. Not everyone's meant to get married, have kids, live a certain way, have certain things, get everything they want. (Holy crap, really? That sucks!)

No matter how many people you date, sleep with; having a relationship with, you never give up the hope that he's/she's going to be *IT* although the *IT* changes the older you get. As your needs and wants change, so does what you decide you're looking for; if and when you ever are able to decide exactly what it is you are looking for.

Most single people are still waiting for their Perfect Prince/Princess Charming to arrive on their doorstep.

(In my fantasy, I'm in a doorman building in New York City; so he'll have to charm the concierge to get to me.) Just because you get older, doesn't mean you feel less likely to fall in love and stay in love. (Possibly more cynical, but not less filled with the fantasy of it all.)

The single most said line to people over the age of 35 who still aren't married? Maybe you're too picky!

STAGES OF PICKY...

1. Super picky.
2. Horny, whomever will do.
3. Even pickier.
4. Logical, Moralistic, Boring, Practical.
5. Screw it. Bring me anyone.
6. Are you kidding me? I'm only getting what I want, or I'm going back to sleeping with hot/young/nubile (fill in the blank.)

When you get older, because you've gotten older; because you've been picked through/as well as thrown back several and are still out there...you may need to change what you want. (I.E# You aren't being realistic. I.E.E. You aren't 25, anymore.)

The truth is, the fantasy of love never goes away. Sure, you may get roughed up a bit; smashed, picked through, even a little bruised; but somehow, somewhere it comes back around, and around, giving us hope that with the right person(s) by our side, we can accomplish anything.

WHAT TO PACK FOR PRINCE CHARMING

(1). A croissant and a latte. He's galloped a long way. (2). Matching bra and undies. (Remember what your Mother always said.)

PRINCE CHARMING SHOULD NOT BE

1. In debt. (Since you may be.)
2. Secretly married to another.
3. Pretend to be one way, then surprise us by not being anything like the person you created.

Please keep your horse groomed, we've got friends to impress.

AFTER THE WHITE HORSE

Okay, at some point, you should probably give up on that theory that a wonderful, prince charming (or princess charming) is coming your way. Not that you can't marry a wonderful person and have a perfectly nice life.

God, that sounds boring.

It's just that, at some point, the idea of being swept off your feet becomes a little less likely.

(Or too difficult with that extra 10 lbs. you've added recently.)

At this point, you may or may not have a child (of your own/with an ex/with a stranger/be knee deep in debt/ living high on the hog/extremely well-off/running around like a chicken with your head cut off...which means that dating to find someone to spend the rest of your life with just got less attractive looking and well, you now have less time to drive each other crazy. Yes, you're not going to have 60 years of wedded bliss if you marry at 40, even if you live to 100. On the other hand, will probably spend the last 3 to 5 sitting in front of a TV show trying to remember your own name. Even if you do still decide to go after the one that you want/need/have to have, going after them will take on a different approach. Since everything you were doing up to this point, didn't work (exactly like you planned) so you may need to come up with another genius idea.

A FEW GENIUS IDEAS

1. Let it go.
2. Exhaust every friend/relative/total stranger to set you up because, "you're such an amazing catch".

3. Marry for companionship. (You can't legally marry your dog.)
4. Give it up and start to date several men in many states.
5. Take a hot bath and relax. It's only love.

CHAPTER 2

Women Are Idealists, Men Are Realists

Women want love. Men want lots of love.
Men want money. Women want lots of money.
Women would give it up on the first date IF the
man would propose afterward, before or during.
I do.

CHAPTER 2
WOMEN ARE IDEALISTS, MEN ARE REALISTS

Several men read this book. They all said the same thing ..."*You're wrong!*" My reply? "Write your own book, I'm sticking with my theory."

Men think they're idealists. Reality is...they just want a nice pair of tits (to look at), a beer and some porn; A nice hit of pot wouldn't hurt either, in no particular order. Women think they are realists. Creating a 'bucket' list that no man on the planet could fulfill (at least in one lifetime). Nevertheless, someone has to settle. Down, that is. Into that thing we call 'married life'-You know that real part of life where you have to do things you don't even want to do in front of your dog.

REALITY CHECK, PLEASE!

A MOTHERS ADVICE...always marry a man who loves you more than you love them. (By them I don't mean plural, unless you want to!)

This theory never worked for me, because if I love a man less than he loves me, how am I going to want to marry him? If I'm not feeling a passionate, ever consuming love, what is "love" for, anyway? (Ah, perhaps the reason I'm not married. Just a thought!)

Although, marrying a man who loves you more than you love him will ensure that he always has a challenge and has less control over the relationship, may also grow tiresome for you. The fact that you didn't do very much to earn his love may feel too easy for you, and although easy sometimes nice, may lead to a lack a sexual spark that well, is kind of important in marriage. (At least, in the first 3 to 5.) Most women (by most I mean all) have fantasies that never go away.

Women from 8 to 80 are still waiting for their personal Prince Charming. Yes, men have fantasies, too, but they usually involve Pay-Per-View and a bottle of vodka. Most men secretly know they aren't a woman's ideal fantasy (because most women tell them). Even if she marries you. She still may be wishing and waiting for Mr. Perfect Prince Charming to ride up on his white horse and carry her off. Most men think this is ridiculous and that she wouldn't go.

Think again.

Even if you think she loves you more than you love her, she'd go in a heartbeat. She's been waiting for this guy her whole life. She just never thought he'd show up, so she married you. Oops, sorry to burst your bubble, she just wanted the wedding. Oh yeah, she may have loved you, but she loves her fantasy more. Don't feel bad. It's not that you're a bad guy; you're just not her fantasy.

Yes, we know, we know.

She may not be your fantasy either; you married drunk/lonely/horny/rich/happy/sad/out-of-your   mind and now you're stuck with that rambling nut-bag. Should have listened to your lawyer and done the Pre-nup.

SEND SOMEONE STABLE

Women like to have some sort of stability in their lives. So, when you fall in love and slip that ring on our finger, we realize that our PPC may never be coming

(We've also spent all that time changing your hair, your wardrobe, how you eat, your snoring) so we decide you'll do. Word to the not so wise. Just because we marry you, does not necessarily mean we are madly in love with you. We could actually have very screwed up taste and decided every other person out there was the wrong choice, are lousy at making the right choice and you came along at the perfect time.

I'm sure most of us did the same thing for you, too.

It's not the same fresh feeling everyone has in there 20's or 30's when they marry the dream partner.

Madly in love and think I'm wrong? Just wait, you're times a comin'. Not that you don't spend your time trying to make that person fit your dream, and perhaps they even end up (miracle of miracles) being exactly what you thought you didn't even want! How fun is that? Brings a whole new meaning to the term "I don't know I'm looking for." Marriage in all it's glory should be filled with dandelions, puppy dog tails and sheepskin rugs (well, some people may enjoy these finer things in their marriage) but all too often; a year or two in, and it's more likely filled with over-stuffed closets, bad breathe and a shared bathroom. Sure, there's some fun thrown in there for good measure, like a sex act you've never tried before or learning how to make linguini in clam sauce together. But other times, it's probably just like the things you do alone; just with someone to bother you in the same room. (At times you'd **rather** be alone.)

REALISTIC MEN STILL CHEAT

Even though your man has sworn his devotion, vowed to love, honor and cherish you (till whenever your mutual love contract expires)…men cheat! (Though most, when IN LOVE; in the dating stage, usually stay faithful…hmmm!). Although, they may still be sending pictures of their penis to random ugly girls they've never met. Even though both parties may cheat, Men and women have very different views on what cheating means.

WOMEN'S IDEA OF CHEATING=KISSING (even without tongue-Cute tennis instructors exempt)

MEN'S IDEA OF CHEATING=VAGINAL SEX (anything else is fair game when he's horny).

Once a week, once a month, once a year or once; if they can get strange, they'll get it.

(And by strange, I may mean someone they will never/infrequently/once a month/on-going-see again.)

When he comes home wanting some random sex act he's never mentioned before, that he says he saw on pay-per-view in the hotel room, might be a clue he's getting some.

Some are pickier than others. Some men won't go for every Sue, Betty or Jane they meet. But they may go for Betty and Jane, or just Jane. Gay men cheat. Straight men cheat. Ugly men cheat. Fat men cheat. Men that are happily married, cheat.

YES, THESE COUNT

Top-off, Rub Down and Happy Endings.

(Although, I have to say, what's a little rub down between strangers on a quiet afternoon?)

MEN = DOGS (not intended to insult dogs)

A DEFINITION OF CHEATING

Sticking one's tongue in another woman's mouth that isn't your wife, even if she has the same name as your wife. She **isn't** your wife, end of story. (FYI-women cheat, too, but usually it involves flattery, gifts and a large penis.)

A BRILLIANT IDEA

Join an acting class. Give yourself a make-out scene with the hot girl/guy in the class. Free pass.

HOW DO I KNOW MOST MEN CHEAT?

My father told me.

Oh, yeah, and I walked in on him kissing his secretary, Teresa. I also walked in on him holding hands several years later with a beautiful blonde. I should have had an idea after he dropping me off for school in the 4th grade, noticed my friend Robin and said, "Who's the broad with the boobs?"

Here're some facts I've learned. Tonight. In a bar...

1. *Men love food*

2. *Men love pussy*

3. *Men love porn*

(I jotted this down as several tongue-wagging frat boys surrounded a nearby table watching the The Hooters waitress drop off nachos).

A RANDOM SURVEY

After spending two eight-hour days sitting in a vacant parking lot at the end of a deserted road with several randomly selected men and women, these are the answers we came up with. (Okay, that was a lie. I never did a random search with anyone. Who has that kind of time to organize that sort of gathering?) I called a few people, who called a few people and the rest I just made up.

1. Men-Granny pants Very large white underpants. I am told this is not an attractive form of undergarment on women and all pairs that you may own that resemble these "granny pants" should be thrown away immediately or given back to Granny.

2. *Women-Hairy ass and hairy back (shoulders included)* Let me just say that unless you are a member of the monkey family, this is neither attractive or fun.

3. *Men and Women-The Freak out=stalking.* The freak out usually occurs after one member of the relationship has fallen more in love than the other member. Usually it has nothing to do with the less-in-love member. Usually, the stalker/freak is simply an obsessive person to begin with. Once the more-in-love member has fallen and can't get up, he or she will do everything possible to make life a living hell for the other member.

Phone calls, unexpected visits, non-stop texts, online stalking, yelling, screaming, crying…are all accepted uses of entrapment practiced by the freak.

Oddly enough, even perfectly seeming normal human beings, once they've fallen in some sort of weird vortex they think is love, can turn into complete freaks.

This freak-out can go on for years and can even last a lifetime. Most of the people I spoke with pretty much feel the same way…*"if I don't like you, leave me alone."*

Random Turn Off's-Men

*Women, who don't shave, wax or exfoliate. (Men who like Burning man and Coachella may be exceptions.)
*Women who don't offer money on a date.
*Woman who are social snobs. (Unless the man is secretly gay, and/or snobbier than the woman.)
*Women who don't like threesomes. (Unless the man has reached a certain age and is willing to give it up for the woman he loves.)

Random turn Off's-Women

*Men who don't walk on the outside.
*Men who take money from a woman on a date.
*Men who don't watch sports.
*Little bugs in strange places on the body.

DOES ANY OF IT MEAN ANYTHING?

Not really. Although women are idealists, when they choose to marry you, they most likely get real and put their heart and soul into the marriage.

Although a man is a realist, once he marries his wife, he may suddenly decide to worship her, grow increasingly bizarre and do strange things; like idolize and place her on a large pedestal.

Hypothetically. In most cases.

He usually puts her on a pedestal after he's knocked her up and decided his penis has no right being inside her vagina. Although he worships her, she now may just want to get...far, far away.

And...

2 happily married people enjoying sex, having a fabulous time, equally dependent upon one another and equally smitten should be placed in the zoo and observed for testing.

Or, locked up somewhere never to see the light of day, because they're making the rest of us look bad.

For some men, the simple fantasy that they can cheat is enough.

Some reasons it may be enough...

(1). They're too tired (2). They've been married too many times and h. gone through all their money. (3). They finally found the one. (Who threatens to kick their ass if the DO cheat.) (4). They aren't as hot as they once were, thus not able to get play like they used to. (Please! Don't feel sorry for them. They got plenty when they were younger.)

CHAPTER 3

TWO TYPES OF MEN

My brother is straight. He married a girl.
My mother is straight. She married several
boys.
My friend Michael is gay. He likes my brother.
My brother likes Jimmy...as a friend.

I'm still single.

CHAPTER 3
2 TYPES OF MEN
(I Don't Mean Gay And Straight)

Random studies show there are two types of men...

1. Powerful man + needy woman = *CAVEMAN*
2. Needy man + powerful woman = *CAVEMAN*

MEN WANT NEEDY WOMEN

How do I know? My father told my mother and my mother told me. So did every one of my ex-boyfriends. Well, maybe not verbally, but hey, anytime I had to be at a back-to-back meeting, and couldn't make it home until midnight, there he sat, quietly sullen, wanting to know where I'd been all night.

MEN WANT TO FEEL NEEDED

Okay, let's dispel the myth right here: They may tell you over and over again how much they love independent, successful, powerful, self-sufficient women.

Don't listen. Close your ears.

It's a trap!

If you are powerful, you are a threat to a man's job, which is to take care of a woman. The minute he gets you, he'll try to change you. Unless of course, he wants you to continue climbing the career ladder, so he can quit his job and be a stay-at-home sloth. He will still try to change you. And because you're successful, he will assume you cannot do domestic things - like cook, clean, vacuum, arrange flowers. Yes, you can do them.

No, you don't want to.

Yes, domestics can be hired for that sort of thing.

(If forced, you can do them; It's just like riding a bike, isn't it?)

He may want you to take a cooking class (assuming you can't cook) and you probably will because after you fall in love with him, you're in his web, and he knows it.

Men that are truly independent and love a woman with a lot going on, may eventually start to resent her because she's not making him a priority. Sure, they'll act impressed with what you've accomplished. Then, notice how the conversation turns right around back to him? That's because he's heard enough.

He doesn't want to be impressed with you. He wants you to be impressed with him.

Hint: Try spending your life in-transition and helplessness, and see how many men flock around to save you.

WHAT MEN NEED

Men need to feel like you can't live without them, even if you can. Men need to feel that no matter what you do to them or how many times you do it to someone else, you'll be there for them. And so they start to test you. It's kind of unfair because you always did well on tests…when you had the time to study! This is a different kind of test. You know, this is a pop quiz.

Today.

Now.

In a myriad of ways.

You'll be asked all sorts of weird questions that make you feel like there's a right or wrong answer. (Trust me, there is.) They will take you somewhere to make sure you know enough about any given subject to be able to listen to them talk about it. No, they don't care how much **you** know, they just want you to hear them give you the information. They may make snide comments about your non-marriage status. They may try to find things wrong with you, really quickly, so you feel like you're being judged. (Yes, you are being judged.)

His mood may go from into you, to not, very quickly...in one felt swoop. Never mind the fact that you didn't like the way his pants were riding up his ass, it was never up to you.

Nope, if he wants you, he tries to lure you in, and just as quickly can decide he was incorrect. He may cheat on you, blame you and then beg for your forgiveness. If you don't forgive him, He'll surmise that this makes you weak. Men have a very backward view of relationships. They will only love you conditionally if you love them unconditionally.

You should try to be the perfect woman, but he can be a complete selfish slob. You will still be subtly tested throughout the relationship to make sure you are up to snuff. Your feelings about him don't really matter. As long as he wants you, you should be happy and keep quiet. For God's sake, you talk too much.

THE LEMONADE STAND-BAKING THEORY

Successful women may say, "Why can't he just be there for me emotionally?" If you bring home the bacon, he doesn't think you need him emotionally. He just thinks you need him for sex. (Where's the problem?)

Then he becomes needy, you know, just like a woman, which then turns you off. Men are programmed to be the breadwinners. Facts show they're given fewer hugs as children (yes, I may have made that up) and studies show they had twice as many lemonade stands growing up (no, I didn't make that up). That's because their mothers were trying to teach them how to earn a living, while the girls were in the kitchen learning how to bake.

The cross gender/gay situation occurred because of this. Whoever crossed the line became that sexual preference. If a girl preferred lemonade stands to cooking, she became gay, or extremely successful. If a boy preferred baking? Well, you know the rest. This is a much easier theory to follow than born that way.

Of course there are exceptions. If you'd like you can use the comparison of boys who play with Barbie dolls and girls who play with trucks.

THE SHUT-THE-MOUTH THEORY

When you are dating and needing a man, you need to shut-the-mouth. This only works one way. Silence.

You need to be able to communicate to your man in one way. Looking good. Never complain. Never tell him off. Never have an opinion. Never raise your voice. Never question him. Never lecture him. Never scold him. (The bedroom can be an exception, depending on the kinks.)

Come on, I'm not serious here. You certainly can talk about him behind his back. But not doing these things to his face will help a great deal in making sure that your relationship goes the distance. You know, for life; or until he meets someone else.

Don't worry, if he cheats on you he may tell you, "it has nothing to do with you," or "I still love you," or "a man can be happy with someone and still want to cheat," or, finally, "she's just a friend." This doesn't change the fact that you will still need to act needy. Don't ever let him think you don't need him.

If you let him think you don't need him, he'll run for the hills to be with one of the affairs from above. Make sure that you act like June Cleaver, to ensure that he will always come home. Just don't hold dinner.

The point is this. Every time I (or any of my friends) dated a man, the man went on and on about how much he loved a woman's independence and ambition. He loved the way the woman had her own life, her own friends, and plenty of money so he didn't have to support her lifestyle. So, what's the problem, you ask? Who do they end up marrying?

Think back, you independent successful, ambitious "broads." Guaranteed there are a lot more of you reading this book then needy ones.

The needy ones get the guys.

Men may say they love your independence. Sure, for a week, maybe a year. Then one day, when they get home from the office and you're still at work, they will begin to resent you, deep down (We really don't need to dig that deep). A man wants to feel as if a woman can't tie her shoelaces unless he leans down and does it for her. I say, let him.

FACT: Women suffer from calcium deficiency more than men. Why bend over if you don't have to?

I have a friend, who has a friend, whose friend was very ambitious and independent. She starting dating this guy and began taking cooking classes, French lessons and knitting classes. Although she broke up with her boyfriend, she now knits for the whole family and dates a French cook.

ALWAYS ACT LIKE YOU CAN'T FIND YOUR WAY

Since a man has to feel like he's always needed, you're going to need some needy lessons…

1. Waitress. Not well.
2. Get fired a lot.
3. Cry a lot.
4. Get lost a lot.
5. Pretend to forget everything.
6. If you can, really do forget everything.
7. Have the perfect body but don't work out.
8. Don't lift anything heavy.
9. Grab and read every Geisha guide you can. Tell him you aspire to living a Geisha life.
10. Don't talk.
11. Work for lawyers. Don't be good. Wear short skirts.
12. Be a hooker. Pretend you had to do it to survive.

POWERFUL MAN + NEEDY WOMAN = CAVEMAN

Deep down (not that deep) a man wants to own a beautiful woman. He wants to conk her on the head with a club and kidnap her. He wants to bring her to his cave and make her serve pretzels and beer, to his poker buddies, for the rest of her life; regardless of the size of the cave and that you may be asked to clip toenails (with your teeth). You must always have your capped-tooth smile ready and waiting for any request. This is what needy women do.

They also take care of the man when he's too old to do anything for himself (except when the Pre-nup is too generous, thus leaving her to run off and leave him with nurse care). If a powerful man chooses a needy, much younger woman, he's doing so because he realizes once that little blue pill no longer has any effect on him, the stares from the envious other men, will have an effect. As long as she's thin, looks good on his arm and helps him in and out of the car, he's content.

Positives and Negatives

POSITIVES

1. You won't have to work.

2. You'll get to shop (all the time) but you'll be "on call."

3. You'll get to talk on the phone all the time (but probably be monitored.)

4. You can bring your mother to live with you and buy her nice things.

NEGATIVES

1. He will treat you like you're dumb. (What do you think Dumb Girl chapter is for?)

2. He will control your every move.

3. He will promise to love you, even while he loves another.

4. He will take control of all your credit cards (if he gives you any).

5. You will be on an allowance directly proportionate to how much sex you give him.

6. You will not be allowed to have any friends (except your mother, if she's not a nag).

7. You will not be allowed to gain weight; but you can't go to the gym.

He won't trust other men around you.

NEEDY MAN + POWERFUL WOMAN = CAVEMAN

Needy men love powerful women for the same reason that powerful men love needy women—it makes them feel wanted. Powerful women spend all day working, making deals and generally trying to better themselves. The last thing they want after a hard day at the office is a really intelligent nerd to talk to them about finance. They want to relax and be happy. They want a great massage from a really beautiful, dumb, quiet guy, who looks great in a tux. Needy men want powerful women for great parties, great sex and good food.

Powerful women want needy men because they usually look like boy toys. This way, women get even with the powerful men who don't want them. Powerful couples usually don't work. They clash, unless both spouses are clearly secure (happens around 80 years old, when you're too tired, anyway) or one acts less superior. This is why the above scenario's work together.

A powerful woman feels needed by that hot young thing because he worships her, compliments her and makes her feel like she's amazing. Powerful men don't do that with powerful women, because they cannot dominate them.

TWO POWERFUL PEOPLE MAY LOOK GOOD TOGETHER, BUT GET THEM BEHIND CLOSED DOORS AND ONE'S SUBMISSIVE.

Or, they're both beating the crap out of each other. But one's still stronger.

The more powerful spouse usually controls the relationship.

That being said, if the sex is good, the really screwed up, needy partner controls the relationship.

The needy man is perfectly happy with his powerful broad bringing home all the bacon. The powerful broad is perfectly happy having incredible sex with this God, because she's in her prime and he makes her feel good. Men her age don't appreciate her. In fact, it's the same for the powerful men and needy woman syndrome. Each must be sure to be complemented and taken care of in some way. Money, sex and lots of attention are usually the key factors.

WHAT THE NEEDY MAN MUST POSSESS

1. Must be well endowed and a great tongue.

2. Must be dumb, but never act it. (Note how this is the opposite of powerful men + needy women.)

3. Must be willing to squire from party to party at a moment's notice.

4. Must be gorgeous. Must wear cashmere and look great in a pair of jeans.

5. Must have class-or act like it (Take a learning annex class if need be).

6. Must love to 'give'.

7. Must not work, in order to have time free and available for powerful broad.

8. Must act in love/lust/hot for.

CHAPTER 4

DATING

See Dick Spot Jane across the gym.
See Dick check out Jane's ass.
See Jane turn red and run.
See Dick chase Jane into the ladies room.
See Jane fly out the back window to her car.
See Dick run faster and farther until he catches her.
See Jane jot her number down and speed off.
See Dick smile and saunter off.

CHAPTER 4
DATING

Ah, dating...isn't this fun? Everyone looks great from...far away. Or first glance. And then, something happens.

You actually have to get to know that person. Spend time with that human, interact, fondle and possibly share space. Some people date simply to find 1 person to love, honor, cherish and spend the rest of their life annoying. For others, they simply date for the sport of it-the intrigue, drama and yes, chaos. Going on the actual date, in fact, pales to the comparison of the fantasy they have built up; the thrill comes from just being chased, wanted and/or stalked. (Within reason, of course.)

Some women date to get married, have dinner paid for, have things bought for them, have their toes licked (you know who you are, David) waste time or otherwise complain about and/or gush about: Dating. Men date (If they have to) to get laid (along with masturbating) waste time or doing things they wouldn't normally do; All because they're horny/lonely/horny/getting older and less attractive so snapping their finger and grunting no longer works like it used to.

Dating advice from my Mom: Keep your options open and your legs closed.

Dating advice from my Dad: Keep your mouth closed and wear a short skirt.

Most women would like to date several men in many states—if only we could find them. In the meantime, we don't want to let you down, so some play that whole damsel in distress thing. Remember that you need to think we are needy creatures. God forbid we should disappoint you.

This actually works better when you *are* needy and/or in distress.

SOME DATING ADVICE FROM ONE DATE TO THE NEXT

1. Wear a dress or very short skirt.
2. Shave well in advance. (This way all cuts dry.)
3. Drink heavily. (Vodka doesn't have a smell.)
4. Talk about *him* and only *him* on the way from the door to the car.
5. Don't eat. God knows what your etiquette habits are like.
6. If you must eat, try to impress him with your knowledge of vegetables.
7. Slip that breath mint in while you still have water.
8. Don't stay too long in the bathroom. He'll think you're bulimic.
9. Don't return his text or call after the date.
10. If you run into him, claim answering machine breakdown, then accept a second date.
11. If you like him after the second date, marry him. (Do you really want to go through all that dating bullshit again?)

Dating Advice from My Mom: Always date (And marry) a man who loves you more than you love them.

Dating Advice from my Dad: Keep your nails clean.

Dating is a tricky game. Some love it and some hate it. Some just want to date for the rest of their lives, while others break out in a cold sweat at the thought of meeting the one.

One small problem.

You have to date if you want to meet your future husband. You're other option? Continue to go to bars and get drunk, you're bound to meet someone there.

But isn't that where you met every other ex-boyfriend? *"Being taken care of. I don't need a guy with money, but I want to be taken care of"* Basically means the same thing.

This leaves a guy pursuing you with one of two options: (1) He either has (or makes) money thus ensuring he has the ability to afford the lifestyle in which you fantasize about becoming accustomed to-Or; (2) He steals/borrows/begs in order to keep you in the comfort of the lifestyle you are hoping to become accustomed to. If, in fact, you already live a certain lifestyle and are really just wanting a guy to take care of you so that you don't have to spend all your money-you actually still want him to have money. Either way, you'd prefer a guy with money. (Or a large body part, but that's a different chapter.)

Some useless, yet helpful, dating tips to talk yourself into. (In the mirror, over and over, before you go on that next date.)

Don't give away everything up front.

In fact, don't divulge most of your stuff.

Ideally? Share nothing.

The relationship may have a better chance of survival.

Come on, how many survived on truth and total honesty, anyway? Being needy and over the top (even if you think you're being you) is just creepy for anyone. Remember, date several men at once (not on one date-unless you can quickly go from one place to the other without getting caught). Take your pick.

Relax.

Sleeping with the guy isn't the problem. It's just that weird way you start to act after you sleep with him, that's the problem.

Just remember. You're the same nut-bag wherever you go.

Let the guy take the lead. Yes, this may mean the relationship has now officially ended.

The saying "just be yourself and he/she will love you-only works if everybody loves you-just the way you are. Remember, you still give a great blowjob, and there is plenty of penis around the corner. Make sure that guy you're so hot for is really that great. After a few drinks, good or bad-the truth comes out. Want to know how he feels about you? Get him drunk. Roofie him, then ask all the questions you want. I may not know what works, but I certainly am an expert about knowing what doesn't.

Wanting to grow old with your partner, probably won't happen if you're already old when you've met them-That's okay, a short

love is better than no love at all and if one dies early, then you can idealize that love for the rest of your life. Just because you want to fall in love, doesn't mean it will happen. Tell God you need to be in love. (Lie. You can always apologize once you're in heaven).

DATING AS A SPORT

This could possibly be the best way to approach dating. Remember when you decided to take up tennis? Yes, it was possibly because of that hot tennis instructor, but you had an intention of learning the sport of tennis, and to some degree, you did. You took a bunch of lessons (until you slept with the instructor and realized all he talked about was tennis) and you had to move on to another instructor. When you couldn't find one that you wanted to date anymore, you gave up learning the sport. It's okay, this is the way dating should be. Very little emotional energy should go into it, remain objective, learn what you need from every particular person and move on to the next, taking what you learned from one to the next. Yes, this should not only make you a better tennis player, but if worked correctly, may make you very good at dating.

DATING FOR CONTROL

When a guy likes you, but secretly feels that he will never be good enough for you-or be able to keep up with you, he will probably start picking on you, leading to him being in control. If you're really into him-this is fun-For about a minute. After that first 60 seconds when it feels like playful banter, it will start to feel-well, just odd. Kind of like someone putting you in your place for things they don't even know about you. Instead of complimenting and making you feel good about how wonderful you are, they go out of their way to get control and find some way to make you feel less than so that they can feel more of, or good enough. It's a strange, vicious cycle and the only out is to possibly date someone more successful than yourself. But finding someone more successful than you can be a challenge, which is the reason you started having sex with the 23 year-old Brazilian soccer-player to begin with. He not only makes you feel attractive, but he has absolutely no difficulty telling you how great you are and not because you're paying him or even emotionally involved.

No, the fact that you will never become emotionally involved, while having great sex, is the exact thing you're looking for. That guy that you do like, that you do see hope in, if he secretly feels intimidated, will torture you. He'll make you feel 'small' somehow because this way he always has the upper hand. (Unless he's really just not that into you, in which case he will still torture you.)

If he secretly thinks you're too good for him, but stays around dishing out a brand of humor less than flattering, you'll know he's just trying to 'not play all his cards' because he's just sure that if he shows you the 'whole deck' you might just go running for the hills. And he may just be right. You probably would. He may think that the only thing, that's keeping you around is the fact that he's hard to read, treats you like crap and doesn't kiss your ass like he thinks all the other guys do.

Or, maybe it's the opposite. They're a complete pushover because they are completely into you within the first five minutes of meeting you. Finding a guy that has both masculine energy and confidence seems to be a tricky combination.

Yes, pour yourself a drink, you know you need it about now.

If a woman has her life together, has a good job, some level of success and is smart; for some men, they find a need to push the woman down and belittle them in other ways. If they don't they can never figure out why the woman would want to be with them in the first place. They secretly don't think they're good enough for the woman, so they think they'll be the one to 'put her in her place'. Whatever happened to the good ole' compliment? And when did a compliment turn from, "you're amazing" to "I don't know what kind of guy would be able to handle you?". Telling you you're smart, witty and too quick has become a detriment for our society. On the other hand, you just simply may not be as amazing as you think you are and should probably see a shrink.

DATING TO WIN

If you are dating to win, you want to be the best at everything. You are like this with everything in your life. You must have the best-looking guy in the room/party/planet...because in your mind, you think this makes everyone envy you. You may be right, but not for the reasons that you think. Dating to win is all about one-upping everyone else.

Which is fine, if it lands you great dates. But if you're dating to win, you don't even really care about the person you're dating. You just want to be better, bigger, stronger and hotter than everyone else.

Go for it. Most of us are just too tired for that kind of competition anymore, but the Bachelor has plenty of openings.

DATING AND BEING FULL OF IT

Is there really the perfect person out there?

Really is everybody as amazing as they make themselves out to be? And just because you're single doesn't mean you're unhappy, lonely-   Shallow and/or vain. (I threw in the last 2. They actually may be a reason you're single) but most people are self-involved, so that doesn't give enough credence to the reason you may be.

How is being single any different than all those married couples that are currently in therapy because the *OTHER PERSON DOESN'T FULFILL THEIR NEEDS?* It's like saying the person you're having an affair with is so open and honest. Of course they are, they're screwing you and their wife. They have an amazing life. And you possibly do, too. Especially if he's bought you the condo you're currently living in. Actually, you're better off buying your own place, so he can't just show up whenever he wants. When two people are single and someone wants to impress the other, it's easy to be full of it. It just happens. Things can fly out of one's mouth that one never had the intention of saying- things that aren't even true. But, if you don't know the person, you won't know what's true or not. So, when that person suddenly isn't around anymore, you will never have known which parts were true or not (unless you've gone through his rolodex and set up a lunch with an ex, which is just downright stalk-erish, but do-able).   No, you really have to take someone at face value and believe the hype they're selling you, one hard-to-believe-story at a time. The problem begins when the relationship ends. Then you start to question well, everything. "But he said this", and "he promised me that" or "we were going to go (fill in the blank).

None of it ever happened.

For whatever reason, one of you moved on. He left. You left. You both left. You're still waiting to hear from him. Why? Because you believed the hype.

He's a good salesman and you bought the sales pitch. It may have happened after you've slept with him, or it could have even happened before the second drink. Regardless, something about how he spoke to you, things he shared, places you went, time you spent, blah, blah and blah, led you to ----believe him. Forgive yourself. Move on. Get your shit together already, will ya, dummy? By the way, women do it to men, too-Yes; we were lying when we told you how crazy we were about you. We were…at that moment…that second. Yes, we've disappeared. Yes, we've moved on.

DATING OUT OF BOREDOM

(I'm tired just thinking about it). When you date out of boredom, it's mostly because you're sick of everyone asking you about your 'dating life'. If you are making up stories and creating dates that don't exist, just so you can keep everyone off of your back, you may want to actually accept a few of those dates, just to see what all the dating fuss is about. Don't worry; you probably won't like anyone anyway since you're always soooo bored with everyone, but at least you got your ass out of the house.

DATING FOR DINNER

Many people date for a dollar. (I'm not referring to hookers, who if they are dating for a dollar are way more hard up than the gals actually dating for dinner.)

When you date for dinner (this means that you have mutually agreed to go to have a meal with this person you are considering spending the rest of your life with, or at least the next hour to hour and a half) you should be open-minded and optimistic. (Yes, sometimes this takes mediation, working out and/or a hit of pot). You probably will want to have drink(s) on the date, depending on the size of your date's gut; (compared to his photo) height (which did or did not match how he described himself) and long range goal plans (which may or may not include telling you about all his horrible ex's and what he plans to do in the future to get even).

Dating for dinner can be jolly good fun, if you've had enough to drink and/or your date actually turns out to be someone that you would even go on a second date. If this is the case, you should have very little regret about accepting a dinner date vs. a drink (which you can worm your way out of pretty easily).

Worming your way out of your dinner date once you're already on it...

1. Excuse yourself-don't return.
2. See him, text from street that you aren't able to make it.
3. Accident/sickness/death.
4. After a drink, apologize and make up some horrible story about probation, abortion, having to head straight to *AA*.

No, none of these are nice/reasonable/respectful, but will get you out of there quickly.

Dating for dinner only becomes tedious/horrendous/depressing/miserable-when you actually get a good look at the person; suddenly see them in a 'different light' or 'was three sheets to the wind when you hooked up the night/week/month before. Now, you find yourself stuck all the way through eating hell. The good news is that you can practice your etiquette, which is never lost on any good meal-and can benefit you, in the future, when you marry into royalty.

ALL YOU NEED IS ONE. FOR EVERY SEASON

It seems almost impossible to find just one person who will fit everything you're looking for, for the rest of your life. And if you knew exactly how long the rest of your life is going to be, it would be a heck of a lot easier to know what it is you're looking for. Otherwise, we change. Yes, it's natural. Just like wanting to wear something different for lunch and changing for dinner. Just like when it's a bit chilly outside and throwing on a sweater.

People change.

They change their minds.

They change their eating habits.

They change careers.

They change their underwear. (Hopefully.)

What you were in your 20's isn't essentially the same person you become in your 30's. Who you grow (painfully) into your 30's evolves into that (hypothetically) amazing person in your 40's. (Or not.) It doesn't matter really, because grow or not, you do age; and as you age, you sometimes change-Your mind. You change your ethics. You change your habits. Unfortunately, no matter how hard you may try, you usually cannot change your character flaws-

But you can learn how to hide them. Going after one person for every need in your life is Ludicrous. (No, not Ludacris the rapper, Ludicrous the adjective.) Ideally, the perfect situation would revolve around choosing a mate-For the season. This way, you can enjoy one particular type of person during one particular type of season. That person would ideally enjoy the same things you enjoy at that particular time of year.

They also would fit your needs as you're going through that season and match energy, state of mind, in-flux of thought. As the seasons change, so does your partner. This does not work the same as with pets. We do not need to change our pets every season, because unlike humans, pets DO fulfill every need at any given time of year. Although, in the dead of winter no one likes to walk their pet(s) but because they love their pet, they do it (or hire a dog walker to do it for them). It doesn't matter, the pet(s) still loves the owner no matter if they pick up after them or not. Unlike human beings who generally yell and pick on each other when either one does anything remotely wrong. This is why it's best to change as the seasons change. You can certainly rotate and keep the same partner(s) year after year.

I'm not implying that every year you pick four

different people for the four seasons (I mean you can if you want to), but the whole point is to have options. And when you have options, you aren't desperate.

And when you're not desperate, you're more fun to be around. And when you're more fun to be around, you draw more people to you. And when you draw more people to you, you get to have more than four people. (If you can find the seasons.) This does become a problem in Los Angeles, where there generally are no seasons.

Even odder, no one settles down in Los Angeles, so perhaps because there are no distinct change of seasons, no one feels the need to pick – anyone – ever. There are the occasional couples I see flitting about in Los Angeles.

They throw dinner parties, attend school gatherings and go out with other couples. They occasionally come out to single places and stare and point at all the strange, plastic, single people at places they used to go when they were single. They have picked one mate, perhaps, because the weather never changes-they feel secure in knowing that some things do stay the same and thus their partner they've chosen will be good for the long haul. I suppose never seeing your partner in a parka/never shovel snow/doesn't understand the concept of chains for a vehicle- has its positives-this will be a new experience and you will eventually see your partner in a different light.

At some point, couples from Los Angeles must venture into the cold. (I'm not referring to the Valley in December). The couples that are already coupled up are not in this equation. This is for single people who are out there thinking they need to pick just one person. It's too much work. And sometimes, it's too hard to choose.

Life is a schmorgasboard. Life is a tapas menu. Life is extra cheese, lots of salsa, side of guacamole, extra sauce.

Why shouldn't dating be the same?

Limiting yourself to one person certainly puts a great deal of pressure on oneself. And when that one person doesn't live up to what you thought they would live up to? You do that thing called crying.

And you cry some more.

Then you beat yourself up.

Then you tell yourself what a loser you are. Then you get pissed. Then you try to get even. Then you cry some more.

It's really all a waste of time and energy, *and cute clothing.*

The truth is, you should just date. Just live. And learn not to care. Learn not to be attached to the outcome (unless they buy you something-take that with you). You should try not to hopelessly romanticize the situation unless you've already become betrothed. And even in 'betrothed-dome' you should be careful, because any complacency on either part? The other person is running for the hills. Unless of course you both become lazy, fat and happy, then by all means-enjoy your life. Finding a mate for all seasons at least allows you to open your mind to what you think you want, even if you don't find it in one human being. It also opens you to a new way of thinking. You can't make yourself like someone, but you can certainly make yourself get good at being social and learn the art of dating. (So that you can learn about yourself) see what you like and give yourself the opportunity to not limit yourself. Okay, okay, so you might end up with 1, not 4.

On the other hand, you whittled it down from four to one; so at least you chose whom you wanted without desperately trying to land someone.

DATING SOMEONE FOR THEIR SOCIAL CIRCLE/FRIENDS

Dating someone because of the people they know is just downright...

Awesome.

The fact that you are smart enough to pick your circle to engage in –Learning about a particular species of humans that you normally would not be able to infiltrate is not only brilliant, but also calculating. This may work for a while, until you are found out to be a fake who's not really into there friend-the person you supposedly are supposed to be into. If you are well liked by the group, you may be in trouble if you were only using the person, because at this point-You now have an entirely new group of friends that may suddenly hate you, or hate the person you were dating, if you're cunning enough to turn that person into the bad guy/gal. This wasn't really your intention. You really just liked that group of people and when you were around the person you were dating, with their friends, you loved him/her. It's just that alone thing and that sex thing that got in the way. Sure, they're terrific around other people, the life of the party, cool to be around, interesting to have a conversation with-even the hand holding is nice.

But when it comes to the 'my place or yours' part, you realize that 'Oh, I have to now be alone with him/her' and inviting everyone over every night becomes tedious-

And redundant to your significant other, who may have a moment (or several) of asking, "Are you just dating me for my friends?" in which case you can either lie (absolutely not) or tell the truth (In which case you will no longer have that group of friends). It's not that the person is bad, you just aren't into them the way you should be and you know it. You're basically using him for his/her social connections. The only ending that can work in this situation is when they dump you because you 'just don't fit in' or you fall for another person in that group and basically push the original person out of that group.

Don't feel so bad. That person depended way too much on their social circle, anyway, and needed to get out in life and experiment. Don't you feel better? You did him/her such a favor.

And stole all his/her friends.

Way to go.

DATING WHEN YOU'RE YOUNGER FOR SEXUAL ATTRACTION

This isn't really called dating, it's called 'hooking up' and it's the same thing you do when you're older, just hopefully not through text, but probably so. If you do happen to go on a date that advances past a text that reads, "what up?"

Which eventually (17 minutes later) leads to a knock on your door, you may run out to a fast food or cheapie restaurant, inevitably leading you right back into -that bed you've been sharing for most of the dating relationship. It's okay, you really have nothing else in common with your significant other, other than great sex, so to see them eat a burrito-   And run to the bathroom, isn't going to be an experience your interested in, anyway. Keep it simple, keep it moving, keep on texting. You're young, hot and hopefully not pregnant in the near future.

DATING WHEN YOU'RE OLDER, TRYING TO EXPAND YOUR SHALLOW DESIRES

This is tough. Understanding that older people need to have open minds –a deeper understanding of what they supposedly really need/want/desire in their life, looking past looks, finding deeper meaning through –(that thing called life) experience, shared interest, morals, boundaries and ethics-Really can take the wind out of your sales.

When one…

(Not me. This absolutely does not apply here) leaps into that dating pool past a certain age, at some point. They possibly take a deeper look into themselves to see 'what the hell they're doing wrong'. This may or may not work. If it works and you do manage to crack open some huge jackpot of spiritual awakening, you may actually meet someone and marry from Kabbalah class.

On the other hand, you may actually find yourself going on several dates with several different (and by different, I mean people you 'wouldn't in a million years find yourself even looking at, let alone going out with) but this is what happens. You tell yourself that 'I've got to be more open-minded' which led you to date a paleontologist in the first place.

Never mind, you have absolutely no idea what a paleontologist is. Or, what they do, but you find yourself not at all intrigued, even though you knew you wouldn't be, even though you told yourself 'I should try to be intrigued'. What you may find by expanding your horizons on the dating front, is that you are still that same shallow, like minded, 'I like who I like' person that you've always been.

Which is good, because at least you know who you are. Which happens to be…still on your own.

OPENING YOUR HEART AND MIND TO OTHER POSSIBILITIES

Not sure what I mean by this, but pretty sure it does not include Bestiality. Perhaps there are other 'things' to fall in love with/date/feel passionate about, besides the opposite/same sex. Perhaps dating yourself may be a good choice. Would you date you? If not, you may want to open your ideas on what turns you on in life (besides reality TV) and sharpen your mind, so that you will attract and desire other things than simply meeting someone who probably won't fulfill all your desires anyway and probably will take up more room in your closet.

BLOWING OFF THE GOOD GUYS/NICE GALS

If you're friends/family/Podiatrist have ever asked you if you're ever going to like a nice, normal guy who treats you well, then you probably are guilty of doing this. It's okay; half of the population of the world does this everyone thinks they can do better once they've got someone.

(Unless you're super needy, in which case, having anyone is terrific and you will hold on for dear life, no matter what.) When you're younger, blowing off someone who's not a challenge (I.E. telling you you're the one on the first date. Unless, of course, you are the one, which only works if you actually are, and become the one) should be avoided at all costs.

On the other hand, if you're dating a really nice person and yet they don't turn you on (too pale/too dark, wrong hair color, eye color, too politically incorrect, too much of a pushover) you may actually have real reasons to move on to the next person. On the other hand, just because you dated a hot, dark Latin lover before-And now you're dating some pale, Irish Caucasian, does not automatically give you license to 'kick them to the curb'. Give yourself some time. They may actually grow on you. Once you actually let those sweaty, hot fantasies go of your ex-you may actually find that pale, Irish, Caucasian now does it for you, just like the next one that's falling under your radar of 5'8" to 6 feet, but sexy.

Being open minded to a different type, even one that treats you like a princess when you really don't want to be catered to, can be a learned characteristic.

This may turn your way of thinking into, 'Wow, nice guys/gals are great'. Finding someone nurturing, loving, caring and trusting can be a lovely thing shared by two people; unless of course, you just want who you want, at all costs, and gotta make 'em mine regardless of how they treat you. Learning to like a nice person should be a positive.

Liking someone that actually likes you in the same capacity that you like them is what we did in fourth grade. If you can remember back that far, you probably will remember a great love affair, lots of mushy cards and tons of gifts, like Love's Baby Soft perfume, roller skating and funnel cakes.

When you were in love at that age and he/she was so nice, kind, generous and honest-you loved it. Channeling that inner 4th grader is probably the best thing you can do for yourself if you want to get out of your letting the good ones go mentality.

(That, and check that ego of yours! You look half as good as you did at 30 and your hands have way more lines on them.)

TAKE A LOOK IN THE MIRROR

I'm sure you've been looking at yourself all day-You know your hot. Several experts say that we are so narcissistic that all we really want is someone who looks exactly like us. That is, if we like the way we look. Some couples look alike. Some couples look like they actually came from the same family (don't ask if you don't want to know the truth). There seems to be something to being attracted to similar looks, it creates a familiarity-Even having a similar nose can make you feel more comfortable. Just be sure that your nose and his nose are the real noses they were born with, unless you've both had nose jobs and therefore, you'll need to pull out pictures from before to make sure you really do look alike. Plastic Surgery can change everything so who really knows if you really do look alike or not?

Maybe you've both got the same plastic surgeon and you've been manipulated into liking each other because you think you look alike.

Deep, huh?

Well, actually it's really superficial and shallow to base everything on looks, anyway; especially when most of us will lose them at some point in our lives. Oh, what do you care, you'll just buy new looks.

IGNORING OBVIOUS RED FLAGS

Sometimes you may get hard up/desperate/horny/bored/intrigued and end up dating below your normal set up standards, which includes, but not limited by…

1.   Several marriages that led to divorces when you said you would never date someone who's had more than one.
2.   Felonies, misdemeanors and tax liens.
3.   Triplets under the age of 3.
4.   Widowed at 35. (Unless they show cause of death so that you know it wasn't murder.)
5.   A sob story on the first date that can include one spouse having full custody of the kid(s)/pet(s)/possession(s).
6.   Going through a transition that you find out has been on-going for the past five years and continues to do so with no way out.
7.   Bragging about one's past when one's future looks bleak to haggard.
8.   Hearing any story that includes gunshot wounds, beatings, restraining orders and/or -Recurring rehabilitation visits (all while drinking a shot).
9.   Telling you they need bus/cab/a ride home because their car just broke down on the way to the date.
10. Wanting/needing/begging any prescription medication from you, even before asking if you take any of the prescribed medication.

TRANSITION DATING, WIDOW, DIVORCE, SEPARATED, CHEATING, DATING MANY, DATING ONE, TAKING A BREAK FROM

Transitional dating is what happens when you aren't really sure what you're looking for (or doing in your life, for that matter) which could be most of your dating life. Or, the opposite happens. You think you always know what you're looking for-sometimes you're able to find it, other times you just keep on searching until you do.

There comes a time in your life where you are between some sort of defining moment, and find yourself 'stuck' and unsure of what you're looking for and/or what kind of person to date.

This is a great time in your life and if you can get over that small thing you're experiencing called depression/confusion/non-committal- taking advantage of this preciously screwed-up time is a perfect excuse for you to date whomever and whatever you want.

In fact, the crazier your choices, the more leniency your friends will give you. They will chalk every decision you've made to, "He/She's just going through a hard time and trying to discover what they want." Take all the time you want, because once they realize you've re-found sanity, you will no longer have a leg to stand on.

Dating in transition can be pure bliss. You don't have to come up with any excuses as to why you've suddenly decided to not shave your armpit hair, why you've decided to sleep with several guys/gals at once, or even switch teams. You're simply 'trying things out' and even though you aren't 22 anymore, you have been given a 'get out of jail free' card because of the difficult time you've recently been through. This transition thing comes about because you've finally broken up with what's his name/changing a pattern of thinking/re-evaluating your life/Having a crisis of some sort (made up *or* real) not sure what to do next.

Note to self...that difficult time you've been through technically has a shelf life of maybe 6 months, and that's even pushing it. So this seven-year 'transition-dating thing' is getting old and many of your friends and family aren't falling for it anymore.

WIDOWED MEN

Ah, the merry widow! Although 90% of women file for divorce from men, when it comes to dying, men seem to bounce right back. They're the true needy ones. While a woman may mourn for days/months/years/a lifetime, the man wastes no time on that sort of nonsense.

The quicker he can get into a relationship, the better.

That being said, dying is the way to go if you truly want respect from your spouse. (Unless, they've had a hand in your demise, ala the black widow.)

It's probably best to die when you're in a particularly great place in your marriage. This way, you will have left while on a pedestal, which is great because you probably didn't get that much respect while you were alive. The best part of dying is that your husband (although married/in love/procreating with another) secretly (or, not so) harbors fantasies about you, your life that never will be, and a future without you that the new wife/lover/whore-will never be able to fill. The new filler probably won't mind because she's off spending your life insurance policy that you never thought would need to be cashed.

If she's only in it for the moolah, chances are once a season of clothing has passed (as well as the bank account) she will be off and onto someone else from the Country Club/Yacht Club/Parcheesi tournament. Your husband just needs coddling and as long as there is another woman there to show off to his friends/colleagues/enemies, he's a happy camper.

When the husband dies, the woman tends to mourn much longer. She can go on forever crying over the loss of the husband…whom she berated/picked on/talked about behind his back and yet suddenly all you have to do is, well, die and she's suddenly decided you were her hero.

Dying is good for marriage. More people should try it. Be forewarned, once you try it, you ain't comin' back and the grass isn't always greener.

DATING TIPS TO MAKE YOU FEEL BETTER...

I said better, not "floating on cloud nine because 'I'm so amazing" better.

QUIT BLAMING YOURSELF FOR ALL THE SCREWED UP PEOPLE OUT THERE.
They became that way all on their own.
MAKE SMARTER DECISIONS ABOUT THE LUNATICS YOU LET INTO YOUR LIFE (or quit complaining about dating them).
BEING OPEN MINDED DOES NOT MEAN LOWERING YOUR STANDARDS (unless you want to try S and M).
JUST BECAUSE YOUR PARENTS MADE BAD CHOICES DOESN"T MEAN YOU HAVE TO (but you can blame it on that, if you want to).
NEWSFLASH - YOU'RE SINGLE - NOT NECESSARILY BECAUSE YOU'RE A LOSER (don't get so excited, you actually may be a loser for other reasons).
EVERYONE LIKES A CHALLENGE (I.E. everyone likes to feel like they're getting someone worthy of getting). Even Monkey's don't like the monkey that like them; preferring to chase the ones that ignore them. Blame the monkeys!
EVERYONE LIKES TO FEEL NEEDED (I.E. Some more than others.) (I.E. (2) Some way more than others).
EVERYONE LIKES TO FEEL LIKE THEY'VE BEEN SAVED (no, not from the back of your truck with that sticker).
PICKING WRONG PEOPLE DOESN'T REQUIRE ONE TO LABEL YOU WITH INTIMACY ISSUES (but you may have them, regardless).

SOME PROBLEMS WITH DATING

(1) You have to go out with people you have no interest in riding on a subway with.
At least on a subway, you can get off on the next stop.
Once you've ordered a drink, you're stuck with them.
Learn to guzzle quickly.
(2) You have to shower (unless you don't mind how you smell).
(3) Kissing several frogs has lost all its meaning-
(4) You are no longer looking for the one, but have decided on several different ones.
(5) Finding something wrong with every potential date happens before you go on the date as opposed to during the date (this saves time and energy).

Meeting guys at night when you're younger

When they say you don't meet anyone worthy 'after midnight' they aren't talking about 22 year-olds who are just getting started with their evening.   In fact, when you're 22, it really doesn't matter what time you meet someone. Midnight is perfect, because at 22, the likelihood of your attention span 'spanning' longer than a week or so doesn't really exist. Why? There's always another one around the corner; especially after midnight.

How can you go wrong? Why is it necessary to be in your right mind when being with someone you like? I mean, when was the last time you were in your right mind, anyway? That's only for grown-ups and you've got plenty of time to just have fun! A bit buzzed, feeling happy, everyone looks hot. When you meet someone that late at night, you've already moved beyond your list of must-haves stage to, 'who's left now?' to "I'm so drunk it doesn't even matter." On the other hand, it was so easy to have a relationship when you were that age. Things just seemed to click, and the next thing you know, you were in a relationship.

Meeting guys during the day, when you're older

As you age, the thought of meeting someone after a certain time becomes not necessarily less exciting, you just may not have an interest in staying out that late. So, you start to realize anyone you want, anyway, is probably asleep around the same time you are- and he or she can't stay awake for any late night hook-up, either. The thought that you are already in your business 'attire' and can hook a fish at the same time (or several) becomes the obvious thing to do. No more having to get all decked out at night just to hopefully meet someone, you can actually put more effort into your daytime life (when you used to think daytime was just for business) you now realize all those people actually going to and from work-are dateable. Wow, this opens up an entirely new dating field and one not fueled by Vodka. (Unless, of course, you drink during the day.)

Happy Hour

Happy hour is the grown-up's way to date.

At some point past 30 and before 90, you find happy hour. The presentable place to drink, drink some more, flirt and act like you are only there to un-wind from your extremely stressed out day. Drink # 2…while you're relaxing, you're really spending your time scouring the bar for potential dates. While single people populate happy hour all across the country, married people also love happy hour. It gives them a chance to see what they're missing. They either go home happy, realizing they are missing nothing, or quickly put the wedding ring into their pocket as they try to pick you up.

You actually don't know if you should get excited by happy hour, or not. Many people are desperate at happy hour. They only give the illusion that they're really there to drink. And yes, some are really there to drink. In which case, you should probably stay away from happy hour because you look pretty stupid drinking your soda water, and you may be mistaken for a hooker.

Come to think of it, why are you wasting your time at happy hour?

Get home! Your dog needs a walk!

The Gym

The gym is a great way to meet someone, as long as it's not in the middle of the day. If you want to know what someone does for a living, go to the gym at 1 pm during the week. When you see them, be sure to follow them to their car. If the car is older than your Mother, run fast. (Unless you're into vintage.) This has nothing to do with being materialistic and more to do with the fact that not only does your potential crush not have any ambition to work, but he's perfectly content where he/she is in their life and unless you're lazy too, this won't work. By the way, what are you doing at the gym at 1 in the afternoon? The best way to meet someone at the gym is early, way early-like 6 A.M, because these are the business people and as they say, the early bird catches the worm.

This is great for everyone except me.

(I'm still 6 dreams in at that hour.)

WALKING

Walking anywhere is great. Except Los Angeles-Where people don't walk. In fact, if you are caught walking in Los Angeles, you might just get some odd stares. In New York City, London, Paris, Chicago, Boston, China, it's quite natural to walk everywhere and you're not alone in this. There are hundreds, thousands; millions of people all doing the same thing. Moving about their lives, just living, doing their thing. Which is a great way to meet someone, because they're not trying. Walking down the street and seeing someone you like is kind of like shopping. Some days you just window shop, other days you go into the store; same way with meeting a potential stranger (kind of like dating online, only you get to see if they're pigeon-toed). If you get really desperate, and have lots of money, fly to any big metropolis and…walk. You're sure to meet someone!

WHERE YOU LIVE VS. HOW YOU DATE

"There's no one to date!"

Since we all say this wherever we live, we assume there is no one decent to date. There are truths that larger cities give you more options, thus making it more difficult to make a decision, and living in a smaller town/city (although less options) may make you, "settle down and pick 1". If you're single and want to be in a relationship and/or dating-you probably need to be less picky, and realize that unless you pick from the available choices you have (or wait until someone turns legal) you may find yourself masturbating to magazines for the rest of your life.

Calm down! Don't cash in those frequent flyer miles and move to Plano, Texas. (I just got off the phone with my friend. She said there's no one there to date, either.)

IF I DON'T ASK, I DON'T WANT YOUR ADVICE

Everyone thinks they know the reason why 'You're single' and they're not afraid to tell you. Just head to dinner with a group of friends (that are all in a relationship). They are all experts on relationships, what makes a relationship work, what you're doing wrong and will point out specific reasons why you are not with 'the love of your life'. Never mind, they, themselves are unhappily with the 'not love of their life'. Of course there are exceptions, the couples that really are in love.

And if you ask them what makes the relationship work? You will usually get a pretty simple answer. "We just clicked".

In fact, those happy couples usually don't tell you what you're doing wrong, but encourage you that "the right person is out there, you just have to keep looking" or, "You're amazing there's a lot of weird people out there" and "I don't know how you do it, if I was single, I don't think I could handle it". Which is nice, because, well that's why they're your friends.

It's the other 90% that think they have it perfectly figured out as to the reason(s) you are a mutant gene in the dating pool of life. In fact, it probably has no real bearing at all on why you are actually single. No matter what they will instill in you, their ideas on exactly what the problem is. All the while complaining about their own love life.

OTHER BAD ADVICE...

(1). Getting advice from a 65 year-old who still texts for dates. (2). A friend who's cheated on their significant other for the past five years 'on and off' and/or the 'run me over like a Mac-truck because I can't stick up for myself against my pushy, overbearing wife, aren't the people you want to be listening to. Regardless of whether the happily married couples are being honest or not, they are at least on your side. Walking away from a dinner where everyone gangs up on you thinking they have the answer for your single life is only going to make you feel worse. Being lied to will remind you of dating life in the first place, so it's more natural and comfortable. Asking advice from someone who really does know what they're talking about makes sense. You're asking them.

Asking someone's advice usually means that you truly are interested in whatever knowledge they may happen to know. You value their opinion.

You respect their advice. You acknowledge that they actually may know more than you or may have a different and yet appealing way to have you go about trying something different in the dating world. Getting advice from someone you didn't ask and don't have any respect for in the first place, doesn't make any sense. Do they know that you secretly think they suck as a human being?

Have horrible taste in there own spouse? Do they not realize that you think their husbands' job 'killing roaches' (although not beneath you) isn't the ideal person to spew rhetoric about compatibility, morals, romance and ethics?

Do they lack the understanding, that perhaps, when you got married 10/20/40/100 years earlier...

Things were different? You probably got married because your parents told you to. You had to dig to find things to like about that person you're still sharing a dinner table with, night after night.

Nowadays with dating, one might have to dig a little deeper than 'we shared Geometry' or 'he was my neighbor'. Besides, there are so many more serial murderers these days; you could easily have grown-up down the street from one. On the other hand, you may still be madly in love with your significant other-just because, you grew-up together.

Good for you.

And, quit rubbing it in our face, we've already called up/texted/stalked everyone from the old neighborhood and there's no one left. Or at least, returning our calls.

Things Chicks/Guys Do to Screw Up A Good Thing

Freak out. You should at least wait until after sex and preferably five months into dating (after you've lured him in with your awesome sexual techniques) 3 months is so obvious and so yesterday.

Neediness - Acting/being/pretending/actually being needy. Only works if the guy gets turned on fixing the damsel in distress. (Acting like a damsel in distress is fine if you really are independent and testing someone.) Although, if you actually are needy and it's worked for you, I wouldn't change a thing.

Fake pregnancy... that becomes real pregnancy. Try to do this only with someone wealthy (unless, you have your own money). Taking sperm from someone who cannot support the baby is a bad idea. (Unless you're using them for sex and/or sperm.)

Pay or Play- making it obvious that you are only going to sleep with someone for lots of gifts, cash and trips. I take it back. This is a wonderful Idea.

Sleeping with someone too soon (for free) is the bad idea.

TYPES OF DATERS
THE SERIAL MONOGAMIST DATER

The serial monogamist dater goes from person to person to person with no break in-between. You date for a long period of time, getting very seriously involved very quickly spend all your time, energy and emotions on that person and yet, for whatever reason, you don't end up married to him/her.

He either dumps you or you dump him. The serial monogamist easily suffers fools and bounces back quite quickly. Just as easily as he/she "fell in love" she falls right back out and moves right on to the next Tom, Dick, Harry or possibly Sally.

The serial monogamist (God love her) loves love. Essentially, you could just spend the rest of your life doing this dating thing.

Hey, there's always a new guy.

Who invented marriage, anyway? Oh yeah, the love part. Well, when you're a serial monogamist dater, you learn to love that person and only that person you're dating at the time; kind of like marriage, only shorter.

DUMPER vs. DUMPEE

Remember in pre-school when you had your first crush? And he chose a prettier/funnier/smarter/dumber girl than you? (Yes, it may be because you spilled orange juice all over his brand new velour shirt on picture day, but maybe not.)

If you're the dumpee, you may feel sad/mad/betrayed/rejected/belittled/unwanted, even left out (i'm sure I left out a few emotions, feel free to add your own). And, no matter how many times it happens to you, it still feels impossible to understand. Let's take a moment here.

Go ahead. Cry.

Shout.

Scream.

Bang your head against the wall.

Feel better?

Now, get over it. Move on!

You're going to have to face the fact that relationships end. This is not the time to mourn. This is the time to start planning your next victim.

The biggest problem with having to start over is that you feel some need to re-evaluate (again) every stupid past relationship(s), the things you did wrong-why you picked so and so, and so on. This is not only a waste of time, but re-hashes old baggage you really didn't need to bring up, ever again. Bury it along with that diary from junior year.

If you're the dumper (just so you know) you're ruining someone's life. That's okay they'll get over it and move on. Unfortunately, when you're the dumper, you figure your better half is right around the corner. Dumpers sometimes spend a great deal of the after-dump regretting their choice. You may actually try to get that person back. Chances are, by the time you decide to go after them to get them back. They've moved on...to someone else.

Don't worry about it. Go to the gym. Go to some parties (sex parties if you can find them). You actually may be able to get back with the person you dumped for some great "break-up" sex (which is actually better than you remember-until they open their mouth and you remember why you dumped the person in the first place).

THE FLITTER

The Flitter is the girl who dates around. She flits from place to place, room to room and guy to guy. She'll go on eight dates a week, sometimes three in a day. She is constantly being set up, yet she can't remember the last time she had a relationship or a conversation with someone that didn't include-

"So, what do you do for a living?"

(Unless you live in Los Angeles where it's the first question out of everyone's mouth.) The last time a man got *this* close to her, he was leaning over her with a dental tool, cleaning her teeth and wearing rubber gloves. The Flitter rarely gets involved with anybody on a deep level, but is always seen on a date. The Flitter is a great first date, she just sucks at anything longer.

Even if she is asked out on a second date, she'll probably decline because she has nothing deeper to share. A Flitter is all show and she'd have a nervous breakdown trying to come up with something resembling witty repartee, intellectual stimulation and a knowledge of current events, which is usually standard on a second date (or sex, which she isn't any good at either). The Flitter is nice, upbeat and doesn't hurt children (or animals) but, she's boring and she knows it. The Flitter is only good at one thing: flitting from guy to guy and date to date. (She's secretly still in love with her 11th grade anthropology teacher.)

THE BORE

The Bore rarely, if ever, dates. When she does, she bores her date to death. Keeping a façade is what dating is all about, and the Bore is way too pragmatic to fake anything for anyone. The Bore has no idea how to play games and in fact, you'll know the Bore by his/her response to dating; "I don't play games."

Dating *is* a game and understanding the rules of dating are something the bore has no time for.

You have to play coy, be manipulative, lie and cheat (and sometimes you have to play strip poker). The Bore will not fall weak at the knees for her date, will insist on going Dutch, open her own doors and demand to meet you at the restaurant instead of being picked up.

This is not because the Bore is nervous.

The Bore doesn't know what to say to you in the car. Blurting out quotes from Descartes just may make you turn around and take her home.

The two or three things they do come up with to talk about include; economic status, love statistics or latest health issues. Most likely, during the course of dinner, she will have worn the topics out, so getting in the car with you means she will only repeat the same stories. The Bore will tell you intimate details of her life without you asking. She will immediately break every rule and talk about her ex-boyfriend in prison, her erratic weight gain and the history of herpes. Although she'd probably be willing to sleep with you, at this point, you'll be thrilled you brought your own car. The Bore may not understand what she did wrong, which ensures her cynical behavior for the rest of her life. Bores think they're a lot of fun. Yeah, so are PMS and bed bugs.

I CAN'T LEAVE MY APARTMENT

The "I Can't Leave My Apartment" girl refuses to leave her apartment, which can pose a problem when one wants to…leave the apartment. She's been single for so long that the thought of venturing out sounds like a wild, crazy party she's too old to go to. She claims illness, death of a pet, loss of hair, nail problems or "I'm in the middle of a good book,"-And you cannot convince her to go anywhere. If it's a Friday, she'll claim she had a horrid week at work. If it's a Saturday, her manicurist "put her through the ringer.

"The I Can't Leave My Apartment may "peruse" the online dating sites and she may even have a few on line flirtations going on, but it will never lead to anything.

Everytime someone mentions meeting up, she clams up and stops the on-line flirtation.

The I Can't Leave My Apartment Girl always has an excuse why she can't…

Meet-up/go-out/be set-up/go to a party/live a life outside of her apartment/abode/house/bathtub.

Don't take it personally. She hasn't been fun since 7th grade. She just wants to sit in front of the TV and watch life. She, of course, thinks the right person will be knocking on her door any day now. She's still a hopeless romantic, but to do any work to try to get a man? Forget it. That would be pushy. I Can't Leave My Apartment girls aren't pushy. They're agoraphobic and usually end up sleeping with the pizza-delivery guy.

I KNOW HE'S THE ONE

Every guy she's been involved with is the one. This started out innocently enough (when she was twelve). Every boyfriend since then has been the guy. She has no idea what she's looking for, but luckily for her, all of them have IT.

"Have you gone on a second date?" you will ask. She'll probably say, "It doesn't matter". She's already picking out china patterns and planning weekend getaways. Just be her friend and go along with it. She has a short attention span and sometimes it's better to be able to move on quickly and really believe your own BS. (She also has a lot of leftovers, which may be just perfect for you-just fish in her waters for a while and see how you do).

I ONLY WANT TO DATE YOU IF EVERYONE ELSE WANTS TO

They have to be the center of attention-All the time. It's like they were the prom queen/king in college (10 years later) they're still holding court. It's all about them and if it isn't about them, they'll do something to ensure that your attention does land on them.

Every time you go out with your friend, they automatically make you feel like you're on an episode of the bachelor.

Even worse, you didn't even try out for the stupid show, nor do you watch it. You had a long day at work; you just want to hang with your friend. Then you see a cute guy. God forbid you tell your friend you think he's hot/cute/fun/schtupable, even if she didn't notice him before, she' noticed him now and regardless of whether she really wanted him or not-your competition has begun. It's all about what she wants/has to have-even for the moment. Don't worry about confronting her, she'll deny everything with a bat of an over-extended eyelash, and go all victim on you, "Me?

I would never do that to you" I was only trying to help you". Really? Did I look like I needed help? I only want to date you girl really just likes everyone looking at her/talking about her/to her/with her and anything else, just won't do. When someone does pay attention to anyone else but her, she will find a way to make it about her, anyway.

Good or bad, she'll cry/pout/yell/whine/stomp her feet until attention is on her no matter what. Then she'll talk badly about the guy to make you feel like he's suddenly not worth having. Either way, if she wants him, just step out of the way. Chances are she's younger, flirtier and has more energy and patience than you. You know you could have him if you really wanted him, but really-If she's that intent on getting him-let her. You can always go after him behind her back after they've started dating and he realizes she's a little nuts.

I'LL MEET YOU THERE

She's mysterious and independent.

She will never let you come to her apartment/house/condo/car. Guys love her because they think she's a challenge.

The problem with the I'll Meet You There girl is that she doesn't let anyone into her head, let alone where she lives. She's pretty much a closed book and asks lots of questions, yet anytime someone asks her anything it gets deflected back to the guy, which a guy should love because it's all about him. He/She is dating you for more than your blank expressions, one-liners that go nowhere and mysterious places that you came from/going to.

He/She's most likely hiding some hideous secret-their apartment's a pigsty, or they still live at home with their parents.

Can I Have Your Sperm, Please?

The Can I have Your Sperm girl only wants to date you for one thing-your sperm. Your ivy-league education and/or square jaw/chin-dimple is highly impressive, combined with that thing called-

Youth, stamina and good genes produce a healthy baby. When a woman decides that dating for a baby daddy/sperm donation is cheaper than actually going to a sperm bank. She will scope out her prey so that he can impregnate her with a healthy embryo. Usually women that do this have money and don't need a guy to financially bankroll them, or the baby. If all goes well, they may even want you for baby #2. The only unforeseen problem is 16 years from now, when you get a knock on your door from a few kids looking for a hand out (and probably wanting to move in with you-its about the time they hate their current parent(s).

I HAVE TO GO, MY CAT IS DEAD

This girl will go on the date, but come up with an excuse to leave early. Not believing any guy is really right for her, she'll concoct some outrageous story so he will have to take her home or end the date pronto. She's still comparing every date to her old football player boyfriend from high school. She probably will never get married.

The I Have to Go, My Cat is Dead girl ends relationships and dates for no reason except that none are good enough for her. When you ask about an ex, you may get an answer such as, "I didn't like the socks he wore with his tennis shoes." She's not kidding. She really didn't like his socks. To her, this was reason enough to break up with him. The I Have to Go, My Cat is Dead girl is a perfectionist. She's looking for perfection. Her football player high school sweetheart was perfect. Until he got another girl pregnant and was forced into marrying her; Thus making the I have to go my cat is dead girl send out cancellation notices 3 weeks before the upcoming wedding. He still calls her every weekend, drunk and reminiscing about the good ole days. She's still hanging onto the thought of him, so no one else will do.

I'M SPREADING MYSELF TOO THIN GIRL

She has a lot of balls in the air. His name is Steve, Mike, Randy, Nicola, Pete, and probably another Steve. Some days she'll do a lunch and dinner and even squeeze in a coffee date. The problem with 'I'm Spreading Myself Too Thin Girl' is that, she is. Because they're all appetizing in their own way, she can't choose just one, so for a while, she juggles them. Then, one ball drops and he's gone. Then another. For whatever reason, they're in-they're out. She moves on. When you ask "I'm Spreading Myself Too Thin" girl about "Mike" she may say "Mike, who?" or "Oh, Mike, I'm not into him anymore" or "Mike I or 2?" She's serious. You might respond, "But you were just dating him, Tuesday?"

Please don't try to dig deeper. If she's moved on, so should you.

I'll Put All My Eggs In One Basket GIRL

Sure, why not? When you buy eggs at the grocery store, you certainly don't take the eggs out and put them in separate cartons, do you? She's a bit of a romantic.

She's actually still in love with her boyfriend from kindergarten. (Okay, I got over Paul Finkelstein last summer.)

He was over me the day of 'picture day' – When I sloppily spilled fruit punch all over his velour shirt. (Yes, that was me I was referring to earlier.)

The I'll put my eggs in one basket girl never falls in love until she is 'absolutely 100% sure that the old love/crush/unrequited somebody really does not want her. This includes him/her marrying another–Being carted off to witness protection and/or a certified letter telling you to stay away. He/she is such a romantic, that all they remember are the wonderful times you shared and she cannot fathom being with anyone else-

Ever.

Really.

She is alone because she cannot find anyone who fits everything she is looking for…Now/currently/this reality/today-If she could combine every quality from every one of her ex's, she would have the perfect guy that she would most definitely stay faithful to for the rest of her life, or until he's hit by a truck. Even then, she'll mourn his loss for 10 years before finally moving on-with her ex-boyfriend from 4th grade.

Does This Guy Make Me Look Fat?

She's always about appearances. Anyone she dates; she's all about what he does, what he can get her, where he can take her, what he can do for her.

And the problem?

None that I can see.

It's just everyone else may think she's a…

A.   Social Climber.

B.   Call Girl.

C.   A User.

D.   Quite Smart and followed the likes of many well known (and lesser well known women who snagged wealthy, powerful men).

You became one of these women after…

(1) You've been treated badly (More than once).

 By a guy less attractive/smart/funny/inspiring, who did nothing for you except break your heart.

(2) You watched other people do it and decided why not?

(3) You decided you weren't going to lower your life-style, so whomever you add to yours, better up the ante and allow you to enjoy the finer things in life.

(4) You are attractive/You know it/You use it to your advantage.

(5) You decided Love only got you nowhere fast and what's the point, anyway…

(6) You realize you better act fast now before your looks/talents/smarts/wits expire and all you have left is remember when…

FUN FOR THE MOMENT GUY

He's a hell of a lot of fun.

Really!

Right now…

For the moment.

Oops, it's gone. Wow, that was fast.

Well, it was fun while it lasted. There's really not a lot to say about fun for the moment guy because chances are you thought he was so freaking amazing and now, well, you're just embarrassed. What were you thinking? It's okay.

You're entitled. Guys do it all the time to chicks. Usually it's after sex, but sometimes we can't even stay around – that long.

HOT SEX GUY

Hot sex guy is great if he doesn't get in the way of your normal, everyday life. Even if he gets in the way of your normal, everyday life-He's pretty good. As long as you compartmentalize where this guy -Fits in and remember to not…

A.   Fall in love.

B.   Give him a key to your place. Chances are hot sex guy has a sex addiction, which is fine for great sex.

But once he has a key; you just might come home to naked bongos and candles everywhere. Hot sex guy has now turned into too much romance guy and overstepped his boundaries. As long as hot sex guy is just for hot sex and he knows his place, this little romp can fit very nicely into your life.

HE'LL BUY ME ANYTHING GUY

Damn, where do you meet one of these? I have several friends who have them, but that invisible leash they're being kept on would make my neck itch.

THE 'I CAN BUY MYSELF ANYTHING I WANT ANYTIME I WANT AND NOT HAVE TO SLEEP WITH HIM' THEORY...is much better if you can afford it. On the other hand, when a guy simply wants to shower you with gifts because of the amazing creature you are-simply for just spending time with you and wants to show you how much they like you.

There's certainly nothing wrong with that. Just no gift over $10,000 or you have to claim it on your taxes.

HE MAKES ME LOOK SMART GUY/How To Impress Your Friends/Boss/Mother

The fact that he goes/went to Duke, Northwestern, Brown, Dartmouth or KU (not the last one, just wanted to see if you were paying attention) can certainly impress everyone around you, even you. A nice degree followed by an amazing job, can be a turn on. Wanting to be around that person you are dating who is not only smart; but can impress everyone, is an added bonus. Theoretically, you should only date someone that you like. (I said theoretically.) Sometimes you have to push yourself to date someone because they are smarter, better, kinder, more intellectually stimulating than you. There's even a chance you actually do like this amazingly smart guy that impresses all your friends and if not, you can always use him to hook the one you really want because being seen with this catch will up your standing in the dating pool and possibly make you more desirable.

I CAN'T DECIDE GUY

I can't decide guy dates you, but drives you crazy. He cannot make a decision, about, anything. This includes you. I can't decide guy is great if you can't decide, either. In fact, most of the population cannot make a decision about anything anymore because there are far too many choices so you probably don't feel too alone in your confusion.

If you both can't decide, continuing to date is probably working out just fine. You may spend the next 50 years going back and forth, as the wishy-washy two-some. If you are trying to bag this guy, best to drug him, get him on a plane and force him to live in the wilderness. At least now you've made a decision for him and happy or not, he's stuck.

And he's yours.

BLIND DATES

Everyone thinks they have the perfect person for you. And there you go—Another night of makeup and clothing wasted on that financial guru that Sandy and Bob just had to set you up with...

Even though they never set up anyone. But, the minute they met Stanley at H and R Block and saw how funny/charming/smart/quirky he was-they just had to set you up with him. They just knew that you'd have a blast and most likely be inviting them to your wedding in six months. You've never hit a man before. Stanley was your first. Did it have to do with him touching your breasts that he called 'supple' through that clingy shirt you were wearing?

Either that, or it was blind date meltdown. Either way, you'll never listen (or talk to) Sandy and Bob again. This isn't to say that some blind dates don't turn out well. I'm sure there are thousands of happily betrothed blind couples married today, living in bliss.

Just don't let Sandy and Bob set you up…again.

SOME POSSIBLE WARNING SIGNS YOUR DATE IS GOING BADLY-

1.   He calls you 'Dude'. (Unless your name **is** Dude. Blame your parents, not your date.

2.   He asks you about your friend, even though he asked you out.

3.   He wants to know if you have a younger sister.

4.   He only wants to talk about when you were a cheerleader (15 years ago) and if you still happen to have the uniform.

5. He asks you what your mother looks like.

6. He goes to the bathroom and never comes back.

7. He makes you pay for valet parking, but says he'll pick it up next time. (Or, he'll cover the drinks).

8. He takes you straight home after dinner, even though opera tickets are in clear view on the dashboard.

9. You call to thank him for the date. He doesn't remember who you are.

10. He spends the entire date fawning all over you and everyone else.

EVENTS

Singles-events/political/social-fundraisers/Meditation groups/Yoga class/Cooking Class/Swapping Clubs- Supposedly finding what you're passionate about, leads to the person you're supposed to be with. Attending a set of classes that teach you something new that you've always wanted to learn (like macramé your mother a scarf for mother's day) will lead you to the man of your dreams.

One small problem-if you really did meet him in macramé class, I'm not so sure he's the man of your dreams (but he may be your brothers').

Meeting someone at an event is great if it's something that you're both really there to witness/learn/experience and/or participate.

If you're both pretending to learn how to make a Vegan quiche, meeting this person started out with false pretenses and chances are, you are both just hard up.

You were never even interested in learning how to make a Vegan quiche in the first place. What makes you think you're going to like that kind of guy? At least take up something you really want to learn how to do, even if you don't meet anyone. At least you've learned a new skill.

A PLACE WHERE YOU MAY WANT TO MEET SOMEONE, BUT YOUR JUDGMENT TELLS YOU IT SIMPLY ISN'T THE PLACE—LIKE A FUNERAL

Yes, I was flirting with the son-in-law of the deceased, may God have mercy on my soul.

Actually, I don't think dead Ed would have minded—he wanted to set me up with his stepson; he just died before he had the chance. Which brings up the question, "Is there a time and place that wouldn't be okay to meet the right man?" In a word? No. You're 30 something. Take it where you can get it.

SOME REASONS WHY A FUNERAL COULD WORK

1. You're wearing a great dress.

2. You can see him at his worst if he's related or close with the deceased.

3. You get to see how he interacts with large groups of people.

4. You get to see how he looks dressed up.

5. You get to see if he gives up his seat to the old lady breathing heavily with the walker.

SET-UPS/DOUBLE DATING/THE FIFTH WHEEL

Before you let your friends set you up, take a look at their significant other. Would you have gone out with them?

Remember, beauty is in the eye of the beholder. You just may not have the same taste as your beholder, so be careful what you behold to them. There's nothing worse than being set up with someone unattractive whom your friend finds attractive.

Unless they secretly think you're not that hot and thus this is all you can get, or should be able to get at this point-Because you're still single and can't afford to be picky.

You can still afford to be picky, even if you're old. (This may mean you will have to wait longer to find your significant other. If everyone is being picky, no one will ever settle down.)

They may be setting you up because he/she is secretly hot for the person (but they can't follow through because they're married) so they set you up. The person setting you up may insist on tagging along on the date. Fondling the third party under the table is a good indication there's something going on between them and you were only asked out as a cover. It's okay; this is where the hot bartender comes in handy.

I'D RATHER BE ALONE

You're screwed! Just pack it in. Give it up.

Refer to giving up/letting go chapter. I'd rather be alone girl is at her wits' end. It's not so much that she loves her independence; it's just that she'd rather not be with any of the men she's ever met. According to her, they all sucked; she'd rather be alone. And so, guess what? She is. Don't try to set her up-she's busy organizing her jewelry. Don't bother inviting her to parties, either. She's eating. Leave her alone. She'll come up with any and every excuse as to why she doesn't want to get back out there. She's too old/fat/needs Botox/too tired-She really just wants to be alone. Let her.

She'll come around when everyone becomes widowed. That's good. By then, she should be ready to date and will have her pick of many options.

PLACING THE AD

Yes, you realize that a lot of people meet this way-But do **you** have to? You've worn out all the normal ways to meet someone; bumping into him on the street, going to a

bar-
Drunk while singing Karaoke at Aunt Sally's stupid annual piñata party.

You had to resort to writing down all your likes and dislikes (that normally you reserve for yourself)

Along with your profession, religion and other personal details, including your age (minus 5 to 7 years) you could treat this dating thing like a business. Lucky you! Remember what your mother said. "Treat the man you marry like a business partner." How romantic is that! In truth, once you get to this point, you aren't so concerned with romance. You've flown way past romance, straight to e-mail me your credentials.

The weird thing about placing an ad, or using a dating service, is that it makes you feel like you're pathetic. (Nothing to be ashamed of.) Start telling yourself, "I'm not pathetic, this is a perfectly healthy way to meet someone. "Since I'm so busy, this helps me meet Mr. Right, and we've cut through all the garbage of finding out if we're compatible." Another approach–have a yenta or a matchmaker set you up or try to get set up into a fixed marriage. This way, you'll have no choice. You're stuck. You have to marry that person. Why be presented with a choice? Choices lead to confusion. And why be any more confused than you already are? And what are you going to do after you've dated everyone from the dating service or ad and still haven't met anyone? Go to Aunt Sally's party. Maybe this year she invited your Prince Charming. (Oops, you forgot! You met him last year, got drunk and made out with him in the broom closet.)

UNLESS YOU'RE KRISTY...
Who's been to 4 Countries in 3 months…

Met several interesting men (and bought several new clothes at ½ the price).

Kristy is always meeting new guys online. They're

all amazing and she has options, options, options!

I was never really sure what Kristy did for a living, but she does seem to be meeting lots of guys. (And has really great clothes!).

THE MATCHMAKER

Although they are the first to brag/emphasize/tell you/lie to you how many couples they have set up/married off/watched fall-

In love-They quite possibly are not telling the truth! I know, hard to believe-but my cousin was the casting director for a reality dating show. She did the matching, not the supposed matchmaker.

In real life, they can tell you they have the perfect person(s) for you at a small fee of (fill in the blank) which inevitably becomes a sliding scale (the more you complain). Most of the time their idea of hot/gorgeous/fun/successful/athletic men are not the same scale in which you look at the human form. From where have they been comparing their goods?

Yes, compared to the average person, these people that feel the need to be set up/allow someone to match them-may have good intentions, really want to meet someone, trust in someone who themselves, cannot find a second date-That's okay, they still hold out hope that this person (that they spent three months rent on) will find them their happily ever after. I suppose if you add up all the money you spent on vacations/food/wine/clothing/cabs/gas over the years, this could actually be a less expensive option.

Who knows? You may just get lucky on the first match, meet the love of your life and live happily ever after.

On the other hand, you may just end up more depressed with the people you've been set up with-which then makes you call and ask the matchmaker, "Am I really that unattractive?" And "They're nothing close to what I asked you for".

Most matchmakers are running around looking for cute/fun/presentable people for their database-
For hard-up guys they take money from, say they can set them up with the love of their lives and then never follow through-With any of the people they initially promised. (For one lie or another.) If the matchmaker is single and they think the guy is hot, she will try to steal him for herself (kind of like the stay-at-mom, who's sick of charities, fundraisers and volunteer work-so opens a consignment store, just to have the pick from everyone else's closet-courtesy of her bankrolled husband; who, FYI, probably sleeps with one or more of the consigners) which can be awkward if the guy isn't into her and truly paid her money to meet someone.

Now, this will backfire, as the matchmaker is now vindictive, steals his money and sets him up with psychos. On purpose, so that he'll run right into her arms.

Grab a drink and take a breather. This may be a lot to take in.

SOME WEIRD, FUN AND TRUE ON-LINE DATING EXCHANGES COURTESY OF MY BROTHER, CRAIG
RE: (Millionaire Match.com)
Subject: Hello Dark and Handsome
Good Morning Craig!
I think your profile is great and if you live in Georgia, I would enjoy getting to know you better. I think you are very handsome, But I have a confession-I have a sister that I'd like you to meet.
She will not be amused that I'm doing this, as she just got out of a terrible relationship (That she let drag on too long)-Her name is Christina, she is way more -Spirited than me, as I'm the most conservative!

Roxanne
P.S. We all had dark hair once upon a time. Tina still does, she is recalcitrant and a hair stylist!

(Plenty Of Fish)
RE: Hey There Craig
Craig,
I did read your profile, and I believe it was this morning or yesterday, can't remember. I enjoy all animals with the exception of cats, and if you want to know, I don't think of them as animals really. I do like birds, tho-

RE: Hey There (Millionaire Match)
Good Afternoon Craig,
I know there are allot of crazy people in this world and there are a few on this website, I encountered a man that did not like the words "Not Interested" And he went off on me and sent me several ugly emails, so I blocked him.

I don't understand, because I was very nice about it and we didn't have anything in common plus he was 68 years of age and I don't want to change a grown mans diapers in the next few years, I would like to enjoy my life before I got to that part of it.

Match.com
RE: Hey There
Craig,
I'm sorry I didn't get back to you, as there was a weird smell in my hallway all weekend. Well, we found out what it was on Sunday night. There was a dead body in the apartment down the hall. Anyway, hope you are having a fun weekend!

RE: HELLO
Hi There-
My weekend was so, so, worked most of it-As for my experience on here, none of it is good, but not bad either, it's seems like all the men are only looking for one thing, someone who is perfect and willing to follow them where ever they are with no consideration of maybe we have a life, work, family etc.

Dear Clothesking,

I'm Beverly. Thanks for your email. A little about me...I have been married 3 times 1st was a drunk-

2nd a cheater with a big sex problem and 3rd very nice guy (long time friend) but has had a lot of ex-wife problems. We all get along now, except for the first two.

Beverly

Hello Craig, how ru. So cum get some kisses☺ x0x0x0 Star

(Craig's response)

Can't stop at one kiss...Better pucker up more than that!

Millionaire Match

Ohhh my God!! I really enjoyed reading your profile and it's hard to believe why such a handsome looking man like you be alone over there without getting ladies chasing on you. I need a man to buy me things-lots of things, so I can be pretty and there for him. I'm 35, so I hope you understand that I would like to hear from you soon...sooner, rather than later.

RE: About Me Marie

Hello, thanks for keeping in touch with me-I am Marie, by name. How's this online thing working out for you? I'm new here-I am looking for a man to make me happy again and be there for me always. I have fully decided to be a role model to my future children (When I have them). Please let me know of an embarrassing moment that you have had.

MATCH.COM

Morning Craig,

Wow, I don't think I have 11 best friends! U must be a very social person, not that I'm not. However, I just have a couple very close friends. Montana is a beautiful state. Haven't been there in many years. I once stayed at a cabin in the area they filmed "A River Runs thru It.

"I haven't had an interest in fly fishing, but I have been on many hunts and, if I say so myself, am an accomplished hunter. My second hunt I ever went on was a bear hunt in Montana. However, I really don't see hunting in my future anymore. I've lost interest, not that I wouldn't go on one with someone. I just don't think I want to be the primary hunter. I do not have any birth kids, but I raise my nephew. He is 26, has high functioning autism.

I've had him since he was 12, when his mother, (my sister) passed away. She was in the first Golf War and died many years later of complications from injuries she had sustained over there. I'm currently going thru a divorce. Okay, that's all for me. What about you?

AND, A FUN TEXT...

Craig
Want to get together for lunch sometime this week?
Girl
Silly, I work Monday through Friday..
Craig
You don't each lunch?
Girl
Lol
Craig
Dinner Friday?
Girl
No, dinner Friday doesn't work either.
Craig
Good luck on your search.
Girl
Oh really? Just because I don't want to have dinner or lunch

with you, "Good luck on my search?"

> Craig

Have a nice day.

> Girl

I was only comfortable meeting for coffee, so now forget it.

> Craig

Then why didn't you just say that when I asked you for -lunch? "I'm just comfortable meeting you for the first time for coffee?"

> Girl

Good luck on your search.

(Yes, these are real exchanges courtesy of my Brother).

A USELESS, TRUE STATISTIC

Millionaire match may not be the answer-But according to the experts, 35% percent of people date online. (Somehow, this does not make me feel better about online dating.)

A THOUGHT

Expecting flowers from a straight man (after sex) is possibly asking for too much. Once he's had sex with you, he's already won you. You want flowers? Make him work for them. (And really, flowers? You're likelier to receive flowers from a gay man than a straight man.) So, if you receive flowers after sex? Make sure you've had a history of his sexual orientation. Straight men just aren't that aware.

I'LL MARRY YOU, BUT I'M TOO OLD TO DATE YOU

By the time we hit our 30s and 40s, we've dated most everyone in our state and quite possibly, surrounding states. There's always recycling, but isn't that what you did with the last four boyfriends? You may be worn out/tired/hung up to dry and just not into doing it anymore. You cannot take another night of bad sushi and groping with that guy your best friend swore looked like that *a list celeb.*

(Yes, a much less attractive, shorter, thinner, poorer version of *that A list celeb.*) We are bored, out of our butts, from bad dates. So, here's what we decide: we're going to get married. We will get married. We just will not date. Period. It's the perfect answer. Just set it up. Pick the guy. We see him. We like him. He's fine. Marry him. What do you think divorce is for? No more dating. Dating only leads to more dating, and more dating only leads to more sex. And more sex? Break-up's, fights, boredom, passion. We don't have time for that.

We have to get on with it before we're too old to get married without help from a nurse's aide.

(I was rooting for getting married before menopause, but that's just me.) So, let's cut to the chase.

CALLING IN THE ANGELS

These are last resort rituals that may…

(1)."Hey angels, bring me a guy/gal/donkey/fish/monkey/hot young thing".

(2). Sit cross-legged on floor, chant current movie stars name over and over again until groggy-

Or, someone appears. If you see actual people and there is no one there, you've done the chant too long.

(3). Stand in favorite yoga position and yell out Mother Theresa's name.

RESPONSES TO FREQUENTLY ASKED QUESTIONS…

You took the last great guy; have you taken a look around lately? I've joined an ashram. They believe celibacy is the only choice. I'm still in love with my last boyfriend.

He's on his way over (you don't have to specify from which Country).

Where's your boyfriend?

He works nights. He works days.

He's away on a business trip from 5 to 7. He works out of town/country/planet. Where's yours? I prefer other people's mates. He's on his way over.

Why haven't you met anyone?

I'm pickier than you are. I've met several.

Anyone is a pretty harsh term, don't you think, Mom? No one measures up to my father.

I've recently acquired a dog.

Do you like being single?

(1). Is this a trick question?

(2). In June, July and August.

(3). When I'm dating several men in several different states.

(4). When I add up all the money I've saved since I stopped dating my ex.

(5). Every other Sunday.

(6). When I'm in shape and getting lots of attention.

(7). Yes. (Pause). Do you have anyone to set me up with?

CHAPTER 5

BOYFRIENDS

It was fun seeing you again
With your arm draped on another woman. While I sat
Wilting in a corner, calling your name.
It was FUN seeing you again.
    Making out
With that girl we used to make fun of.
Now you two are making fun
Of me.   It was FUN seeing you again.
    Just like old times.
Me wanting you.   You wanting her.

CHAPTER 5
BOYFRIENDS

Chances are you're dating the wrong guy and you know it. It doesn't matter, it's not like you let go of Mr. Right. As far as you're concerned, Mr. Right hasn't come along, and if he does, you'll blow off Mr. Wrong in a New York minute. (Unless the sex is really good, which makes it much harder to expedite from.) Here's the dilemma: that slob on the couch eating all your food? The one you bought that stupid video game for? He's possibly keeping you from meeting, ah, dare we say it, Mr. Right

Or at the very least, Mr. Better than what you've got right now.

(Not to say that Mr. amazing is out there-have you been out there lately?) Before we send him on his way and give him a proper burial, however, let's establish some of the things he is... *VERY GOOD IN BED*

Now, let's discuss the things he is not... *HUSBAND MATERIAL*

Because you're afraid/can't quite get it together/have fun with him for now/can't stand the idea of dating-you've allowed Lazy Larry to take over your life, as well as turn your apartment into a sports bar and video arcade. You feel safe. You feel comfortable. He's seen you without makeup and still likes you.

At some point or another, you're going to have to wake-up. (You don't have to, but it's helpful to). Remember that you're interested in conversation beyond the ingredients in fruity cereal. Buck up, get out there and date.

On the other hand, you could be dating Mr. wonderful. He's so fantastic, that you (and everyone else) can't stop gushing about how great he is. He's attentive, respectful, the sex is good, he has a good job and you enjoy most of the same things, everything's great.

So what's the problem?

You don't want to marry each other. This is only a problem if one of you wants to get married and the other does not. It could be you. It could be him. Doesn't matter.

For whatever reason, one of you ain't it; and both of you agree on that fact.

WHEN DO I DUMP MY BOYFRIEND, AND, BETTER YET, WHY?

You may not want to dump Lazy Larry. (Or Wonderful Willy.) If anything, he's been fun, even if you feel like his mother. He makes you feel needed, and it's been a long time since you've felt needed. (Your drunken best friend calling at 2 A.M. just to talk doesn't count.) When you reach a certain age and see all your friends settling down with the men you never thought you'd date, you may panic.

You may go after every wrong man out there. It's not too difficult to do. Apparently there are more screwed up weird ones than good ones out there. They sense you're searching for them, and they appear. Even though you're saying you're ready to get married, the very fact that you dump every available guy for every unattainable or unemployed/still searching for anything, is a sign that you're searching in the wrong pond.

And, you may realize that every amazing, put together, successful guy you meet doesn't last long- for one reason or another. (Yes, dating your best friend behind your back may be one of them.) You go after the wrong man. You woo him without really understanding why. Then you get him.

6 months later, after the great sex is still great but you aren't so thrilled about him anymore, you'll be wondering, "what am I doing?"

This is common. Don't spend the next year feeling sorry for yourself and still sleeping with him.

You need to get out because you've now cut another six months out of your search for Mr. Right, and now Mr. Right has gone off and married someone possibly less attractive/ambitious/better connected than you. He was waiting for you, but you chose the wrong guy. Now you have to cut a few corners and get back on track. First, you're going to have to get rid of him.

Here are a few steps to take on your road to recovery:

1. Stop sleeping with him. Now. In an hour. Soon.

2. Stop sleeping with him when he calls you drunk a week later.

3. Forgive yourself for sleeping with him after you called him drunk 2 weeks later.

4. Forgive yourself for sleeping with someone else, just to get over him.

5. Take a yoga class and give up sex for six months, or until you meet a better guy. Or start sleeping with your yoga instructor. Do not fall in love, even if he knows "tantric sex."

6. Fall in love with your yoga instructor because he knows tantric sex.

WHY AM I PUTTING OFF THE INEVITABLE?

This is easy. You don't feel like there are even a few good men out there. You see what the potential "good" men are dating. They are dating women that you've seen get beeped, run off for an hour, and then return. This isn't true for all good men. Some good men are not interested because they're busy working. They want to meet you totally by chance. Women can never do this because we're always thinking about that meeting.

The saying, "It happens when you least expect it," is not true for women most of the time. When in the world are women going around, not expecting it?

Anyone we happen to meet, we think, "This could be it." Doesn't matter if we never lay eyes on him again. So we stay with Lazy Larry to ease our souls and relax our bodies. Isn't too complicated, is it? Lazy Larry's great in bed, has a tight ass, doesn't talk too much, complain too much, whine, demand or yell, and he's good to look at. (You have friends for deep conversation.)

When a woman reaches a certain age, she thinks about marriage. Often. She sees everyone else doing it and wonders about her own lack of "other half," She may even start thinking about pets. She may begin to wonder, "Will my computer and his printer be compatible?" "My dog and his dog? "Will he want to sleep on the same side of the bed?" "I wonder if he has a walk-in closet or would be willing to build one". (You don't think he's moving into your place, do you?)

The innocent first questions women ask themselves when they are young and silly enough to dream won't matter anymore-Because you may or may not be able to have kids and/or may or may not care.

You'll be more concerned about whether you can be on his health insurance plan and finding out how to bring up a life insurance policy. This is why you forego all that heavy baggage of worry you were lugging over your shoulder and go out with Lazy Larry. He makes you forget about all those things you thought you wanted in a man. He doesn't have your level of education; his parents sleep in twin beds (separately-just like every TV show from the 70's) he's a different religion and he maimed several squirrels when he was a kid. You don't care.

Morals! Hogwash! Out the window! Ideals! Please! Who's going to know? So what if he says, "Ain't nothing." You do too when you're really drunk. (Okay, you said it once, in college, high on 'shrooms.) Okay, you never say that, but this is what you will do: you'll start to stand up for Lazy Larry.

Your friends, business associates and parents will begin to say, "What are you doing with him?" In which case, your first response may be, "He opens the door for me."

In the beginning, no one else will understand what it is you see in Lazy Larry. They won't understand that he makes you tea at 2 A.M. when you have a tummy ache. They won't understand that he puts the toilet seat down. They won't understand that he will fix your brakes on your car, free of charge. They won't understand that it's exciting for you to have sex with him in that greasy overall outfit.

Don't try to make your friends and family understand. They won't. They're still hoping and praying you'll come to your senses and dump him. You have to be ready when you're ready.

I said maybe!

WHY MAYBE?

You're in your sexual prime and probably aren't ready to give that up yet. You may never be ready to give that up. Don't make the mistake of thinking about marrying Lazy Larry and changing him. He's never going to be any different; unless you've come to terms with his 10th grade education, the fact that he's 15 years younger than you and looks it, has a tight ass, has the ability to fix cars-and actually knows a lot about-well, nothing-stop looking. You've found your Prince Charming. But you can't fool us! We know he's not good enough. You know he's not good enough. That's not the point. You've told yourself you're fed up with trying to wait for Mr. Perfect, and are settling for Mr. Right-Here-Right-Now. Either that or you can be celibate. Up to you. On the other hand, that Mr. perfect you've been waiting for may start out amazing and turn into a nightmare worse than Lazy Larry could ever be! This is the hard part. Once you've dumped LL, you have to start over.

At this point, you've basically given up on meeting any decent men. You're sitting around with your single, successful girlfriends (for some reason, you've cloned like a pack of wolves) and talk about men. You have (once again) sworn off the wrong men and decided you will only date eligible men.

Married women think it takes absolutely nothing to meet a wonderful single man.

Never mind that they met their husbands when they were 23. "It's so easy to meet a great guy. I see them all the time," they will coo, thinking this makes you feel better in your search when in actuality, it makes you feel like an even bigger loser for not spotting what is your obvious oversight at all the perfect men. If you could just live in your married friends' dream world, you'd be fine. In the meantime, everyone will pick on you for the boyfriend you've chosen. Forget going to the track, they'll take dibs on how long it will last, betting you won't make it to the end of the month. This is where they fail in their assessment. Simply to save face, you'll stay much longer than you intended with Lazy Larry, just to show everyone that you really felt something for him. You don't want the wolf pack to ever be right about the guy you picked, even if they are. "Well, he's just a filler, anyway" you tell yourself.

Or you remain single and celibate until you decide you can't take it any longer—sitting here, waiting and waiting for your soulmate, which is what got you into this mess in the first place. All of a sudden, Mr. Hottie Filler comes along and you say, "Why not!"

This is probably where you screw up. Not the sleeping with him part; the caring part. It becomes nearly impossible to do what men do and just have sex. Sure we can start out like we don't care, even do our power trip,

"I'm more successful than you, so you can never hurt me", but deep down we know we'll get emotionally involved.

It's part of our genetic makeup.

It's what we do.

Even when we don't get emotionally involved-we become addicted to the sex and being addicted to sex with that person is just as dangerous as being emotionally involved. The trick lies in separating our current Lazy Larry from any other men we are set up with, or are to meet, while frolicking in our new "pressure free" fun relationship. We lie and tell ourselves, "This is perfect. I'll sleep with LL, still have my weekends free to meet Mr. Right, and have a blast at the same time." That lasts for about a week. After that, the incredible sex you're getting from Lazy Larry becomes more important than going out to some stupid single's bar; or being set up with your sister's ex-boyfriend's younger brother's college roommate. Please! Who wants to have to work that hard at finding Mr. Right? Let him come find me.

In the meantime, I'll be in bed with you-know-who.

Besides, I have a friend who has a friend who's friend knew a girl who tried to date only nice, available, not as attractive, but good "catches" that are ready to settle down, and after two months, he dumped her for a Playboy Bunny— from Sweden. And interestingly enough, her current friend of the friend of the friend, was actually sleeping with the ex-lover of the playboy bunny from Sweden, so it all worked out!

YOUR EX AND EVERYONE ELSE'S
Remember high school? When everyone inter-dated? That's exactly what happens when you're in your 30's.

You've dated everyone there is to date.

You have no choice but to date your friend's exes, even the ones currently being indicted. You've waited for your friend to break-up with Mr. Finance for three years; so by the time he's single again, you do everything you can to make sure you guys finally date.

If you can set-up the ex your poaching Mr. Finance from, it saves getting lecherous stares from her that you are now happily enjoying her seconds. She may even chill out enough to share intimate secrets about him that would otherwise take months to learn.

Although it may seem incestuous, you'll appreciate getting those little tidbits of information. You don't want to have to meet a stranger. It helps a great deal if someone you know has dated the guy. Like baseball cards, you're trading boyfriends. The problem is, your friends all ended up with one of your ex's. Now, after Mr. Finance goes off to do a hard three to five, you're once again on your own.

Having gone through all your ex's and everyone else's exes, you are in this position which is called being alone. Perhaps you've been too picky with your choosing? Your friends who stayed in it with the ex that got passed around is still with him. Why? She put up with him. You spent far too much time analyzing everything that could possibly be wrong with him-until he leaves. You thought you made the right choice being done with him, until you got the solid gold embossed wedding invitation. How does he suddenly look so much better than before?

You've now decided he was the best thing that ever happened to you. You might even try to win him back-showing up everywhere they go, dressed to kill-probably to no avail. He will remind you how you treated him like dirt. "I thought you liked that," you'll yelp. It's no fun being kicked when you're down. (I thought men had lousy memories, you'll remind yourself.) Here's the truth about exes: they only look good when they're on someone else's arm.

You had absolutely zero issues with kicking him to the curb and moving on with your life, until you see him with another woman. We can't believe how dumb we were. How foolish to let him get away. This is the same for your friend's husband.

You could have cared less about him when he was single. He didn't even look good to you and you even had the chance to date him. You convinced yourself he wasn't your type, until you're friend married the geek.

All of the sudden, that geek looks good. Really good! You start thinking, "What was I thinking? That guy's a winner!" And he was right in front me the whole time. You should be ashamed of yourself. You only want him because your friend has him. Now, every time you see them together, you say to her, "He's the best guy. Where did you find him?" Like you didn't know where he was the whole time. The enticing part of all of this is simply: you don't have them, so you must want them. All exes, and everyone else, suddenly look very appetizing; and there's no shortage of men, just available ones.

But who wants an available one?

No one wants you when you're available, so why should you want him or her? Sometimes, you'll blow off an available man for that very reason. You will not be able to figure out why he's still single for the same reason he can't figure out why you are. This is a very damaged couple. Two single available people should not date. Pining for an ex is brilliant. It is in keeping with the romance of the Prince on the white horse; only, when you dated him, he was more like the court jester who couldn't get into the castle. But once you've broken up and he's found another princess, you idealize him as the perfect man.

It's okay; this makes you normal. (Normal but alone.) We're attracted to everyone else's man, because we figure that if we're still single at a certain age, there must be something desperately wrong with our 'picker.'

We need to make sure other men want us, especially men who want other women. This isn't about cheating with a married man, or stealing one, it's about pure adulation from the opposite sex. (In a sexual-way.)

If we can still get a rise (so to speak) out of our hooked-up exes, or any other unavailable men, we feel that at least there's hope for us. Most of the available men don't give us the time of day. What are they looking for, anyway? 21-year-olds who kiss their butts, that's what! Which would be easy for you to emulate if you weren't so damn lazy (oh, and smart).

You are too much pressure for an older guy. They want to be able to play around. Yes, he may remind you that you're eggs aren't so hot anymore; but it's okay, his sperm ain't so great, either.

Neither one of you should want the other!

THE EX

The guy you thought you'd marry a long time ago but didn't. Now he's married with 2 kids and laughing at you. It's fine. Once you see how he's currently living with three kids; a lot of stress (which has added to his waistline and hairline) you will take a nice deep breath and treat yourself to a martini. "Moving on", you tell yourself. That month of stalking his family to make sure "I'm not missing anything" was well worth it. And remember, there's always someone else's ex. At this point, no matter whom you date, there's a great chance he/she is someone's ex. (Unless they've recently reconnected with their Monk status.)

FALLING QUICKLY

Falling in like or love quickly is great, if you make sure that you can fall out of love just as fast. Meeting someone is great, especially when you really think you like him or her. You go on one date-and you click. 2 dates-click. 3 dates. So on and so on. When it works out as opposed to being a nightmare, you really think you may have found the person that is going to change your life. If you have the ability to think that someone can change your life immediately after meeting them, they are the answer to your problems.

(God, we hope so) and/or is that missing link (not anthropologically) then you better just as easily believe that, well, you might have been wrong.

Especially when that perfect person disappoints you. Not to be pragmatic, but there's just no way a perfect person can keep up to that ideal forever! Well, unless you're that married, gay couple, that one that say's they are "perfectly aligned", never argue and completely happy.

The thought that you could actually meet, be perfectly aligned and spend your life with someone is a fabulous dream; a dream which most people strive for, some achieve, most chase. Some give up the chase, allowing real life to filter in, hoping for some semblance of happiness, fulfillment and great sex. Others do seem to find what they are looking for (even if they have to marry several times to find it). No matter, you only go around once (on Earth-This time-Now-As yourself) So, you might as well do whatever you can to make yourself happy; which for some, includes picking people that inevitably make us, well, miserable.

Misery should not be a part of your dating syllabus, but sometimes it is. Why? Because we set ourselves up. We believe our own hype, we believe other peoples' hype and we meet someone who we inevitably is going to be the answer to what we think we're looking for (at any given time this can change) put all our eggs into their basket and hope for the best. All this is great, until you wake up in bed next to that person one morning and see how they really look (inside and out) in the light of day. At this point, you may even find that you are still enthralled with that special someone. You think you've found the Holy Grail Of Love!

5 months, 6 months down the line, you still realize

you've never quite met someone like this before! Something just 'clicked.' Something just 'worked'. And then it just…didn't.

Actually, if it did (or still does) you are probably walking down the aisle as we speak (which is weird, because the fact that you're reading this book while walking down the aisle in your off-white, or red wedding dress-is just strange timing, period). If you are one of those people that really did find the yin to your yang, then go for it. And for God's sake, don't ask too many questions. The more you ask, the more you'll find out and possibly the less you'll like.

On the other hand, this perfect person, you may come to find; sooner or later (hopefully sooner the older you get) isn't so perfect, after all. Mystery is the great mediator of life. We all want to feel that rush of excitement and freshness when we meet someone. Then, the stories start. History. The past, baggage, family, friends, ex's, rehab, etc. It's amazing what someone you've never met before will tell you and it's amazing what you initially see as a red flag –so easily gets swept to the side as you convince yourself what initially was "wow, not good" turns into "oh, big deal. Everyone's been married 3 times".

Having ideals, standards, morals and ethics are something you create and find out as you go through life. Picking a partner is supposed to fall into that same mold (this is apparently why That woman who birthed 10 babies at once met her boyfriend in church).

Sometimes, our ideals, morals, ethics and standards fly quickly out the window when we meet someone we've just got to have, even if they don't fit one thing we think we're looking for.

Sometimes, someone can come out of left field and shock us. Sometimes that's a good thing. Other times, it requires some serious soul searching and "what the f was I thinking?"

At the end of the day, it's not much different from when we were kids having a crush. It happened pretty fast.

You knew whom you wanted to follow home from school, send a valentine card to play doctor with. (Oh, that was just me?). It's pretty much instinctual who 'conks' us over the head and tells us to go there-I like him/her. There isn't much deep thinking involved, and although we aren't necessarily aware of the reason we like that person(s) We are just simply drawn or pulled to them. This is what happens when dating. (Unless you've been forced to marry-then you'll "Learn to love him/her".) So, how can it be that you can immediately be drawn to someone and think they are going to change your life and ever so suddenly have it turn on you? How can something so amazing turn so quickly into crap?

Because we only think we know that person we are sharing our most intimate secrets with. We only think they are everything we ever wanted in someone. The true test is spending time with someone. The true test is common ground, shared interests, similar sense of humor. The true test is quite possibly, that thing called - A 2nd date.

Dating A Guy For His Potential

When you're younger you can certainly date a guy for his 'potential.' In fact, unless he's a trust fund baby or robs banks as a hobby (not getting caught, of course) the only thing you are dating him for is 'his potential.' Which is great, because he's only dating you for your perky tits. While you are dating him for what he is going to be once he finds his place in the world, be forewarned that he is hoping your rack stays that perky forever.

So, by the time he has made it (assuming you're still together) you had better pre-plan that breast augmentation so that when he does make it, he won't try to trade you in for a better-balanced model. But this isn't about him. It's about you and what you choose.

The nice thing about being in your 20's (besides being able to call your parents and asking them for money), is that you have so much time in the world (or think you do) that you can just explore, play, have fun and screw your way through to your 30's without a care in the world. You can also have several different kinds of relationships to try and figure out what the hell it is you actually want.

But that's fine. Because you don't have to know what you want, right now. It probably won't matter anyway, because you'll probably end up falling in love with someone just like your father; whether you like it or not. So, just go with it. Sometimes potential is a lot better than what they become.

Dating A Man For His Money

Let me start by saying (although, I have several friends who are pretty good at it) I am not. I graze toward the 'hopeful', 'dreamer', 'when-I-make-it', 'on the way up' or 'on the way down. Which, by the way, if they're on the way down, you have a pretty fair shot of every former narcissistic maniac being suddenly amazing to you because they've been through 'so much' and 'finally know what it's like to love, nurture and respect someone. Who has the kind of time for that?

Not me.

Dating a man for his money sounds great, if he's not cheap. And let's go with that. Let's go with a generous guy with money. Picks you up, sends for a car to drive you from destination A to destination B; wines, dines…spoils you rotten. Buys you gifts on a whim, flies you everywhere and surprises you constantly. In fact, he delights in simply taking care of you in every material way he can.

And the problem is?

(I think I'm done writing the book now. I have a rich guy to lasso.)

The problem with dating an extremely wealthy man (or woman) is that (what I've heard) now you are at the mercy of everything this guy wants to do-Whenever he wants to do it. Your career, what career? Give it up! He wants to do things. It doesn't matter what those things are. You better be ready, willing, able about doing everything he wants to do and when he wants to do it. (And yes, no complaining.)

This is probably why an older guy picks a younger, submissive woman; he gets to call the shots. For several thousand a month, some people pretend to let him/her call the shots. This is when those acting classes come in handy.

Or you can watch a friend flirt and copy their behavior. I probably couldn't do it (I talk too much). But I'm sure you can. Let me know how it goes. If you really are dating a man for his money, you know exactly how to rope him in and enjoy all the finer things in life you've probably done this before, so you already know what to expect. I'm sure you will have a great life; at your country club, playing tennis with Alex and Dmitri every Saturday, jetting off to Bora-Bora just 'because'; and furthermore-who cares about a stupid career that took you 2 degrees, 7 years in college, and expects you to get to the office by 7 A.M. so that you can call China?

I mean, really.

What is the point of your career, when this guy has more money than your entire family makes (and town you're from) combined? And at the end of the day, a career can't keep you warm, but he (or his money) can. So, enjoy him and his money. Just be careful if you marry him. He'll take over your life so fast, you'll never know what hit you.

On the off chance you happen to meet a very wealthy

guy who wants you to have your independence, own career, and helps you along the way?

For God's sake, move far, far away and give up all your friends because we are going to find you and try to take him from you. Fast.

DATING A MAN FOR HIS MANHOOD

This is kind of like dating James Bond. (Only without all the money, jewels and suits.)

The thing he does possess is his quick wit, charm and that 'just cold enough to you, even though you know I want you' glare that he only gives to you in a room filled with hundreds of beautiful women.

There's something so alluring about him-he's got a great job, he takes care of business, can even fix your car. He's got a great body, a great head of hair and he's got a core group of guys that he's had since 5th grade. This guy has a great set of ABS. He knows exactly what to do to please you, all the time. This guy can make a great husband, if you don't mind that you fell for the mysterious, strong, charming aloofness; which doesn't bother you once you want to have (what we call) a conversation. He doesn't like small talk and pretty much everything is small talk, so having a great conversation about the world (past a witty one-liner) is a bit too much for him. It's not that he can't come up with conversation, he just doesn't want to. It's all there, in his brain.

Of course, he reads several papers everyday; it's not that he's dumb or un-educated he just doesn't like to chat. Having dinner with a bunch of other couples will not turn him on. He'd rather go away with his group of buddies (from 5th grade) and play golf all weekend. Which is fine, if you're okay being alone with all your coupled-up friends and trying to flirt with their husbands. Not that you want to flirt with their husbands.

But really, how many times can you talk about the

purse at Barney's you've just got to have?

The same thing that made you fall for the guy because he's such a guy is probably the thing that will make you miss someone more sensitive and communicative. But isn't that why you have your gay best friend, Charles?

DATING A MAN FOR LOVE

Wow, what a concept. People actually DO this! They fall in love with someone and actually date, then get married! I know, I know, hard to believe, but you've seen them, they're those happy-go-lucky couples with their arms draped all over each other, all the time; and they seem like they're really into each other. Truly interested. It happens.

I'm not sure if it has to do with chocolate, sex or a meeting of the minds, but whatever it is, tons of single people want it, try to find it and go to great lengths to keep it once they have it.

When you're older and searching for love, you look for the same thing you did when you were younger-attraction–only this time, you may have decided that he can be a little heavier, a little less athletic than you initially hoped, a little less hair (than he had five years earlier) and doesn't have to be the best looking guy in the room (unless you still must have the best looking guy in the room, in which case dating for love probably is out of the question).

Dating for love requires something called patience, compromise, communication, the right attitude and a willingness to share your life (all the good and the bad) with that significant other.

I need to stop for a moment.

It's a bit too much to take in.

Yes, we've all been in love (some even engaged and/or married once or twice).

But, that love thing? Every time you do it, again, it

suddenly feels like the first time. It suddenly feels like it's the only time and it suddenly feels like if you let it go, you'll never find it again.

Dating for Love is great, if you can find it.

If not, there's always reality TV.

The problem with dating for love when you're older is that everyone wants everything to happen immediately. Which is great if you think you can immediately know someone-all his/her habits, make that connection, go on one date and poof-you're in a relationship.

You may think this all sounds great and easy, because who really has the time to slowly nurture-well-anything, anymore? The problem with something happening instantaneously is that it can blow up in your face, just as fast. A person that wants you that quickly has to be more of a control freak than sincerely in love with you. Sorry, I know, you really thought you were that great! Well, you are, just not that, that great. There's a difference.

Trust me, you'll thank me later...after the restraining order. In this case, taking the time to get to know someone before you jet off to a weekend in Palm Springs and spend ten hours a day staring into each others eyes, enjoying fine dining, his snoring and a great golf game...only to realize you have changed your online status prematurely from single to in a relationship may now bite you in the ass.

When you can't get away from this person (even though you've agreed to be with him) you're now stuck. It's okay, you may actually decide that being protected and smothered (pick an adjective) by this insecure person...that he/she cannot be alone, so he/she has decided you (and if not you, then well...you) are the one. And maybe you both are right for each other. Who knows? Love sometimes happens very fast. Like microwave popcorn, which takes about 3 minutes to pop. (Hopefully, the sex lasts a bit longer.)

DATING A MAN FOR HIS SPERM

At least you have decided why you're dating him. Most of the time, you make yourself go on a date, not even excited to go on it. It becomes like a second job. Having to meet someone that you aren't remotely attracted to or finding just that one 'thing' (like a sexy earlobe) that will keep your attention span throughout the three-hour dinner. Dating a man for his sperm gives you a purpose, and who doesn't like to go through life with a purpose? You have gotten to this point because you either:

A. Didn't get pregnant with your last boyfriend. (Even if you wanted to).

B. Tried to trap the last several. Lovers/boyfriends/one-night stands, but didn't get pregnant.

C. Wasted too much time dating everyone until there is no one left and now you must scrape the bottom of the barrel (and possibly end up with an ugly child).

Possibly dating a man for his sperm works best once you've seen baby photos so that you know what you're getting in for. You're not worried about your side of the gene pool; you've seen your own baby pictures. Dating a man for his sperm comes about because you have some sort of game plan and having a child by a certain age, with a fairly decent guy that you've picked (in your mind) is the best way to go. You know him you may know his family and you've actually seen how he behaves at dinner parties and in public places (and still want a kid with him). It's less about falling in love with him and getting married and more about his lineage.

Falling in love with Baby-Daddy-Sperm-donor will only work if the guy suddenly sees you in a different light, falls madly in love with the baby or falls down, knocks his head on something sharp and changes his mind.

Otherwise, chances are good you'll be going it alone. But that's okay, you had baby-man-sperm on the brain anyway, and you didn't really look to him to be husband or father. You got what you wanted, so let him marry someone who really wants him (sperm, penis, mind and all).

DATING A MAN FOR HIS PEDIGREE...

Dating a guy for his pedigree will create that same saliva-like Pavlov build up as the dog you choose. Are you getting hot when I say Ivy-league? How about Martha's Vineyard? Perhaps Brown, Yale, Harvard, Kennedy, and/or any other sweat inducing name will make your ears (and your nipples) perk-up? Indeed, you need a summer place in the Hamptons, a winter place in the Swiss Alps. You must jaunt to Cannes (even if you're not in the entertainment business and/or from a wealthy family)... and in order to do this (so that you can meet/date/procure your man of pedigree) you must either take out an extremely large loan (to cover the cost to chase him around the globe) or come from money/have money/find/steal/earn money. Dating A Man For His Pedigree will ensure your social status right along with his, but will probably (unless you grew up in that circle of friends) make you an outcast at the same time. Be prepared to be hated by all the women that never got the guy (even though they are from the same social circle) and be prepared for icy stares, flirts from his friends and the challenge that understanding four forks on the left side of the plate are all used during that meal.

(Yes, left to right; outside to inside. Didn't know this was a mini guide to etiquette did you?) I may have just helped you land your Pedigree Puff.

I HAVE BAD TASTE

Yes, there's always that. But while you're busy beating up on yourself about all the horrible guys you draw into your life, ask yourself about your taste in say...furniture?

How about clothing? Do you have bad taste about everything? Chances are, you don't. Which is good, because this means although you may sexually still be attracted to the same types over and over again. You can change what you're doing, who you're looking for and even what your idea of a good guy is; even if you know you have bad taste. If you're trying not to have bad taste anymore and you know that you are doing the same things over and over again. It's probably best to take a short sabbatical and re-evaluate what the hell you're doing! No, the short sabbatical is for you…alone.

Do not bring the 27 year-old hockey instructor along. Yes, bringing him along on the short sabbatical is called missing the point.

WHAT I NEED TO DO TO CHANGE MY TASTE

Usually, this requires an open mind. In order to have an open mind, you must tell yourself (or pay someone to drill it into your head). You must experience new things that you normally wouldn't do. This includes dating people that you normally wouldn't date. This includes opening up your mind, heart (and perhaps legs) to new experiences to try to prove to yourself that although you may have a type-getting to know any other breed of the opposite gender can/may/will/probably not produce another type of attraction that comes from the head/heart/probably not your loins.

It's okay. Your job here is to try new things.

Experiment by dating a different kind of person than you normally would find yourself being initially attracted to.

I know, I know, sounds awful.

Strike that.

Stay home and watch re-runs, then text the loser you're currently trying to get over because

This dating crap is just too much work.

DID I LET ALL THE GOOD ONES GET AWAY?

By the term let I'm implying you've had some control over the situation…there's a short answer for this and it's - yes! Quite possibly you did let all the good ones get away. While you were chasing your career/slaying the dragon/having lots of relationships, flings, one night stands, falling in love/ finding out what made you Tick – hanging out over a toilet after one too many good parties/traveling the world/having fun...and enjoying your life. You may actually have let a few good ones slip through your fingers.

Oops. Time to get over it. Think about how much fun you've had (considering you can remember).

Who cares? What do you think photo albums are for? The less time you spend re-hashing those long ago days of what if's, the better. Besides, you need to tell yourself that you had perfectly solid reasons why that person(s) wasn't right for you-then. (Feel free to write down the reasons in the small space below.) Yes. This space. Oops. Used up, sorry…You may not need much space because the truth could be that you really did let several go that could have been great in your life now. (But, not so right for you then.) Here's the good news. There's a huge search engine out there and it lets you find anyone you want. And sometimes, really bad pictures can be found that even they didn't know existed. Try it-you'll be amazed at how quickly it can get you over anyone.

If that doesn't work, just remind yourself…

(1). *"THE TIMING WAS WRONG AND I JUST WASN'T READY; Or, (2). THE TIMING WAS RIGHT, BUT I JUST WASN'T READY!"*
Or, (3). "Crap, I really screwed that one up!"

(I'd pick one of the first two) this last one just makes you feel bad about yourself).

CHAPTER 6

DUMB GIRL

I try to act stupid,   but I'm not.
I try to pretend he's smarter than I am,   but
he's not.
I read, like, the paper.   But pretend like I don't.

I try to pretend not to know what's going on, because
I'm so confused after reading those HOW TO books
that I'm an utter mess.
So, I sit and pretend to know NOTHING, cause that's
what I think those books are saying.
 Am I wrong? 'Cause I could be these things.
For the right guy.
Then again, for the right guy, I wouldn't have to.

DUMB GIRL

SHUT UP

SHUT UP   SHUT UP   SHUT UP

Two things that are helpful in your plight to be dumb girl-
Keep mouth shut. How? Don't talk.

Actually being not very smart helps, too.

Men like dumb girls. That's a pretty general statement,
so I'll try to be more specific. Men like women who don't
talk. Well, they can talk when they have something that's
complimentary to the guy.

*Disclaimer -A gun was held to my head while
writing this chapter. I don't condone acting dumb to
get someone-unless you already have, in which case
this won't offend you because you won't think it's
about you, anyway.*

WHAT DUMB GIRLS DO TO GET A GUY
1. Bat their eyelashes a lot.
2. Smile.
3. Listen.
4. Listen some more.
5. Throw in a few compliments.

A hypothetical conversation might go something like this-

DUMB GIRL

(Looking up at sky)
Oh, the sky, it's so...big!

HE-MAN

(Pushing out chest)
Yeah. I studied Anatomy in high school.

DUMB GIRL

(Gazing into his eyes)
You did? Oh, wow! You are so smart.

> HE-MAN
>
> Yep.
>
> DUMB GIRL

Wow. You're so funny.

> HE-MAN

Uh-huh. I was captain of the football team, too.

> DUMB GIRL

(Feeling his biceps)

Wow, you're so strong.

> HE-MAN

> Uh-huh.

Silence. Looking at the sky as he pulls her closer.

You get the picture. He's in love. In love!

Why? She didn't do a thing but talk to him, about him, compliment him and act not so smart. He thinks she's the greatest thing in the world.

They usually get the guy. Let's cut back to *The Way We Were,* a perfect example of the dumb girl syndrome: Robert couldn't handle Barbra. She talked too much, was too smart and she challenged him and all his friends. She also wasn't his physical type. Every "not pretty enough" girl thinks it's the real reason she didn't get him. He thought she was too much to handle, but Barbra had to have him-chased him down and caught him, made him dinner and slept with him on the first date.

Then, the more she fell in love with him, the colder he was to her. She did not follow her mom's advice of 'The man should love you more than you love him.' She didn't care. Had she cared, she never would have slept with him the first night or ironed his shirt. She didn't follow any of the rules. Then, when he dumped her, she chased him. To top it all off, she got pregnant without being married and followed him out to California.

Marrying a man like this is bound to set you up for disappointment. He'll cheat just because he can.

He doesn't need a woman to want him just because he's attached to another. The problem is, women want him, anyway. There was an underlying theme that Barbara wasn't good looking enough for him, not his type. The bottom line is that he ended up dumping her and going with the dumb, pretty girl who didn't talk. Did you catch that at the end of the movie? She didn't say a word-that I love you no matter what smile was pasted on her face while holding onto his arm for dear life. Barbra touched his face… his hair…they have this entire moment. Dumb girl says nothing. Barbara says, "She's lovely, Hubbell."

Barbra knows.

The dumb girl got him.

Storybook romance!

Beautiful, dumb women are very good at getting the guy.

I didn't say anything about keeping him, but they're very good at flirting and reeling them in.

Want to know how to flirt?

Watch a dumb girl. She'll be the one with the flock of ten guys around her hanging on her every sashay of the hip. What's she saying? Nothing.

Lots of giggling, a smile plastered on her face and some hip movement. That's it. Men who date dumb girls can get away with giving them simple gifts, like a key chain. Dumb girls will act thrilled and surprised. Don't worry; it usually leads to bigger gifts later on. Dumb girls are actually pretty smart. They just play dumb. Men like dumb girls because they laugh at everything the man says and think everything he says is brilliant. When was the last time you acted in awe of a man or gave him a compliment?

Telling a man you like his tie is not a compliment. (But it may mean you have very good taste.) Most men say they want a smart woman, but secretly wish you'd just shut up and hang on to his every word.

Smart women are too are too busy. Even if we want to get married or settle down, we don't have the patience for any of the bullshit associated with that sort of manipulation. It's too difficult trying to remember the fake age we just told our date. Men love to be catered to and dumb girls are great at indulging the man's every whim. (So are hookers, but dumb girls are free.)

He says he wants you to be independent, but then calls you six times a day wondering where you are. Just answer him with, "I'm at the store getting you a fabulous rump roast," or better yet, "Baby, I'm getting waxed. See you tonight."

Hang up with the required yelp, so he'll really know you're at the beauty salon, and not at your job, stuck in traffic or getting ready to make your next business call and close your million dollar deal. The man understands the wax. He does not want to hear about the deal. He loves to be catered to. Toe massage? Sure. Dumb girls will give it wearing a leopard print nightie. You had to have two martinis and a hit of pot before you pulled out that leopard mess. After the first time you dolled yourself up, you hired him a private dancer and went back into your office to work and sent him straight into the arms of the dumb girl who possibly **is** the dancer we put right in front of his face.

Smart girls are sometimes very dumb, but not in the correct way, dumb. Dumb women know how to be smart, but use it infrequently. Smart women spend way too much time trying to be smart.

Familiarity with the stock market and world events may get you a good ten-minute conversation with the head of a corporation, but he won't want to take you home.

You're much better off putting on a sexy dress, show some leg and giggle a lot.

A man doesn't need to know that you know anything-He just wants to make sure you look good on his arm, while he shows off about-everything.

The smart girl is spending way too much time trying to be "smart" with him, thinking that's really the kind of woman he'll end up marrying. Wrong!

He doesn't want to talk about the boardroom in the bedroom. Dumb girls know this. Dumb girls know their place. In fairness, dumb girls may really be smart girls who got the hint.

A smart woman already possesses everything she needs-they're called boobs. A man is looking for a woman who is sexy, nice, cooks dinner, takes good care of herself, is nice to all his friends, speaks seven languages (can say yes in all of them) and can take care of the house; or hire a hot maid. Women know that to get a guys attention they need to lure them in with their breasts, not their balls. Dumb women know how to make men feel wanted. A strong, independent woman-although a turn on to a guy; makes him sweat about where he fits in. (Especially if she's busy being busy-as in real life busy, not 'acting busy, so he'll like me busy.)

Guys that like a challenge and get laid a lot will like this kind of woman. Inevitably he'll find a way to control her and make sure she knows he's the leader. Its fine, dumb girls already know this.

They're busy too. But they're only busy doing four things waxing, manicures, pedicures and shopping. Their entire existence is built upon pleasing their man and making sure they look good for him. Smart women may pick up your dry cleaning-if it's not out of the way. Women's lib and feminism really screwed it up for the smart woman. She ends up splitting the tab on meals. For dumb girls, everything is paid for—she's too dumb to divvy up the check. The man knows this.

It makes him feel needed. There's no way in the world a man would ever make a dumb girl pay. With a smart girl, he gets confused. He thinks if he doesn't let her pay, she'll be insulted. The man has to do way too much work with a smart girl.

THINGS TO KNOW ABOUT BEING SMART...

1. It may be why you're alone.

2. It isn't working.

3. Stop it. Now!

4. Before it's too late.

SOME HINTS TO HELP YOU BECOME DUMB GIRL

1. Let the man lead the conversation.

2. Always look into his eyes like he's Superman. (Helps if you really think he *is* Superman).

3. Let the man ask all the questions. If you're not sure how to answer, just repeat the question like it's the most intelligent thing you've ever heard.

4. Giggle. A lot.

5. Act helpless. (Automatically makes him feel needed.)

6. Better yet, *be* helpless.

7. Smile and nod your head to nothing in particular.

8. Throw in a witty statement about current events, every six months or so. You don't want him cheating on you with a smart girl.

When a man leaves a woman, it is not usually for a smarter girl, unless the current smart girl is legally insane; In which case he wanted out not because you're smart, but because you're crazy and smart-a deadly combination. Although a man may leave a marriage, a live-in situation or relationship for a dumb girl-he may cheat on his wife with a smart girl. But he won't leave his wife for her. She's too independent. The fact that his wife won't leave him helps greatly in his decision to cheat. He can. He knows his wife isn't going anywhere. He may leave you-a lawyer, for his secretary.

He leaves you-a Doctor, for his assistant.

He leaves you-a world-renowned chef, for the nanny. The person a man leaves you for is the exact person you are not—a needy girl.

She will do nothing except stand by his side, praise him and tell him he's the most wonderful being on the planet.

You told him that.

Once.

On your honeymoon. (He was going down on you at the time).

In all fairness, you may have never told him he was that great because he wasn't that great. Oh sure, men say that they want you to be smart, independent and self-assured, just as long as it doesn't take away from devoting a hundred and ten percent of your energy to them. How about a compromise: play dumb in the bedroom and smart in the kitchen; and don't ever talk about your income.

DUMB WOMEN (and a nice wife) DO THIS WHEN THEY MARRY

1. She cooks.
2. She cleans.
3. She takes care of the babies.
4. She's home when the man comes home.
5. She's nice to his parents.
6. She has a part-time job, working from home.

You know, just like in the 50's. (Watch a rerun of any of those shows to familiarize yourself.) Really, where did that Harvard education get you, an affair with your brilliant Morals and Ethics instructor? His wife, by the way, is a stay-at-home mom and part-time needle-pointer. (Yes, an ex-student).

Studies show that a career as a female judge is not as much the way to a man's heart as shaking your booty at the local sports bar. Even though he told you you're brilliant and would have an amazing career, he's still married to dumb girl. He knows he wouldn't be enough for you and he doesn't want the aggravation.

He just wants to have sex with you. The same things that turn him off about you as a potential wife are the exact things that turn him on, in the bedroom.

SO WHAT SHOULD I DO?
(According to my father)

Show off some leg. And show a little cleavage. They're not going to stay that perky forever. (Might as well use them while you can). And for God's sake-quit telling *HR* about that boss who's sexually harassing you! Enjoy it! And if he's single, marry him! On the other hand, I'm sure exactly how you are is exactly how you should be-And continuing to make fun of dumb women with men flocking around them is not a waste of time or energy. Yes, the right man will come along and like you just the way you are.

Even if you're kind of, well, a pain in the ass and a know it all.

Hint: Most guys (at some point before they die) decide they've had enough of the dumb girl and decide they may want an equal sparring partner to go through life with. This may or may not occur later in life. If a guy has married his first wife, divorced her, married a trophy wife second, moved on to dumb girl third-This leaves you.

Aren't you lucky? You get to be wife #4 and take care of that aging octogenarian that wouldn't dream of cheating on you. No, not because he's madly in love, he's just too old at this point. This is where you either decide you're madly in love or keep Ricardo on the side. Some people, as they mature, do decide to stay with one partner and actually have an amazing relationship-And they didn't happen to meet at 15 or 80. This is why you must continually take care of yourself because some cougar is one step ahead of you, trying to take your man and his AARP card. Do not befriend any women if you are married/living with/dating when you're older. They are just waiting for you to kick the bucket/get kicked to the curb and take your man, AARP card and all-

Another reason why having a younger guy to keep you young is the way to go.

Yes, he can be dumb, just not in bed

CHAPTER 7
I'm Too Old To Wear White

BUT I WANT TO...

I want to wear white to my wedding.
No matter how old I am, or how wrinkled I am when
I get there. (That's what Botox is for.)
I think it's only fair that I wear white. My sister got
to wear white (although she was nineteen.)
I want to wear white to my wedding, because it
seems like the right thing to do.
By 'right' I don't mean 'I should', but I 'wanna'.

I'M TOO OLD TO WEAR WHITE

In the dream we are twenty-one. Okay, maybe twenty-five; if you went for that law degree and took a summer sabbatical in Europe.

If you want to push it to mid-thirties because you became a mid-level advertising executive and slept with too many of the wrong men that seemed oh-so-right at the time (or, who really cares, because they were damn hot!). Go ahead...or pushing late 30's, look at you! Top of your law firm...now we're pushing into our 40's, perhaps even, dare I say it, 50's? And you still want to wear white? You're really still fondling those wedding magazines and folding over the pages of your favorites?

I have 2 words for you: wake-up!

Why not white?

White is virginal.

White represents new, fresh, clean; all the things you're not. Not that you never were those things, you're just not them, anymore.

White   *adjective,* **whit·er, whit·est,**

1. Of the color of pure snow. Reflecting nearly all the rays of sunlight or a similar light.

2. Light or comparatively light in color.

3. (Of human beings) marked by slight pigmentation of the skin, as of many Caucasoids.

4.pallid or pale, as from <u>fear</u> or other strong emotion: *white with rage.*

Odd. You started with number #1 fitting quite nicely in your life, ending up at number #4-Blame the dictionary. Blame society, blame the color police, but don't blame me. Who really wants to be filled with rage on their wedding day?

That's what marriage is for.

You're in your 30's, 40's, 50's, dare I say you now have your AARP card and you've finally met your soulmate, or whomever you've decided to settle down with because your soulmate is obviously never coming along. (I wouldn't settle if I were you, but do what you want. My advice is what got me to where I am, so ask someone else.) If you insist on wearing white, running off to Vegas is your best excuse. You can lie and say it was a theme wedding. You can wear white if it comes across like it's a hasty decision. People excuse last minute and disorganized behavior more so than what they deem bad choices. You certainly can wear white if you want to, no one's going to stop you; you won't get arrested (unless you have sex at the chapel…in the wedding dress). You may feel an unwritten code of ethics that tell you or, a friend that whispers into your ear, "You can't wear white, you'll look stupid."

I mean, no one will laugh directly in your face, but you may get a few subtle, "off-white with your coloring is best" or "This time of year, a crème is much classier". Yes, although that might be true, I doubt it's being said to the 27 year-old getting married to her college sweetheart.

At some point, there becomes an expiration date on wearing white. (Don't be sad about it, you can still get as drunk as you want and flirt with the best man.) Is it really necessary to loudly announce, "I'm finally here!"

Isn't it embarrassing enough that you're sending out wedding announcements that are coinciding with your best friends' daughters' bat mitzvah?

Keep your dignity, for God's sake-It may be all you've got left. (Well, you still have your teeth.) Even if you finally marry your soulmate (yes, you've met at the assisted living facility) he doesn't need to know you've been holding onto that 'Cinderella' dream all this time, does he? (Or, the wedding dress for that matter.)

At one time, you did run a corporation. You can't fall into a pool of mush, now, can you?

Technically, white represents virgins. If you're a virgin in your 30's or 40's, you need to re-think not only wearing another color, but perhaps the wedding altogether. Don't listen to your Mother. She's just excited that you're finally getting married. She'll be no help, At all.

WHAT TO WEAR

Marrying in a simple suit or Jackie O type dress is probably best. You can get married, dance, and if necessary, go to work the next day. At this stage your husband is not expecting you to give up your job/career/condo/three cars/two closets/four dogs. The most obvious choice is crème, or as we like to call it off-white, which represents 'Yes, I realize that I've done this before/never done it/may do it again –This isn't that big of a deal – let's calm down, everyone and just enjoy a mature celebration. (God, what a way to take the fun out of getting married!)

THE PROBLEM WITH GETTING MORE MATURE...and not being married (until later in life) is that you feel like an idiot telling anyone you know that you do want to still wear white.

If you are that person who say's, "Screw it, I'm wearing white", you might as well put a sticker on your car (or back) that says I finally found someone. Finding someone is great. Obviously, people are going to be happy for you-Just like the last time you found someone, emailed everyone that you were quitting your job, selling your condo and moving to Mexico.

Until 2 days later when you realized that person was nuts, didn't really have a place to live and made up a story about having something called – 2 kids and a company. Oh well, you live and you learn. Just don't do it in a white dress. People think you take things too seriously in a white dress. A crème suit says, nonchalant and I could go either way in this. If it works, it works, if not, I can use this for a luncheon.

WHAT CAN I DO?

Unfortunately, single people still hoping for a fabulous, wonderful, white wedding…get screwed.

It's just not the same feeling as when you're younger, and if it is the same feeling? Time to grow up, honey. That ship has sailed. (Yes, you are now on the ship, but it's a senior citizen 2 for 1, not the 'We're getting drunk and going to Cabo for three days' cruise.) Sure, you **can** have a fabulous, wonderful wedding, but all the bells and whistles a second, third, fourth (and so on) really get tedious and people start to whisper.

Add white to the mix and you'll really be the talk of the city/town/country/planet. Even worse, you waited to get married and still expect everyone else to make a big deal out of it. Don't waste their time. They're over you, your ideals, plans, goals-they have kid(s) to educate and school(s) to impress.

Don't believe me? Ask any other 35ish girl. (Not the thousands I've polled, they've already been asked.) Single, 30 something women will feel like they've missed their time to make a big deal out of such a wonderful event. (At 80, things turn and it's a great idea to wear white, why not, you may not even make it to the honeymoon!) And, whatever you do, don't ask your married friends. They'll lie to you.

Sure, they'll tell you, "you have every right to wear white" and "Just because you didn't get married earlier, is no reason to not enjoy yourself and feel like a real bride". Don't let them fool you-

You are a real bride; just in red, fuchsia or silver. And, FYI, that $30,000 gown they want to lend you that they wore when they were 24? It will not make you feel more like a bride than the silver Calvin Klein number you bought off-the-rack. (Even though they'd like to see someone else in it just to validate that they looked better at 24 in the damn thing. They really don't. You've been working out all these years, while they've been married 10, gained 10 and popped out 2 kids.)

AND ANOTHER THING...

Part of the problem may be finances. Remember when your parents had a dowry for you? No? Let me refresh your memory. At one time, your parents had set aside some cash to pay for all things wedding. Then, you got older. They got older. You went from boyfriend to boyfriend. Maybe you got engaged. Then you broke up. At some point, your parents gave up on you and used the money to re-do the house. They went on a cruise. They gave you a loan (that you never repaid, by the way). And, there goes your 'dowry'. No wedding money, no big wedding. That thing called time goes by. Feelings change and your ideas change about what you want. You've now been a bridesmaid (fill in the blank) of times, have thrown away/burned/sold/given back all of the mostly hideous bridesmaid dresses and vowed that you would never do that to your friends.

Don't worry. At this point, your friends want you to run off to Vegas and get married. They'll come to the dinner party (if it's not during the week, during the school year). At this point, they're even over you getting married. They have kids in high school and you're just starting out.

Although they're happy for you, they don't have time to indulge in the grand wedding you've been planning.

Your time is up for that window where it was okay to want to wear white, have a sit down dinner for 300 and dance until dawn.

You should have done all of that when everyone else was doing it.

And since you didn't, it's fine, but just keep it low key and get on with it, will you?

You'll get over it yourself, too, in time.

If you must wear white and have a large wedding, rent some friends (just like the band). You're just getting married and they've been married for 10 years now and hate their spouses, anyway. They'll spend the entire wedding flirting with everyone else's spouse and getting drunk. May be better to bring in some faux friends and have a good time. Your (paid) faux friends will be extremely supportive of your large wedding and your Poufy white wedding dress, no matter how old you are! (Pictures may seem odd to you years from now when you don't recognize anyone, but you can blame that on the alcohol.)

I CAN'T WEAR WHITE AGAIN...OR, CAN I?

The good thing about being married before (other than all of the household appliances) is that you may feel no obligation to wear white. Come on, you did it once, and the marriage didn't work out. You planned lavishly, spent a fortune of your parents' money marrying Mr. Wonderful and you didn't make it. You kept the wedding dress neatly wrapped and swore you'd give it to your daughter when she got married. Where's the dress now? You got drunk and had that "burn the dress" party last year. "That white dress thing is an omen", you tell all your friends. "Don't do it. Look what happened to me!" you scream. Of course, your ex-husband has wasted no time finding a new wife. (Yes, she's 27. Yes, she's wearing white.)

SCREW YOUR THEORY, I'M WEARING WHITE

There's the chance that I'm full of it and...you may feel the need to defend yourself. You may say "What are you talking about, I'm wearing white, damn it!

I've waited my whole life to wear white! Deciding to wear white isn't going to cause any harm, obviously, and you can wear white if you want to. It's really up to you. Embarrassing your wedding party (and potential groom) is another matter, but it's really up to you.

Wearing white when you're passed a certain age doesn't necessarily scream desperate (although wearing a 15 year-old wedding dress, does) but times are tough. Why spend the money if you've already got one from a previous break-up? Just because you were supposed to wear it once, doesn't mean its bad luck. Or does it? Wearing white for the first time gives the illusion of virginal, clean, pristine, and classy. So, whatever you need to help get you through the day, go for it.

Ultimately, wearing white is a personal choice. I mean, we only get to go around once (In life-not marriage) So whatever you want to do to make that day special-it should be up to you. (Nobody really cares, anyway.) So, wedding-schmedding! Whatever!

The important thing is that you got to keep the ring and now you have an entire set of formal china that cost a fortune even if, you have no current squeeze to impress. If that brunette reality star can do it, you certainly can!

Oh well, you got great presents and when you have the second wedding-you can ask for cash for that donation and pocket most of it. (Oh, you really thought that they gave it all to charity?)

Even though I don't really care about wearing white, personally. For most women the idea of a big, fancy wedding makes their heart palpitate, their hands sweat. Even their eyes bulge. Wearing white has become synonymous with the event of once in a lifetime.

Considering once in a lifetime may now be several times within one's life, I've offered up a few true stats about other options, courtesy of other Countries...

* *Only after Queen Victoria (19th century) wore white, did it become popular.*

(She was the 1st bride to wear white). Before that, brides wore whatever color they wanted.

*When a floozy wore white on her wedding day, the entire town gossiped about it.

*In China, white symbolizes the color for death. Red (symbolizing good luck and auspiciousness) is the most popular choice.

*In Japan, most brides' start off in white and change three times throughout the ceremony. (Much like what American women do throughout their normal day.)

*Other names for wedding white include Eggshell, Ecru, Ivory and Winter White.

*The amount of material used for the wedding went hand in hand with the 'social status' of the brides' family.

*In 1406, the Royal family wore Squirrel and Ermine. Squirrel? Easy to find. Ermine? You're on your own.

*White is known for Purity, but the color Blue used to symbolized purity.

*Traditional Finnish brides wear Black. (Just like some grooms' mothers' who are not happy her son is marrying 'that woman'.)

And most of all...white makes ones teeth look yellow.

CHAPTER 8

ARE YOU MY SOULMATE?

I think you could be my soulmate.
You.
There in the corner.
Talking with the other girl.
I was in the bathroom when you came in. I think you could be talking to the wrong girl.
Hello? Are you listening?
Sorry about the beer bottle, but I needed to get your attention.
I'm coming, officer. Ow, you're hurting my arm.

You could be my soulmate.

CHAPTER 8
ARE YOU MY SOULMATE?

SOULMATE/S-O-U-L-M-A-T-E The person who is perfect for you, your other half, the one who completes you (Even if you don't know who you are) The one you'll spend the rest of your life with (so you don't have to go through this searching, wondering, waiting, pondering crap, anymore).

The person everyone else has found; except you. Unless you already have found him/her several times, yet for whatever reason, moved on-They are that rare species of human beings who actually are happily in love and with the right person.

I know, take a minute. Let it sink in.

Hard to believe isn't it? You've seen them. They're the ones who still gaze into each other's eyes, have a few kids, still hold hands and even look like they like each other. I personally know several couples like this (and no, they didn't just act like they liked each other for the sake of this chapter). Some didn't meet the love of their life until much later in life, which is good because any earlier and they would have...

1.   Scared them off.
2.   Not been interested 2 months/2 years ago.
3.   Busy traveling.
4.   Hooking up with someone else.
5.   Figuring out what they really want.

So, you found your soulmate. Big. Deal. Yee-ha!

So have single people, several times at several different stages of their life. So did your married peeps (you may have had to search outside of the marriage to find him/her/it). Maybe Europeans and Asia have it right. What's wrong with a second wife, a second husband, a lover a mistress and so on? Yes, Mormons do it, but for some reason, it doesn't look like they're having as much fun. What's a little extra-curricular activity among adults?

Oh yes-the love part, the honor part, the soulmate part. Okay, so now you've gotten your soulmate. Is it worth it? Is it everything you ever dreamed of? Didn't you think Scott, John, Debbie and/or Bob were also your soulmate? (I know, I know, "it's different now; I can't explain it, this time it just feels right").

Now that your life is sprinkled with fairytales and puppy dog tails (at least we hope so, considering what you went through to get him/her) you can chill. Is that what you married couples are trying to tell us? "It's out there. This amazing once-in-a-lifetime-love, and you can have it, too; if you just dream hard enough, go to the right places, get set-up with the right person). So, obviously the right kind of love can happen. And it seems that when the right kind of love comes into your life, it sets the stage for you to do what we call…relax. Yes, the ability to breathe, become centered and start to worry about other things (like money, eating habits and a clothing allowance) comes into play. The ability to be happy regardless of whether you have a significant other (the right one) in your life is the goal in life, but supposing you can find another person who really does complete you- could possibly be the icing on the cake of life. People say that after they've met the one; all the others drop off and the pain, heartache, headaches and money spent was worth the wait.

You may find it hard to believe that there is one person for you out there (I was hoping for a few). But it seems that no matter where human beings are in their lives, everyone wants to find their soulmate (or someone really great to have sex with). Everyone fantasizes about that perfect person who simply glides right into our life, fits perfectly, doesn't freak us out/smother us/turn our world upside down/cause our head to spin off. But it's just, well…hard to find. And as you get older, it becomes even more difficult and confusing.

Sure, there are lots of people out there, and even more to date/sleep with/dump/chase-but rarely, it seems, does the person seem like a perfect fit. Rarely, do we feel like we've been zapped by that chemistry wand at the same time, feel the exact same thing, want the same thing, need the same thing. Men and women are out there searching for the answers like love is the Holy Grail. Some find it and act like it's the most natural, easy thing in the world to find.

The rest of us are just picky and weird and take a lot longer to give into the flow of that perfect person. And, to answer you skeptically, happily married rarities? Yes, we are purposely trying to not be with the right one. In fact, we really relish having screwed-up relationships with unhealthy people, because well, it's just fun.

And when was fun not a good time? Oh right, when dating over and over and over again, and yet the result is always the same. Another one bites the dust. Not that you're necessarily sad when it's over (you may even throw a few parties) but it can get tiring. You can even decide you want no one deciding on your own is drama free and so much better than dealing with someone else's insecurities and problems. You haven't even reconciled your own up to this point. (Yes, even after the $$ on therapy.) When people reach a certain age (and watch enough romantic comedies) they begin to ponder, "Are you my soulmate?"

This thought and verbal exchange is kind of like the little chick that walks around searching, asking everyone, "Are You My Mother?" Men can see their soulmate in every woman that turns them on, until the woman opens her mouth. Women see their soulmate in everyone. The man walking down the street that accidentally touches her shoulder. The dentist who says, "open-up", the security guard who makes eye contact. The guy in a passing car who flips her off (no, not as a sexual come-on, for making a wrong turn).

It doesn't matter. She will see him in everyone who shows up on her radar. Each new date or prospective friend is doomed.

A SAYING
Men fall in love with women they are attracted to while Women become attracted to men they fall in love with.

MY SAYING
That sucks!

Some women (by some, I may mean most) go on a date and at some point in the night (first five minutes) think "He's the guy. He's my soulmate." Which is great, if indeed, he happens to be your soulmate. Which entails hitching a ride to fairytale-land, marrying him and popping out five babies-Anything short of that (like a first date) you're just plain desperate; and a little nuts. (Yes, you may very well be psychic, but keep it to yourself. Guys aren't into that crap.) Now don't take this the wrong way. (You can take it the wrong way if you want to.) It's not that we're desperate (okay, not all of us). It's just that we live in this fantasy world that each new man we meet is the one. We can't help it. Inevitably, he will look at us a certain way, and we will assume we are in love.

We've been programmed to believe that there is one special someone out there just for us. Until you get over the whole soulmate BS and decide several men in many states is a heck of a lot more fun (and easier on the heart). We're raised with the theory that our soulmate, our other half, has got to be out there, somewhere. Is he taking his bar exam?

Is he getting drunk in a bar? Did we already blow him off? Will we ever meet him/her/it? We don't care what he's/she's doing, where he/she is, we just want to find him, mold him, change him, dress him up, and get him to say I do/I will/Oh crap/Okay/What the hell.

Primary Soulmate: Lust, passion, physical- Chemistry, competition, sex, insecurity, cockiness, self-serving, head level-

Who we think we should be with-smart, educated, respectful, kind, loving, warm, security, caretaker, good provider, meets our emotional needs, boring, practical… good on paper.

Soul level-joy, feeling good, deeply connected;

Happy, content, fills all the gaps, deeper in love each year. Depending on the type of soulmate you're searching for (yes, we all pretty much want the soul level) but may end up with one of the other two).

WHAT WILL MY SOULMATE LOOK LIKE?

Although you may have been carrying around a photo (that you've torn from a magazine) and think you know exactly what your soulmate will look like (that's the hot guy in this weekend's blockbuster, you idiot). He/she may come in many different forms/shape/sizes/ethnicities/deformities/character flaws than what you originally thought. He can be a successful commodities trader for a big New York City firm or the grocery checkout person you've been flirting with. Whether or not he/she wants you may be an entirely different story.

The point of your soulmate is that he/she's supposed to be the one, so he/she not wanting you, shouldn't be an issue; negating the chance that there's a soulmate glitch in your holy grail chart and God (and/or you were just plain wrong). It's okay, since you're older and been through this 'false alarm soulmate thing before, you'll be able to move on to the next one much faster.

Continuing to chase after someone you believe to be your soulmate (just because they look like who you've imagined) can cause frustration, which may land you in the loony bin or facing 10 to 20 (if they call the cops).

JUST BECAUSE SOMEONE TELLS YOU THEY'RE YOUR SOULMATE DOESN'T MEAN YOU HAVE TO BELIEVE THEM...

Your parents lied to you about the Easter Bunny, Santa Clause, the Tooth Fairy (sorry, if

I've blown it for you) and having enough money to send you out of state to college. If they're willing to lie to you, what makes you think you can believe a perfect stranger (that's charmed you out of your satin dress) into believing they're your soulmate?

At this point, you must talk to God, some friends and call in some angels to make sure they truly are your soulmate. Nowadays, just trusting anyone who tells you things you'd like to believe is simply naïve. It's a big bad world out there and weird experiences happen. You can think someone is wonderful one minute and (after you've sobered up) realize what a complete tool they actually were.

Telling someone they're your soulmate is just silly. If they are, you both should just know it and talking about it just becomes downright odd.

Your ability to just know, I think-Is what they're (The Gods) talking about when assuring you that your soulmate just shows up. (Unlike a stalker who shows up and tells you they're your soulmate.)

*Yes, it can be confusing to know the difference, which is probably why you're in this predicament in the first place.

Completely made-up. No Scientific research done, no people polled, no animals harmed in the writing of this section...

14 to 21...Experimentation, exploration, rejection, lust, love, sex, secrets and Possibilities. (Ah, the good life.)

22 to 25 In the real world, getting a real job and/or smoking more pot. Working on career. Either dumping first love (that you've been over for three years) jumping from boyfriend to boyfriend-trying someone older and swearing you are not going to settle down until you are **old.** Or, at least 29!

25 to 30...Starting to feel haggard (even though you have absolutely no right to!) You are still in your prime, but feeling as though you had better hurry up and meet someone before you're 30. Babies haven't quite kicked in, unless you're accidently knocked up, extremely maternal or just want to go ahead and start already because you've married the love of your life-you have money in the bank and you are ready to start that white house/picket fence journey (be careful; your 40's are around the corner, so you'll be hitting menopause while they're driving you crazy doing drugs, having sex and ditching school, just like we did to our parents).

30 to 35...You've begun to ponder children-unless you've decided you don't want any (until you hit 42 and really start to freak out). You start to look for the love of your life and every guy you date is potential. You can still date a guy for potential, but teetering on 35, you better start to weed them out. That actor that never made it, but still tells you his fabulous fantasies about when and if.

Terrific, wish him well. Tell him you'll search for him in that gossip magazine and move on; it ain't worth-unless you want to be strapped to a dirty diaper 24/7 waiting with him for his big break.

The finance guy you so desperately wanted isn't making the kind of money he used to make. So, he's probably out, too. Unless you ride out the recession with him (which is awfully nice of you; you should be marrying him for love, anyway. So you probably owe him that much). Part of growing up is (ugh) dating the right kind of person. Going after the player, charming, best looking guy in the room is great for ego and sex, but unless he's ready to settle down and be the man you want him to be, he's just gonna be someone who breaks your heart and takes you down the wrong road-again. Unless you turn the tables and break his heart first (which is loads more fun).

35 to 39... You've officially started your freak-out even if/because of/even if you don't have-a great job and dating non-stop, in-between traveling and spending money (of course). (Unless you're bi-sexual, gay or asexual-In those cases, you are more open- minded and still wanting to experiment.) You'll probably be having a blast if you love your life, have lots of friends and get to do what you want-when you want to do it. Don't wallow in your own misery that you are the **only** one in this position who hasn't met the love of your life, because several other million haven't met him/her either. You may start to look into on-line dating/having sex with your neighbor/cousin/agent or ex-boyfriends perhaps may be re-visited.

40-45... You may have an epiphany and decide you're happy right where you are (how dare you!)

And in fact, have decided the soulmate you've been searching for is...you. (Even if you've gotten quite sick of having sex with yourself.) At this stage of the game, you may have decided that you don't even know if you want kids (may not even be able to have them) and not so sure you really want to get married, anyway. If you do decide you want a kid, you'll start to look everywhere to find your husband/lover/sperm donor.

You may talk to therapists, friends, your rabbi/pastor and/or even a stranger you meet on the street.

You'll possibly stop new mothers and ask them if they...
A. Have a husband.
B. Did it on their own.
C. Are happy they had the baby?
D. Miserable and feel they shouldn't have had the baby?

The reason you have these questions is because you are full of inner turmoil about your clock running out, eggs drying up and not sure what to do.

You may not even be freaking out, but because your eggs are, they send you subliminal messages to hurry the hell up. You've realized you have a very short window to freeze your eggs, date, fall in love (the old-fashioned way) and meet a guy who's willing to 'pop' out a baby with you quickly.

By quickly, I mean, whenever you end up pregnant by the massive amounts of sex you will have trying to accidently have a baby the old-fashioned way. If you're divorced and have kids, you may decide you want another. You may run into problems if you fall in love with that boy-toy you're currently in love with when he suddenly tells you he wants children-but, not for about 10 years. Which is great for him, because he's 24, but not for you, because you're 44 and unfortunately are running/have run/didn't have----time. There are several options out there if you still want to have a kid(s). Having someone else carry it, using your hubby's sperm/boyfriends sperm/strangers sperm, adoption or you can always acquire more pets (See chapter 19). A better option is to record a baby screaming his/her head off in the middle of a restaurant/movie theatre/bathroom/elevator/middle of the night, play it back often and you may quickly change you mind about wanting them at all.

You may have had a quiet conversation with yourself (cried yourself to sleep) that you didn't really want any/another/several more children, anyway, and that having none/one/a plethora would only get in the way of those things you like to do in life.

Like live it.

46-50... By now, you may have actually decided being single is a lot better than being in something unhealthy with child(ren) you can't quite put your finger on what the term unhealthy means, but it sounds bad and you've decided you'd rather not do it. On the other hand, you may still be a hopeless romantic/don't really care that you didn't have a kid/meet your husband at the same time all your friends did and are on your own journey. You will meet the guy you are going to be with and live happily ever after.

(Your ever after just may be a little shorter in length than everyone else's, but, not necessarily.)

At some time or another most people fall in love and get married. Then, they may realize they don't want to be with that person –

Anymore.

So they leave.

This is the person that you end up with.

Someone that's been disposed of by someone else.

Oh well, that's what makes the world go round and round and round. The nice thing about never being married at this stage is that you haven't gotten a divorce. (If this makes you uncomfortable, I suggest a quickie wedding in Vegas, followed by a quick 'oops' and there you have it, a divorce.)

Now you get to feel like you've at least experienced marriage; and you'll feel like you are part of a group of species previously foreign to you...

Like Walruses...

Dating at this stage in life can be strange because it can go a few ways...

1.   You may decide you are only going to date younger and hotter, because really, who doesn't like their ego stroked. (And other body parts that someone older may be too lazy or tired to accomplish without the aid of that little blue pill).

2.   You may have gotten to the above stage because you tried dating all the same age, same religion, great on paper and found that you were still single, hadn't fallen in love and/or still fantasizing about that young, hot whomever across the room/bar/country.

3.   This term is also referred to as the bigger, better deal.

4.   It sometimes happens when you are feeling pretty good about yourself, not feeling so great about that other person you are dating/sleeping with/blowing off and want someone else. You can do bigger, better, more. Yes, you can have it all! As long as you're okay having it when you're in your 60's. (Hey, people are living into there 90's now so this shouldn't be a problem!)

ALL The Good Soulmates You May Have Passed Up

Yes, I know, it's probably hard to believe you were enjoying your life so much, that you actually may have passed up a few good ones.

But it happens.

You shouldn't worry about it too much.

If you want to spend a weekend/a night or a month carrying on about all the good ones that you should have married/ended up with.

Go right ahead, but it certainly won't get you anywhere, except for depressed. Of course, if you happen to follow through and take a journey to the past to see how they all turned out.

(You know the one you should have been with) you may be happy to find out that they are now...

1.   Fat.

2. Not as hot as they used to be.
3. Married to someone not as hot as you.
4. Still the same and you pretty much screwed up.

It's okay, No matter what the outcome you can always tell yourself this: You simply weren't ready to take in all his finesse-it's the same thing you tell yourself when a guy dumps you, FYI. Yes, you possibly didn't want him the first time, for whatever reason and now days/months/years later, you have an epiphany that he was the right one all along. Even if you told yourself, 'I will never Marry (fill in the blank). You now realize that telling yourself you would never marry so and so has come back to haunt you. The crappy way you treated him, the way you led him on, the hot and cold games you played (okay, you weren't really playing games, you were seeing other guys-the wrong guys, but you didn't want to fully let him go). Here's the deal. He's now married/seeing/shacking up/gay...with someone else, so you kind of have to 'get over it'
And move on.

Even if you think you screwed up, there really is no going back. Unless you consider stalking/chasing/sending nude photos will do the trick to bring him back into your life. The only problem with this is that when you did have the chance to have him as your own back then, he had much less baggage. He didn't have three kids, a wife and a place in the Hamptons. He didn't have two dogs, another mortgage and another baby (or grandchild on the way). This time around, it's much more difficult for him to extradite himself from his current situation, just to be with you, now that you've decided he's for you.

You probably only want him because now somebody else does. Okay, you may have decided he's the best guy you ever dated, but that's a slippery slope, too. Really?

He's the best guy? I guarantee if you go through your rolodex of paramours you will remember a few other good ones, as well. Never mind that they walked away from you, they were still good ones. You can always go back and try to win them over again, but since they walked away from you once, chances are pretty good, they'll remember why and do it again. No use crying over spilled semen. Move on. Go catch another fish. There are lots of men out there…with baggage that you've never even met!

YOUR SHALLOW GUIDE TO GETTING YOUR SOULMATE TO MARRY YOU

1. When you're on the date, just smile.
2. Never talk about you even if he asks. Always turn the subject back to him.
3. Have the same birthday and time of birth, as he. Act surprised! (Several years later, of course!)
Fake the orgasm at the table (quietly).
5. Laugh at everything, but not loudly.
6. Don't talk.
7. Act coy. If you don't know how to do this, watch cats and very pretty girls when they flirt.
8. Don't act interested if you are.
9. If you're not interested, it's okay to act interested. You can even sleep with him on the first date as long as you really don't want anything other than sex. A true test to see if he really is your soulmate? Sleep with him on the first date.
10. Name drop an Ivy League school you never went to, but pretend you did, even though you don't 'do anything' right now.
Always be seven years younger than your date. If your soulmate is younger than you, you can say your real age. He's into older women. (He also thinks the sex is going to be filled with S and M.)
12. Have parents who are aristocrats, or will lie for you. Pretend not to care that they're aristocrats.
13. Act shy.
14. Learn to give good blowjobs. Feign surprise when he compliments you.

15. Don't show up for your second date. But show up later at his door, with sex toys.

This is the fastest way to ensure that you will marry your soulmate. (Or, you'll scare the hell out of him and he'll never call you again.)

Either way, you'll have closure.

Hey, we're on the fast plan here. We can't be worrying about scared soulmates. If he's not in it for the long haul, get rid of him. This is the way you weed the good soulmates from the bad.

Oh yeah, one more thing, there are lots of soulmates. Don't despair.

Think back to every time you said, "He's my soulmate" What, you think we just say that once? By the time we're married, we're on soulmate # 20. Whichever one wins is our soulmate. We just think every one of them is the one. And not to throw you off, but one date can change your life. On the other hand, one date can make you wish you hadn't gone on that date, either.

JOBS THAT MAY ENHANCE BRINGING IN YOUR SOULMATE

Work as his intern, Work as his secretary. Work as a waitress, Work as a stripper.

HOW TO TRAP YOUR SOULMATE

Sometimes, that soulmate of yours…

(After marriage, I've heard) turns into a caveman, and you have to decide if you actually want that slovenly sloth that was, oh so different, when you were *just* dating - Which includes, but is not limited by: Letting him do whatever he wants. Don't complain about his growing belly. Plaster a fake smile (take a class, learn how to do it). Look through 1950's magazines. (You'll get the gist). No complaining. The social life may no longer revolve around bars, dinner parties, social events, tennis and romantic weekends away. Trapping your soulmate may takes a lot of work and in the end you may or may not find it's worth it.

You may realize that the marriage your friend has that looks so wonderful—isn't really at all.

And if it *is, stop hanging around them; don't they make you sick to your stomach?*

Try to remember everything she went through to get the guy she married. (Or make it up.)

And when was the last time you really saw them dressed up and went out, in the real world, outside of their house? When was the last time you didn't see her husband in sweats in front of the TV? Coming home from work in that suit (then quickly changing out of it) doesn't count. I know, I know, you thought, "I find my soulmate, I get married, have a fabulously rich rewarding social life –fun things to do all the time, lots of activities, events, nights out on the town…

Oh wait, I did that when I was single".

Crap! Then you realize all of that wasn't as fun as you thought.

You've Got Him-Big Deal-Now What?

Sure, you've had a great time (you've been to every event there is) but now that you're about to settle down With that love of your life soulmate you've spent your entire life searching for-the reality of it just may be a little less exciting than what you've imagined it to be. What are you supposed to do now? Back out on your soulmate just because you've decided you're bored?

Come on, you cannot expect the party to continue every single day, can you? Isn't part of the fun of finding your soulmate; the actual daily life you're now going to live with stability, contentment and a lifetime of security? Haven't you dreamed about this day since you were a little girl? Isn't this everything you always ever wanted?

Yes, there's a chance you were wrong.

There is a remote chance you spent your time fantasizing and imagining this wonderful (completely different than the reality of that life). If you'd like to know exactly what you are missing-

I suggest spending some time at your friend's house-you know, that married couple you've always imagined are extremely happy. (You can pick whomever you'd like, but if you happen to spot a certain A list couple that always seem to be in bliss I suggest asking if you can live with them). They would be great subjects for your experiment.

You know, the couple(s) you are secretly jealous of and wish you were living just like them? Go ahead, step into their shoes (a figure of speech-you can wear their shoes if you want to, but that's not the point of the exercise). Step into their life momentarily. See what all the fuss is about. If you can, try not to get roped into any sort of weird babysitting or pet duties; that's not the point of the exercise, either. The point is becoming an observer; a fly on the wall-if you will. You don't want to interrupt the subjects by getting in their way/changing their daily routine/flirting with the husband/being a pain in the ass-what you are trying to find out is how they work as a team. How they complete each other, all that 'soulmatey' crap, and all. What you're doing here, is either becoming increasingly more jealous (which may lead to a restraining order if you decide you want to live with them on a permanent basis) or leave you justified that you were right all along and the grass is not necessarily greener-Just, ah, different.

Before you decide to marry your happily ever after, this might not be a bad idea, in-general.

Go poll a few thousand married couples and find out what it's really like behind the scenes.

Is it really just like how you lived with an ex-boyfriend from 20 to 23 and got kicked out of the apartment complex?

Was it like those amazing four months with that French guy – what's his name – that you met at a friend's dinner party, he moved in that night and never left-until the authorities showed up and deported him?

Is it how you imagined it would be? Is everyone always happy, smiling and playful? Is it just like an amusement park (without the high price for candy). Do I really need to shower, do my hair, look my best at all times, or is the point of finding your soulmate so that you can finally just be yourself? Or, is being yourself what got you into this nonsense in the first place? Is confusion part of finding your soulmate?

Am I supposed to be quirky/weird/just me/ fake it/wear lots of make-up/ try not to be funny/smart/contemplative/complex/anal/A.D.D? Is the point of the whole soulmate thing – That suddenly zap he/she's there – you're suddenly fixed? And by fixed, I mean you suddenly have an urge to keep everything in your underwear drawer color coordinated?

Um…I actually thought I would have an answer for you by the end of this chapter, but all I've got is a headache. I'm going to go lie down.

I'll get back to you with some answers after I have dinner with that A list duo and get some pointers.

An Ode To Finding Your Soulmate

When I was a wee girl, living in a small town, I used to coo. It was my mating call and all the boys would come running.

    (I had a pet bunny rabbit, too.)

    I was 5.

    Things work a little differently now.

    My advice? A shot of vodka for him.

    Rope.   (A little soap for the wrists,

                         also for him.)

    Sexy lingerie.   Yes. For you.

CHAPTER 9
SIZE DOES MATTER
(Yes, women lie)

I don't care how much you weigh; how much hair
you have left; how small your package is.
What I do care about is if you love me…enough.
I can't tell you in percentages how much is enough;
but considering your shortcomings, it had better be
A lot.

A FEW THINGS WOMEN LIE ABOUT

Penis size – "doesn't matter".

2. How great we think you are.

3. I don't care "What you do, how much money you make, or don't make, what your education, parents, background or religion are", as long as you don't cheat.

4. The number of guys we've slept with.

6. The size of your car/wallet/apartment/trust fund/retirement fund/gut/closet/habits.

7. We're lying when you think we're telling you the truth.

8. Just so you know, this is actually entertainment for us.

WE LIE! WE LIE! WE LIE!

We don't mean to (unless it's on purpose).

We lie to make you feel better. I know. It's not really nice of the female species to do that. Here's the truth-we probably really don't like your back hair, no matter how much we tell you we like the teddy bear look. The comment is reserved for real teddy bears and should never be confused with the real human being with hair in unwanted places.

Other unwanted places? Your ears…your balls…your shoulders…your toes. This is really shallow (because men aren't shallow, just women) there are other things…deeper things…that we lie about.

We don't want to hurt you. But our lies are for different reasons than your lies. You want sex out of it. If we're looking for a relationship, we want other things. Like love, security, your left nut. We want to be taken care of. We're looking for daddy, or a facsimile, thereof. It can be difficult to expect chivalry when you may offer (via text) to come over and cuddle (have sex) but don't offer to pay for the valet when you meet at a restaurant. This is called tacky and should be eliminated at all costs. Sure, you can blame women's lib, but I'd rather call it cheap. Taking care of someone should include, but not limited to; walking on the outside, covering to and from a date, paying for valet if you're meeting at the restaurant (if you can't afford valet, you can't afford my pussy).

Her name is Fiona.

She's 7.

Persian.

Oh, you thought I meant my…

Oh, please.

WE LIE

Of course we don't tell you that we lie. That would just be cruel. If we've chosen to fall in love with you, chances are, we're lying about something. We just don't admit it. Please don't ask. It only complicates things.

It's just like what guys do *"Deny, Deny, Deny* (thanks, Dad) only we look at you and lie instead of denying it. Yes, we want you to lie when we ask if you think we've gained any weight. Unless you are no longer screwing us, we won't want to know the truth. If you're getting some on the side, not having sex with us and still telling us how amazing we are there's something not kosher here. Although, you can be pretty good at telling us everything we want to hear and still getting some on the side, while pleasing us at home. Men know if they tell the truth to a woman she's going to cause a teeny-tiny scene.

She'll yell/scream/cry/ignore/withhold/throw things/hit and all of these things are not something a guy wants to deal with, even if he brought it on himself. Keeping the peace should be the goal on both sides; at all cost. What's a little lie going to hurt anyone? Really, where did the truth ever get you?

Time out. Locked in your room for a weekend? Thrown out of the house? When did the truth lead to a romantic dinner? A new purse? A fun Sunday stroll through the park?

Truth and openness really have no place in a real relationship, unless you like sleeping on the couch. (And make-up sex can be pretty amazing.)

WE LIE AND TELL YOU WE'RE NOT LYING

Women don't lie; we are your mother-for God's sake. Would your mother lie to you? So, we wouldn't lie. We don't want to let you down. Do you want us to let you down? If you knew that we lied, your fragile ego couldn't handle it, so we lie about lying.

What would be the point of doing otherwise?

Men count on women to support them. We cannot be your best friend/confidant/help your ego, self-esteem/slay the dragon/bring home the bacon-if we tell you the truth all the time. It may be confusing to tell the difference between picking on you and lying. Picking on you may entail a truth that is hidden in a complaint. Yes, it's like a code. You'll figure it out after you've spent a great deal of time with that person. Remember, we are only lying to protect you.

Just like men lie to us about not wanting to sleep with anyone else.

LYING ABOUT MONEY

We will, of course, tell you that we don't care about money. As long as you're a hard worker and help create a comfortable life. By comfortable, we may be far off in compromising what that means. We will lie about what comfortable means. This only happens the older we get.

You see, when we get older, we get set in our ways-just like you. We already have some of the things we waited for you to provide to us. We already did it ourselves and found that we may have even preferred things that way. It was easier, no one telling us what to do, when to do it, how to do it. We have a boss for that. And that even became tedious, so we started our own company. Now we don't have anyone telling us what to do and we kind of like it. Don't get this confused with you not being established in some capacity.

By established we may mean (but not limited to) a regular job, some sort of title on some sort of corporate ladder, some level of stability with perhaps a 401K, retirement plan and/or savings in a bank/safe/locked drawer somewhere. Yes, we love you for just being you.

By that, we mean, you are not enough...

Just the way you are.

We love you and we love it when you buy us nice stuff. If you want to. No pressure.

By the time we wait around for the perfect one, we have possibly given up the fact that the other person will be our knight in shining armor, so we do things for ourselves. We buy $400 dollar shoes (because we worked for it) we treat ourselves to $100 dinners (because we worked hard all day) we even treat ourselves to a spa day (because we want to). We didn't wait for you to provide all these things for us. But we do still want sex.

By sex, I mean dinner, a movie and then sex.

After a certain stage in life, we've come to the conclusion that maybe we only need someone for 3 on the 20 things on our list. In that case, these three things better fill the gap of the missing 17. Just because you're in love doesn't mean you need to forego a certain lifestyle (which you've become accustomed to because you earned it).

Staring at your boyfriend's eyeballs until you can count the freckly things is not entertainment (unless this is fun for you while stoned).

CHAPTER 10

VACATIONS

All those places you've spent
Money/Bought clothes for/Had a hangover
because of; and told wonderful stories of
debaucheries one-night stands…

Sometimes I need a vacation…
From my vacation…
And then I'll be on *that* vacation trying to
figure out what I'll do on the *next* vacation.
I'm trying to figure out a way to just go
from vacation to vacation
Instead
Of living my life

VACATIONS AND THE SINGLE GIRL

The single girl looks at vacations several different ways. Some of those ways depend on whether she has a great guy and they have great sex. Vacations with these boys/men are fun. There's no problem except for the occasional mature thought that creeps into her head, "I really should be looking for the man I'm going to marry instead of sleeping with this guy." This thought usually doesn't last too long. She's already on the plane joining the mile-high club by the time it's come and gone. If you're single and without the required male companion of the moment, you may be rejoicing that you've finally let go of that no good (whatever you felt like calling him) at the time. You may be taking this vacation because you are finally free of what's his name. (Unfortunately, you do remember his name, but calling him what's-his-name is the first step in forgetting him all together.) Because all of your friends may be hooking up with others, so you may be taking this trip alone. While you were spending the last 2 years breaking up with the dude, everyone else found a partner. You may find that the few single friends you could play with- don't go out. Ever.

Well, occasionally they go to the store when the local delivery service doesn't have the flavor yogurt they want. You can't count on these girls to be fun, anyway. They haven't had a drink since 1974 and it was a Wine-Spritzer. You may find you have few single friends left. The one you enjoy the most may be broke, so you will have to pay to have her accompany you on your vacation. This is fine. You have the money and she's a great wing woman. In fact, she's just a little bit less attractive than you, which means you secretly know you're going to get all the guys.

Don't bring your least attractive friend no matter how much money she's got, she may not attract any guys at all; and no other guy will want to put his buddy through that. Even though he may find you hot, having to hook his buddy up with your ugly friend isn't going to work. Your ugly friend may be fine for dinner, or a play, just don't bring them on vacation. Leave her home and take your broke hot friend on the trip, at least she'll be fun and will attract the hot guys.

On the bright side, chances are, you are one of a fantastic group of single chicks with some amount of money, social status and looks. You have a great time going on vacations, meeting men and having a blast. The problem only starts when you're back home, in your real life.

You may decide to vacation.

For life.

Vacationing, for life-is great, if you have lots of money, time and nothing else to do. You can just fly from place to place; visit friends, bother people that only invited you for a night. Or, better yet, live your life out of hotels. Who doesn't love clean sheets, being pampered and having everything at your whim, whenever you want it? (Uh, that's what you're supposed to be doing with your husband, FYI-Or, having someone else pay for both of you to enjoy.)

GOING ALONG WITH THE COUPLES

You may choose to go on a couple's vacation. This can be a load of fun during the day. At night, you're screwed; you're just not getting screwed. (Unless you pick someone up and then you quickly become the slutty single friend.)

This vacation is fine if you're in your spiritual awakening phase. You just want to make sure you are not staying in any bed and breakfast cottages where the walls are thin enough to hear a mouse squeak, because that isn't the only thing that you will hear squeaking.

Fortunately, if you're the only single one out of all your friends, you'll get to meet all of the available ski instructors, scuba diving teachers, salsa dancers and bartenders at your La-La land vacation.

Hooking up on the sly is the way to go. This way, they don't think you're a slut but they'll be envious (and probably stop having sex with their husband/boyfriend/significant other). They'll all drool over your find and secretly wish they were with someone this hot. Meeting that hot someone on your vacation is great, but it's a catch 22. Now that friends' husband/boyfriend/significant other will decide they're not going to set you up with what's his name when you get back home. If you like this kind of guy, you're not going to be into his friend. Doesn't he understand vacation sex?

Doesn't he get that you are just having fun and this isn't the kind of guy you take seriously?

"Yes, please still set me up with Brad who's recently divorced with two kids and an ex-wife who still lives in his house. This is just for fun." (You lie.) You realize that you may have experienced a night of ecstasy, but you've probably screwed up any chance of your friends' boyfriends setting you up with a potential mate to marry. You should probably just go on this vacation with your friends and meditate (or mediate) the whole time. Listening to them argue with each other will turn you off from meeting anyone; and spending some quality time on your own in the company of miserable people could possibly be the best vacation you could ever ask for. And, look at it this way, you still have Brad to look forward to when you get home.

GOING IT ALONE

The upside? You don't have to pay for any of your friends. You can sleep in/lay out/party/drink/work out/flirt as much as you want.

A group of women can be intimidating and men won't approach you. Men love approaching women who are alone (even when you don't want them to).

So, imagine being on vacation alone! Have a few Martini's to get into the swing of things. Spend your entire vacation looking hot. Exude confidence and vulnerability. (The perfect woman.) You can tell whoever you've met that you're on vacation alone because you needed to –get away/just broken up/recently widowed/in-transition/horny.

Or, you can say, "I've come to be on my own and explore this city/state/country". If you want, tell everyone you meet that you've just been left. Everyone will know someone wonderful to set you up with. You also tell whomever you've met, that you're waiting for your friend. When you're friend doesn't show up, he'll feel sorry for you and like you because you're vulnerable. Later, just lie and tell him your friend got sick and had to leave the city/state/country.

He'll never know the difference. Going on vacation alone, you'll never-not have lots of choices, especially with everyone wanting to set you up (and all of the husbands hitting on you in the gym of the hotel). Make sure not to sleep your way through that city/country/reservoir, thus you've suddenly gone from hot single female on her own to "that skanky slut is still here?"

GOING WITH THE PACK

If you get a group of single chicks and decide to go on a vacation, you're going to have to make sure you've brought cuter clothes than all your friends; this is the most important factor of your trip.

(Much more than getting the window seat on the flight.) Having lots of cute clothes (with lots of available options) is important, because after seeing what a friend is wearing, you may need to make an excuse-run back up to the room and change into something -

Hotter/shorter/sluttier/classier. The cutest girl always gets the pick of the guys, so make sure you bring something else to the table. You need to have the best legs, nicest ass, best hair, best boobs, nicest nails…something. Otherwise you'll be eaten by the sharks surrounding you. (Yes, these are your friends, but this **is** vacation.)

And the rules are suddenly different. Everybody's horny, everybody wants the same guy and everyone will be fighting over who gets him.

Oh God, here comes the contest.

May the biggest bitch win.

Or, the flirtiest.

Or, the one that ignores him.

Whichever works, that girl will get him.

Which will leave the others to fend for themselves from – the rest. This is called-The leftovers. Leftovers are fine. It's a vacation. You're probably going to be drunk the whole time, anyway. You don't have to marry him. You're probably never going to see him again - after tonight. If you feel the need to brag about the hot one-night stand(s) you had, take a picture of some random hot guy and claim him as your one-night stand. No one will know the difference. There's bound to be competition between Packs of single females, so always do your scoping early when you arrive on your vacation. The best thing you can do when your friend spots a cuter guy first is to reply casually, "Really, you think he's cute? He's a little cheesy, isn't he?" This way, she will immediately focus elsewhere, and you can sink your claws into him.

You may find that your suitcase has been tossed into the ocean, but hey, all's fair in love and war.

I'M STAYING HOME

This plan works well if you are into hibernating and don't feel up to partying. While all your friends are planning their next trip to Aspen, you can't even think about what to have for dinner.

The thought that you have to come up with a plan for your next vacation is terrifying. You don't even know where your next date is coming from. You're considering going back through your cell phone and calling **all** the men's names in it, just because you can't remember who they are. Forget the fact that if you can't remember who they are, you probably never found them very interesting. You realize you're on a desperate mission. You've decided you don't want to be spending your next vacation alone and your next vacation happens to be that place you called home while growing up. You can't go back to where you grew up without bringing your significant other. How do you explain to your friends and their five children where you've been? Oh sure, they tell everyone how successful you are.

Please. Deep down (not that deep) they feel sorry for you.

They could care less that you have the entire latest couture collection for Fall. (Yes, the entire collection.) It doesn't matter to them. They're worried about your eggs, even if you're not. If you're too embarrassed to show up on vacation, just skip it all together. Make a vacation for yourself – at home. Spend time pampering yourself with all of the products you spent a fortune on, yet never used. (Try not to apply everything all at once, thus causing a breakout-which may lead to no dates until everything clears up.) Creating a vacation, at home, can be fun. Especially if you turn off your cell phone and take the day to do nothing…but pamper yourself. Whatever you do, do not start focusing on your past. Do not start dreaming up elaborate fantasies about the future. Both will make you feel worse and you'll ruin your at home vacation. If this happens, immediately hop in your car/train/bus/bicycle- and get out of the house.

CHAPTER 11
MARRIED MEN
(You know, other people's husbands)

Okay, here's the deal. You're alone. You're lonely. You're horny. Every man looks good, especially married men.

Why?

Other women want them, which makes them seem immediately appetizing. Single guys? Who wants someone no one else wants? When you're single and out there in the dating scene, No one looks that great. Sure, from a distance they all seem terrific, but up close and once you start talking?

Boring.

Boring.

Boring.

You start to wonder, "what happened to all the good ones?" In fact, you've decided you've dated all the good ones and there's simply no one left. Just when you thought all the good ones were no longer on the planet earth, you actually see some of the good ones. Slight problem...they're wearing a wedding ring. Or worse, they're walking hand-in-hand with they're beloved in broad daylight, like they're the happiest beings on the planet.

This is more than you can bear. How can it be? "How can those two people be so happy?"

"She's not even that hot" you tell yourself about his wife. "I'm way cuter than she is" and even "how did she get him?"

The right thing to do is move on but something stops you; something called jealousy, competition... others call it boundaries. You just call it the way you want it. You want what you want – whenever you want it, no matter who gets hurt.

Then there are the women who do their best to stay away from married men. At first, you pride yourself on your strength at pushing that leech away. You ignore all advances, return gifts and stop returning phone calls. Then you go on a few more bad dates with available men such as Pathetic Peter with the garlic breath and braggadocios behavior.

A few more dates with the guy who orders first and doesn't open your door. A few more nights out with "two minute sorry Steve." Dates like these make it harder to ignore the- married, smart, good looking athletic guy who flirts with you non-stop at the office. "What ring?" you ponder. "I don't see a ring." Okay, maybe you didn't ask, but he's not wearing one and you're the single one. Why pry? It's only lunch. It's only dinner. It's only sex. It's only heartbreak. It's only marriage. While many women do not fall prey to men like this and, even if they did, would immediately run the other way. The ones who get caught in the web of the married man find they're lured into a land of La-La and convince themselves this is better than being in the single's world. They decide married men are more exciting and can offer something single men can't, such as feelings, communication and/or consistent sex.

WHAT ARE MARRIED MEN?

Married men are the guys giving you all the compliments.

They do this because they want what they can't have. They already have a wife and now they're trying to get into your pants. You represent something they don't have in their current marriage. (No, they may never tell you the truth). They will fill your brain with flattery. Married men aren't afraid to tell you all of the wonderful things you know you are-because afterwards, they are going back home right into the naïve and loving arms of their wife. The reason you think you want them is because you find them to be really charming, open, kind and honest.

Of course, they're probably charming to everyone, which is the reason they are so attractive to begin with.

Married men (From your single eyes)

1. Open doors.

2. Let you order first.

3. Fawn all over you without acting like a stalker.

4 Let you orgasm first.

(All of the above can be acquired by dating a European)

Single guys may do some of the above, but probably not #4. Although you may be charmed, you may also be disappointed that this wonderful guy you are about to date/sleep with/fall in love with-is married to someone else and not even available for you to marry.

One problem? This position has been taken by someone else...who? His wife. All of the above is fine if you just want sex, some gifts and have no morals. In fact, his wife would probably be shocked at how great he treats you-because most of the time she thinks he's a pretty big prick. Although a married man is trying to get into your pants as well, they probably have created a fantasy that you fulfill something that their otherwise-amazing wife-cannot. On the other hand, neither he nor his wife is actually that amazing-and you've made the whole thing up in your mind.

By the way, he's still cheating on her...with you.

WHY DO MARRIED MEN LOOK GOOD?

Married men look good because they love to flirt, are open, are confident, charismatic and seem like they have it all together. Although a married man may be madly in love with his wife, thinking of any woman naked turns him on. A married man may look good to you simply because they are unattainable, unavailable and perhaps even live in another state-which is fine with you if you don't want anything that runs too deep. Even if a man is happy and in love, he may want to screw around. This is just the way it is.

Depending on his level of guilt and morals, he may or may not cheat. He may only cheat once. He may have a girlfriend. He may even fall in love and keep her on the side. But chances are, he won't leave his wife. Even if he leaves his wife, this means he comes to you with all of that baggage from that marriage. You're probably better off just fooling around with him and letting him stay married. Statistics show that even if a man cheats on his wife, it's in most cases, the wife who initiates the divorce 90% of the time. If the man you're screwing around even though he vows to love his wife, you're bound for the same outcome. And don't think she's not out doing the same thing? Why do you think she's not up his ass complaining when he comes home three hours late – and wondering why she's taken up tennis with such fervor?

BUT I'M HORNY AND HE'S HOT

I like my independence-
I have absolutely no problem when Jake goes home...to his wife

You may decide to have an affair with a married man because you're bored and/or like your independence. I would suggest getting a pet or taking up a new hobby, but neither of those take the place of sex. You can always hire someone, but a married man won't cost you anything and may even take you nice places. Who am I to tell you what to do when you haven't been laid in months? Just don't fall in love. Fall in love and you're in trouble. It doesn't take a rocket scientist to predict this crash and burn ending. Who needs to spend more nights crying over something that you purposely fell for in the first place? Talk about creating your own mess. Against you (and all your friends) better judgment; you decide you're going to do it, anyway. You better make sure you're better looking than he is (less chance of him cheating on you) and may be willing to buy you things. You want to make sure that this cheater is worth your time, because he will take time away from your pursuit of available men.

This is exactly what got you into this mess in the first place. You couldn't find any available men worth going after. In your mind, the only available men are married. How quaint!

Not only are they willing, but they buy you things. They even take you out to dinner. Wow! What a change from the normal dating scene where the guy texts you at 7:00 P.M. with a simple "what u doing?" A married has set up the date well in advance (Per his schedule, of course) anticipating with desire the mere moment(s) he will get to spend with you; and he'll do anything for it. He'll romance you, dine and wine you; telling you all the lies you want to hear. He may even be telling the truth. What does it hurt him to fall in love? It just makes his marriage more exciting. In fact, think how much you'll improve his sex life with his wife!

OPEN MARRIAGE

This is a group of individuals (à la celebrity A and much younger celebrity B—enough said) that invite a third party into the marriage or seek sexual gratification openly outside of their marriage. (This does not include sacred vows of monogamy, but may include mutual kink and horny-ness.) Not that monogamy is so sacred. In fact, maybe open marriage is the way to go. Most women, on the other hand, prefer that their husband is the only ones to see them naked (sans the pool boy lurking from outside) whom she pretends not to notice. Sometimes, more often than not, wives don't even want their husbands to see them naked. Some married couples decide after they've been married (and run out of sexual positions) mutually agree that they can't find a reason not to try this. This only works if both are getting something great outside of the marriage. Sometimes, they even cheat, while maintaining a great relationship within the marriage. By the time they've hit 40's and 50's, their sex drive may decrease (sans the little blue pill.)

Just because people cheat doesn't mean they don't love each other. In fact, just ask the man. He will even tell you that sleeping with another woman made him realize how much he loves his wife. (No, he may or may not stop sleeping with the lover even after saying this.)

Some pointers if you get involved with a married man, don't share new sex ideas. This will backfire on you. He'll take them home to his wife, which will make her think he's suddenly putting more care into the marriage.

(Which actually may work and leave you in the dust. You've now enhanced their previously dull, lifeless sex life).

On the other hand, your married man comes to you with new sex acts? You can only infer he's pulled them off of the internet, got them from the recent call girl he purchased and/or got from his...yes, wife.

DON'T FALL IN LOVE

The nice thing about a married man, is when he gets on your nerves, you can send him home. If you find you are falling in love and want to marry this specimen, you'll have to wait for them to get a divorce, which includes his wife trying to take all his money and/or ruin his business.

If you really feel the need to betroth yourself to this cad, do yourself a favor and fall in love with one who's been married a few times prior, so that he has a pre-nup with the wife he's trying to get away from. Thus, leaving the only problem (even though you are madly, deeply and spiritually in love) is you having to now sign a pre-nup (if there's anything left). It's okay, you're marring him for love...not that amazing loft or the place in the country. You are marrying him for that amazing loft or place in the country? How shallow and yet devious of you...Marrying a man that has only been married once previously also may pose a few problems.

There's so much life to divide, all those things that once meant so much that you may find you are spending quite a bit of time on his problems. "It's okay", you remind yourself. "Once he marries me, he'll be there for me". You know, kind of like how he….wasn't there for his wife?

YOU SURE YOU REALLY WANT HIM?

Are you really that in love? You may start to realize all the crap you've gone through (for him) and it's just not worth it. You may tell yourself that, "single men are enough of a headache without adding a wife in the mix". You may decide to focus on a single guy and drive him crazy, instead! "Men shouldn't drive *you* crazy, that's your job! Get your priorities straight", you tell yourself.

Although, you may decide that the married man is the one you want and you have done all you can (or are willing) to find that single fish in the ocean and have committed to loving this one (once he becomes untangled in his mess). How do you justify all of this within yourself? A dialogue may go something like this. "I really want to get married before menopause and I've already been through so much with this man. From here on out it will be sunny skies and romantic nights".

Uh….okay.

Sure…

Whatever you say. What do I know? On the other hand, being with a married man may just be a never-ending, vicious cycle. Even women that are married will tell wild tales to the men they're having an affair with. Either way, unless you keep a distance and use these encounters strictly for sex, you may find yourself getting deeper and deeper into the…mess. How deep? Try digging a ditch through cement with a teaspoon. I'm not speaking from experience. It's what I've heard from a few friends that I can't name at this time.

(Well I could, but they'd probably be pissed.)

CHAPTER 12

MEN WE WANT vs. MEN WE SHOULD MARRY

We should marry a man who loves us more than we love him.

We should marry a man who has less baggage than we do.

We should marry a man who is where he wants to be professionally.

We should marry a man who is a little less attractive than we are.

We should marry a man who loves absolutely everything about us.

We should marry a man who loves our family, friends and pets.

We should not marry a man who makes us pull our hair out and jump up and down like a jackrabbit, screaming bloody murder and then have incredible make-up sex.

But we want to.

CHAPTER 12
MEN WE WANT vs. MEN WE SHOULD MARRY

If you had your pick, you probably wouldn't be going after the same man you should be marrying. That perfectly nice guy you led on for six months, but the thought of kissing him made you nauseous? You didn't dump him because you thought he'd grow on you. You couldn't fake the fact that you knew he'd make a wonderful father. Yes, 17 dates later, you realize you aren't going to change your mind. "What's wrong with me?" you feign, out of mere curiosity. "Why don't I date the guys I want to marry?"

And, finally, "Why am I supposed to marry someone that I have absolutely no interest in dating? "If you're waiting for your taste to change, forget it. You may find yourself trying to dress a little Less sexy for that nice guy that you don't want, but don't want to hurt and a little sexier for those dates you really do want to go out with. Although the older you get, the less you may care about the amount of hair on his head (although not on his back). You may even care a little less that he drives that conservative old car instead of that sexy convertible; that his socks don't really match the shirt he's wearing and even those jeans that are acid wash from 1984. Sure, some things will change, especially with a few glasses of Cabernet and a bad run of dates for a month or 2. But, how about sex? What about pure animal attraction? Liking someone, enjoying his or her company-even having a great conversation, doesn't equate with pure lust, chemistry and that thing you just can't quite put your finger on (but, other body parts are fine). That sexy model from Spain you dated for ten months who didn't speak English, but it didn't matter? Yes, you may have wanted to marry him, even toyed with the idea of living in Spain 6 months, states the other 6.

That lasted all of a week or two. Then, for whatever reason (he didn't speak English?) you decided this was not the man to marry. Well, you can you decided, if you want to avoid your friends and family for the rest of your life, or constantly be barraged with, "Really? What were you thinking?" Realistically speaking, if you want to fall in love and do the marriage thing, you're going to have to change some ideas about your ideal mate.

Doesn't that suck?

No one ever said marriage was fun. And those couples that are making it look fun? They're probably doing it just to rub it into everyone else's face. Please, how many sexual positions can you conquer in one life with the same partner? Really, going to the grocery store every week is that much fun?

What are you doing making out in the cleaning products aisle, just to prove to everyone you're still in love? So, if marriage isn't even that fun and you are still interested in pursuing that option in life (just because you can) you probably are going to have to change the way you think about the men you want. (They no longer do lobotomies, so you're on your own).

Just like men have their ideal fantasy of what they want, so do women. Men just don't want to think women feel this way. We do, it just may dissipate with age. The need for deep conversation somehow overrides the desire for hot sex.

Well, maybe not, but how do you explain to your kid how come Daddy never learned English or finished junior high? Four modeling covers do not a husband make.

The men we want, we can't bring home to mother. Oh, not because we'll be criticized, but because she'll have dreams about him for days. The man we want may do things such as...treat us like dog doodoo...and yet we still want him. The man we want may be into us one minute and gone the next, then suddenly back again, like bad fish.

The man we want is probably fun, entertaining, has a lifestyle we may envy and want to be a part of.

Everything about this guy looks good, seems like a great life and one we want to be a part of. Except that he really doesn't want to be a part of yours. He may even be madly in love with you and want to marry you. This creates a worse problem because, since you're so into him, you may actually consider it. You may even actually do it and marry the guy.

All those problems while you were dating? Yes, they're still there and now you're living with them, not just visiting. We should be able to marry whomever we want. Yes it's the law, but realistically speaking we should also be able to make choices based on gut instinct, chemistry that is healthy (doesn't make your head spin-off) and mutual respect.

He can respect you a little bit more, never hurts...

Which brings us to the men we should marry-you bring him home, and what do your parents say? "He's a very nice man." This is a very different response from the man you want, which when you brought him home. Your mother said something to the tune of, "He's built like a brick house".

Or something like that. But it shouldn't matter. You really should be able to mix the two together and have a perfectly happy life with whomever you decide to become betrothed. The problem is, you like all the wrong guys. You like the ones who really don't have much interest in coupling up in the way you imagined. The ones who do want to couple up? You have absolutely zero interest in them. There's something about someone wanting to be in a relationship, who puts it all out there on the line, that just comes across a bit desperate and that desperation is not something you tend to run toward...but away from. When you're single and older you still want to be able to be with someone who has all those qualities you want.

You shouldn't have to be less picky/make other choices/change the way you feel/what you're attracted to/but as the pickings get a little slimmer/ you may have to decide what you've been looking for may be barking up the wrong tree.

But, there are lots of trees, so you're in luck.

MARRYING SOMEONE OOGLY

If you get married on the young side and/or –

The guy you've married is a bit unattractive; and/or on the scrawny side, he may eventually fill out.

One day he will be the hot guy. (Yes, he may be 70, but you will be, too.) If you fell in love with an unattractive guy, you probably valued other things than his looks. Which is great. Or, you actually found the unattractive person...attractive!

Even better. This means you aren't so picky and actually will find lots of needles in a haystack (if you ever find yourself single again).

Remember, looks are subjective, so make sure other people find him ugly before you decide to commit. If you secretly find him cute, marry him anyway. This way you'll want to have sex with him.

Who wants to wait until 70 to have good sex? This way you're not sneaking around behind his back with the pool boy...unless you want to. Rejoice in the fact that most men's balls are sitting somewhere between their ankles and their toes and that before that little blue pill, they were only fantasizing about great sex with the hooker down the street. Don't worry that you're not loved by other 40 year-olds, you can get a 25 year-old because you'll make him feel like a real man. Once he turns 40, he'll morph into a boy again, anyway, having to go through his much-anticipated mid-life crisis. See how much heartache and pain you've already avoided? That unattractive geek you picked on in 7th grade? You should marry him.

Unfortunately, if he has a lot of money and there will be many women vying for his attention. He will think it's because he's hot.

He may realize it's because he's rich, but he won't care. He didn't get laid until he was 23. He has lots of time to make up for.

You must realize if you marry an unattractive, wealthy guy, he will probably dump you (or cheat on you) with a hot bimbo. He'll want ...baggage.

You're never supposed to date a man with more baggage than you, which is fine when you're twenty-three, but by the time you hit your 40's? How do you (or him) not have baggage? We've been dumped/duped/screwed over and done our fair share of the dumping, as well.

It eventually comes down to deciding if his/her baggage will overrun the relationship. Whoever comes in with more baggage probably controls the relationship. Forget two fresh flowers, innocent and young getting to know one another. It's reality time! Kids, previous marriages, disease, financial troubles, criminal record, sexual positions...everything is fair game. It's okay. Would you really trust dating someone who doesn't have any baggage, or doesn't admit to it? What kind of a person are they if they aren't suffering from something from their past? You want to make sure that person had a life before you came along. What if you're his 1st girlfriend? Scary! How about the fact that you're lying about your past baggage? That's another thing. The less you share, the better. Tell the truth and you may never get past the first date, let alone the relationship. Dating a guy with baggage is fine if he thinks you will solve all his problems, which he will until he switches on you and tells you you're making his problems worse. Try to be his therapist as long as you can. He'll think you're a hero. Do everything in your power exactly the opposite of everything the ex didn't do. It's very easy to figure it out.

When he complains about something take notes. Do your best acting. The point? None really. This really has nothing to do with you, just you getting him. (Wanting to keep him is entirely up to you). You may want to dump him after you realize how crazy he really is. But at least you don't beat yourself up for the next two months talking yourself into how wonderful this idiot, with all the baggage, was. Idealizing him into everything he never was just to beat up on yourself, is just. well…silly.

The only point in dating someone with more baggage than you is if you can be his knightess in shining armor; just like you think he is to you, saving you from---well, yourself.

Once he thinks you're amazing and puts you on a pedestal, he'll start to feel dependent on you. This is the time to freak him out. Berate him and then stroke his hair. This is called the punch/hug theory. (It's also called a hormonal imbalance.) The punch/hug theory works like a charm and you'll get your man immediately. Don't believe it works? Just think what the guy does to us: he compliments us and then doesn't call for days. Then, just when we think it's over, he calls and says something sweet. Then when we think everything's great, he blows us off at the last minute. We vow we're moving on…when he shows up with a dozen roses. It's how he got you. It's how you'll get him.

Baggage and all.

Aren't you lucky!

OTHER PEOPLE'S BLESSINGS

A friend of a friend of a friend has a great marriage. She and her husband are madly in love after many years of wedded bliss (imagine that) and are very happy. She loves everything about him except that he has a big gap between his teeth. He has enough money and time to get it fixed. So what's the problem? She won't let him. She doesn't want another woman to want him.

She knows if he gets his teeth fixed he'll be more attractive to other women. It's called her trump card. Women get complacent. We may fantasize about male models and movie stars; fantasize about being with them, but may go for the geek. Why? Our mothers always told us, "Marry a man who loves you more than you love him." Here's one small problem with that universal theory. Once another woman sees you on his arm, she'll want him. It's inevitable. She'll start to wonder, "Why didn't I think of him, he's hot."

This is called the "wanting what I can't have theory." Men do it more than women, even with single women. Women only do it with men who are taken, no matter how ugly and geeky. If another woman wants him, he must be worth something. But here's where the catch comes in. Your man will leave you, even if he's a geek. When other women go after him, he'll realize he's not such a dork after all and go for the other women. Now, here's where that geek turns into a cheese-ball that can't get a date. He's the one you see at the bar every night-high hair sprayed to his head, three-piece sport suit and white loafers. He's always smiling, "hey, baby!". Forget him **you** can't even get him.

He's after a 19-year-old virgin, a dumb virgin.
She may go for him because he's older. You're still alone. See what you've done here?

You've taken your perfectly respectable geek boyfriend/husband, made him appetizing just by being with him, and gotten dumped. Now he's out there in the singles pool, trying to make it with anyone he can, and you can't even get him. Suggestion? Marry the cheese-ball. He's the geek who already went through his wow I never got laid in high school phase and his, Now-I-make-a-lot-of-money-so-I-can-get-laid phase, moved on to his, I'm-so-alone-and-trying-too-hard phase, and has come full circle back to his, I-guess-I'm-just-a-geek-after-all phase.

In essence, it's no good getting a geek before he

realizes he's worth something. Let some other woman marry him and have him leave her. Let her go through his ridiculous shallow mid-life crisis, then get him on the rebound or keep looking. Hey, no one said this process was easy! Pant, pant, pant…this year's sexiest man alive, the top ten male movie stars, several dozen sports star. Well built men who spend all day playing with balls. We want them, but we prefer them faithful. We fantasize that they are faithful. We want to get them, have them marry us…then obsessively think we are the only women on the planet for them for the rest of their lives. The men we want are wonderful for our egos.

No matter how old we get, there will always be some gorgeous guy (he may be in another country) to stroke us and make us feel irreplaceable.

Never mind that it's for 2 days in a motel room, or that he just said the same things to your sister. These men have charm and we want to run off and marry them, but they don't want to marry us. They just want to sleep with us.

So who cares? Go for it. All you do is work, have some fun, for God's sake! The problem starts when you begin to fall in love with one of these men and think you can get him to marry you. You fantasize about this great life you'll have-living in Tahiti, running a kayaking business. Never mind that he's a bartender, he's hot! Women may try not to think like this, but sometimes, we just can't help ourselves. It doesn't really matter if the guy is realistic potential or not, we fall in love. It makes it that much easier to explain how we ended up in your bed after the first hour together. How else would we be able to explain the unbridled passion we felt? Or, the tears over our Prince Charming dumping us for his next conquest?

Even as sleazy it may seem, we must sleep with you immediately because we've decided you're the one, even if we know, deep down, we'll hate you in a week.

It's our feminine way (hardwired) and part of what attracted us to you in the first place. The mere fact that we have met someone so seemingly incredible in this godforsaken, single world momentarily steals our hearts and makes us forget about the real world. We hate the real world!

We hate taxes and most of all, we hate our apartment and we don't ever want to go back there. Even if we just met you, we want to run around the world with you and chase apes. Or whatever it is you do. We can always wake up, get on a plane and go home. At least we have our memories. Now, we're back to looking for the men we should marry. What a drag! You are so much different from who we want. You are responsible, anal and dependable. Although we may know that we should want to be with you, we really just want to go back to Tahiti and be massaged. But the man you marry isn't going to do these things. Okay, maybe on your honeymoon night, if you're lucky and he stays awake after you give him his blowjob. In Tahiti, you never even had to give a blowjob. He devoured you. The man you should marry? His job should be to serve and protect, but his motto may be a bit more, "serve me and I'll look into getting an alarm system".

When The Woman's the breadwinner

You may not be the **only** breadwinner in the family, you just slay the dragon a bit more than your man. It doesn't really matter who brings home the bacon if Larry cooks it up in the pan. Sometimes Lisa is more comfortable rolling calls and dealing with clients. Sometimes Leisurely Larry is happier playing 18 then frying up some scallops in a nice white wine sauce. Many men prefer the female duties, while the women are more comfortable in the manly duties. The fact that I've even generalized to this degree, I'm sure will get me in trouble with feminists, gays and even happily married couples who's yin and yang have gone a bit topsy-turvy.

Some of these relationships work amazingly well.

The woman hustles off to work in the A.M. leaving house-hubby to take care of the kiddies and stocks, not necessarily in that order. House-hubby may even work with the wife at her current job, although this isn't always recommended; not only because the man likes to feel in charge (even when he's not) but to be bossed around by someone one is married to a woman in charge (outside of Bondage Month) is a no-no. If two people meet while going through a transition at the same time, it can lead to chaos. (Unless of course, they're both extremely wealthy and have nothing but time to explore every Country.) Otherwise, two transitional people are likely to bore the crap out of each other. With no defined roles in the relationship (other than complaining) there's not much to achieve or do. Neither will want to cook. Neither will want to go out. Neither will want to slay the dragon. Both will want to sleep in until 11 A.M. (taking up most of the bed) both will want to 'contemplate their futures. Which never bodes well for married couples, let alone single ones trying to explore having a relationship.

Ultimately, this can lead to an affair, divorce and/or a cooking class. The latter is best, because that ultimately puts one person in the yang position, which only leaves the yin.

 If the yanger learns to cook, the yinner

(Assuming they stop complaining after a period of time) will most likely find their bearings and go back to work. Either that, or you will have two people in cooking class, which isn't so bad, considering you now have two chefs in the house cooking dinner. When a man marries a woman with some amount of success while he struggles to find balance or is going through his own transition, he make start to instinctually take the place as the wife. He finds himself okay doing the things we generally have assigned to the woman. The woman in this instance hasn't done this role for years because she's been into her career.

Which means, she's hired a maid do her laundry, a cook do her cleaning and a personal shopper to pick out her clothes.

If she marries you while you're in transition, this is now your job. Once you've figuring out what it is you really 'want in life' you can resume your normal husband position and she will once again bring back "Lucia' to pick up the pieces. Your wife really doesn't care that you are not working. She's off to work, whether you are or not. She doesn't really put much thought into the fact that you slaved over the stove for 7 hours to created the perfect Foie Gras soufflé (just like if you were working and she were slaving over the hot stove).

Although your true motive for cooking Foie Gras soufflé had much more to do with showing off for Lucia, than it was to impress your wife. Women and men really just want attention. As long as the man is happy taking care of things on the home front while the woman can keep up with her career plan, neither is worse for the wear. This being said, we're talking about a well-adjusted house husband, not some sniveling baby who cant seem to not only get his career choices in order, but can't button his pants. The last thing a businesswoman wants is that strong and confidant he-man she married suddenly turn into some emotional girl. Oh God, there's nothing worse than (believe it or not) a man that needs to talk. Remember all those times you told a guy, "I need to talk" and he looked at you like you had 3 heads? That's what you're going to have to deal with now. You were fine with your man when he was okay in transition, you were fine with him when he learned how to clean the carpet with fresh lemon and caper sauce, you were even fine when he took up ballroom dancing; but this? This emotional baggage of needs is going to be too much. Immediately send him to a boot camp for men. Immediately let him get arrested for some minor infraction.

Immediately have your brother beat the crap out of him. Anything to toughen this pussy up! The last thing a strong, smart businesswoman wants is some man that's falling apart right before her very eyes.

Buck up, mister. Hide those emotions! We don't wanna see you sweat! (Unless it's from sex.)

Marrying Wealthy

Women who marry men with mass amounts of wealth (besides having had plenty of plastic surgery) always know what they are doing. They have a plan.

Problem is, that plan when they're 25, its way different than when they reach there 40's.

When a woman reaches her 40's without getting married, usually something like a career got in the way. This is fine because she was too busy running around the world (even if she did want to get married). In order to put marriage as a priority, she would have done something called…slowing down her…life, oh…and pick a person. 40 something women who marry wealthy men (unless they are completely burned out by their career and suddenly want to be taken care of) may face a few problems. That pre-nup she's expected to sign? The one where he asks her to give up her career so that she will always be available on his G5 to accompany him well, anywhere? It will have to be signed. Forget the money, it's the lifestyle she's marrying into; and usually a really needy guy, which means she better be prepared to be arm candy at all times. If you're lucky enough to be arm candy and land one of these fishies (I don't want one, too much trouble to shower and wear a dress everyday. I've also chronologically expired, I'm sure). You will have to love standing in front of the mirror almost as much as he does. He will expect nothing less than perfect. However you got there, it must be maintained. At some point, he may exchange you in for another, younger and/or better (found at the local plastic surgeon's office) you.

If you decide to go this route, you have to decide if, in fact, after all this time of building up your business/career/friendships, that you will be willing to just let it go and go with the flow-

(I.E. take what you can get) which is fine, if you are able to 'get it back' when he's done with you. Some marriages like this last. (Check your pre-nup, it has the date of expiration somewhere between vaginal rejuvenation and butt augmentation.) In this relationship, someone has to compromise and my bet is, it's probably not the guy.

ON THE OCCASION...

You meet an amazing guy with an amazing career, who fully supports and loves what you do, and encourages you, he should be a keeper. Unless he's secretly hooked on coke, has 3 children from 3 different women, or is a registered sex offender.
I've got the dough…nuts! In this case, you have given up on the idea of getting married altogether.

In fact, even if you've been engaged a few (4) times, you now realize that chasing after the idea of getting married and living happily ever after doesn't even sounds so great, anymore. The thought of up-rooting your life/house/shoe collection to move anywhere for anyone sounds not only un-appetizing but is way too much work. You've just spent the last two years getting the color of your kitchen exactly the right color. What you really want (besides several men in many states) are, well… yes, several men in many states. You want to just have sex, because the guy is hot. And for no other reason. If he's dumb, it's fine; you weren't planning on spending that much time with him, anyway.

When a woman gets to a certain age and has money, she may suddenly decide that looking for love isn't even what she wants, anymore. She may ask herself, "Why do I have to want to get married? Why do I have to find someone?

Why can't I just be single, enjoy my life and live exactly how I want to.

You can.

You will.

I Do. (See, you thought you'd never get to say those words!)

You just might want to be careful the next couples dinner party you're invited to. Your man of the moment…that hot guy you're schtupping? It's probably the reason you were invited to dinner in the first place, and he'll most likely be drooled over by all of your girlfriends. A cockfight of husbands is sure to ensue.

I PICK YOU (Oh, God, now I'm stuck)

The problem with choosing someone to marry is that you are now stuck with him or her. Well, not stuck with them forever (if you don't want to).

There's always divorce and death. I know, I know, some people marry the love of their life and 'til death do us part' and are as happy as little clams. I'm not talking about you. You may proceed to the next chapter. Or, forge quickly through the book all together to the bio page. I doubt you'd be able to use this paper (if you're not reading on a kindle) to clean your house, as the paper is recyclable, but not necessarily the right ply for that sort of thing. Anyway, back to the point. Which is; when you choose a mate, you are now stuck with everything that goes along with him/her. This is fine if you like most things about them, or you have the ability to get away when they drive you…

Up a tree.

For those who do still want to marry the love of your life (or someone within their family) you may have to do some things you wouldn't normally do. No, not go out every night trying to find him/her, you already do that and all that's led to is a hangover. I know what my problem is, I pick the wrong men. I spent my 20's and 30's chasing my career, the wrong guys and spending money.

I now find myself fresh out of picking, which is leaving me with the scraps, the leftovers, the ones that have been thrown back into the sea-of dating pool'.

But you, you probably *did* choose someone and now you, who thought you were so in love, are forever stuck dealing with the daily ins and outs of their problems (along with your own). It's okay, isn't it nice to be in the swimming pool of life together? Someone to complain with/manipulate/cajole/control and/or do weird things all over their naked body while sleeping?

HAPPILY EVER AFTER...BUT WILL I LIKE YOU IN HEAVEN?

You may run into problems if you share the same religion, belief system and you have betrothed yourself to not only earth-love, but eternity as well.

That's a long time! You better make sure you know what you're in for. Heaven's a big place, you never know who you may meet. And, if you're going to Hell? Well, just think of it like spending eternity in your teen years. No conscience, do whatever you want and yet get away with it; just imagine doing it in Las Vegas in August.

If you vow to love, honor, cherish, respect and stay monogamous to that person in the afterlife-you are now doomed from ever having your own space. Isn't it enough to devote yourself to that person-on earth? I mean they gotta have you in space, too? If you have different religions and/or belief systems, you're probably safe because your Gods don't match up, and since your separate Gods won't be able to agree, this means your souls will separate in eternity-no matter what you asked for...on earth. If you want to be together...up there...you better do something about picking the same belief system...down here, before you get there.

PICK THE RIGHT GUY

Hopefully, this entails someone with way less problems than you. My mother always said to marry someone with less baggage than my own.

(Working on trying to forget your baggage, can't hurt either). This is why purging baggage (past thoughts, behaviors and actions) is smart to get rid of. Simply forgetting about them, allows you to no longer have that baggage. So, when someone starts to pry into your life to pretend like their trying to know you and understand you, they will see you are clean of any past dramas; thus leading an extremely healthy (manipulated so nicely by yourself) life.

*Besides the supposed baggage of never being married (at all) by a certain age.

**Not including actual baggage you will need for your clothing.

A few requirements that I will need upon marriage, but you may not:

1. A walk-in closet. (My own, thank you! Build your own).

2. My own bathroom. (Really, I need to watch your morning routine? I didn't even do that when we we're dating. (Why do I want to share spit in the same sink?)

3. My own room for an office. (You know, that place one can go for ones own personal business, pleasure, or boredom.)

4. My own apartment (or house). (Yes, I understand this defeats the purpose of living together, but me moving in with you where you lived with your ex-wife/ex-girlfriend/ex-anything, which was probably decorated by her, will not be good for our new fresh marriage. If you insist that we live under the same roof-in which you've already experienced every sexual position you are planning to re-do with me-you better be prepared that your ex will somehow lure herself into my mind, thus creating moments where I remind you, "exactly how my ex-whatever used to act".

(Just be forewarned and ready with a fly swatter. I have sex ideas, too, you know!)

HOW AM I SUPPOSED TO KNOW WHOM TO PICK?

You aren't. Does that help? You may not have to pick just one. Does that make things easier? Chances are likely that you (or whom you are avoiding picking) are either....too picky, too screwed up, too tall or too something. This makes the choosing process very difficult. You may have already dated every guy there is to date (and are currently hitting on friends' fathers) or you're still actively dating to see which guy fits you best, which is confusing because fitting one best-changes through life. What may suit us at one stage of life doesn't do a damn thing for us in another. Perhaps a guy for every decade is the answer? When you are picking your mate, I suppose it should be like picking an avocado. Too mushy will be too needy, too firm will be a controlling prick, just ripe is the perfect fit. But unfortunately we're not making guacamole here, we're making love and there is really no exact formula. (And that was also a lousy example considering avocados go bad after a day or 2).
On second thought...some relationships do, as well

Some people want their significant other to have an education, some want money, some want fame; some want kindness, some want honor, morals, ethics (you know, all those shallow things); whatever reminds you of your father (good or bad) is probably, subconsciously, what you're searching for. On the other hand, a man subconsciously ends up with their Mother (or as far away from her as humanly possible). This may lead him down the same road of problems he experiences with his mother (just wrapped in different packaging). Maybe we need to think about what makes you happy on a daily basis.

Do you like the same TV shows? At least you know you've got a similar sense of humor.

Does he laugh at your jokes? He doesn't have to.

You have friends for that, but it helps. You certainly don't want to go through life with a humorless douche. I suppose you should pick someone based on their experiences in life and how well they match up to yours. Things you feel you're missing in your life that they will somehow, magically fill; and someone who will treat you like a rock star. The feeling like you're on a pedestal part is great. The falling off part? Not so much so. If you haven't chosen by your 30's and met your mate in high school or college (which comes with their own set of problems) you will be starting over and searching for the one through work functions, social circles, events, the gym and anywhere else you feel comfortable (or, not so comfortable) seeking them out. You certainly can meet a mate anywhere. I said you, not me. I go around most days in sweats, brain fully immersed in 'what ifs, why not's and how come? But that's just me. You, on the other hand, shower every day, get decked out and go into that rat race of a world pumped up and ready to go, ready for mating action. (Which if you think about it, you spend way more energy and time than me on the dating/find a mate thing, and you're still single. Wow, I feel better already!)

HOW TO KNOW WHICH ONE TO CHOOSE

Considering you have options, I'd go for the tall one.

You want to have tall babies, because tall is better overall. Tall can see over things, they usually have longer legs and they seem more in control of chaotic situations.

Pick someone with good skin, good hygiene and not too full of himself/herself. Pick the one who still opens the door for you, still gets embarrassed when they fart in front of you and, oh yea, if they still look at your adoringly (sans that stupid zombie gaze) choose them. What you don't want is that desperate lass that hang on everything you say, everything you do and doesn't have a life of his/her own.

You definitely want someone that won't smother you (your sexual life withstanding).

We all need/want/desire…space.

So, when you're picking a mate, make sure they understand that a 24 hour day includes 6 to 9 hours of sleep, showering, food, walking, driving, work/play, etc. So really, you are looking for your mate to fill maybe 3 to 4 hours a day. Which is perfect because it's like a built in date, with the rest of the time on your own to do as you please. If you're needy and require your mate to be the thing to fill all your time, you become a problem, anyway. If you're getting married to have the guy fill all your time, I suggest you should get a dog and hire a personal trainer. When picking a mate, I supposed -one should pick another with similar qualities to ones own, or complete opposite to fill -The void.

If you've gotten to I do without figuring out if that person drives you bat-shit mad, then I can't help you. In fact, I can't help you, either way-   Considering I'm still single, still 'kind of looking' and probably more screwed up about what I want than you are.

SALVATION. We all want to be saved…and that's the bottom line. Everyone wants to find a significant other who will be everything/complete us/save us. From what? Ourselves, natch! We want that other half to fill our otherwise dull, shallow, boring, stressed, contrite life. If you're busy and happy, you generally don't need anyone; which is usually the best time to be with someone. But to wait for that to happen? This means you have to be fully ensconced in your own life, your own happiness and generally not even want anyone for anything other than, well, sex; and probably opinions about things you don't need the answer to, but ask because you're trying to make the other person feel needed. (How nurturing of you.) The problem with wanting to be saved is that you are then asking the other person, to not only take on all your bullshit; but expecting them to have none of their own.

Which would be great, if not realistic. Being saved also can suck if that person does save you, is wonderful and then suddenly walks away, dies or otherwise becomes engaged with someone other than you.

SEPARATED AND DIVORCED MEN

They may want to re-marry immediately because they can't fathom being alone after being married. Or, they will date you forever and never marry you because their first wife put them through the ringer. You already know that they can commit, because they have (and perhaps, still are). How many times? Find that out sooner rather than later. It can't be much fun being wife #9. (Unless you're part of a harem and #9 has the least amount of responsibility, yet the most attention. Men newly separated are looking for love because they're absolutely sure the ex did them wrong, in every way. You can jump in, play nursemaid and try to be everything his little heart desires, but you'll just have to realize if it wasn't you…It probably would have been…well, anyone else. Chances are, you're going to have to give up who you really are and try to be everything his last wife wasn't. How do you do that? Listen to all his complaints, which will be a-plenty! He's telling you right up front exactly what his wife didn't fulfill for him. That's okay. Get him while the iron's hot. You don't want to be girlfriend #2 after his divorce. There may be no girlfriend #2 if this guy is dating material; chances are he'll marry the first woman who satisfies him after his divorce. So, if (you) the new girlfriend plays it right, you can manipulate the situation and satisfy him in all the ways his wife did not. Just make sure that your true colors never come out. Never let him hear you calling people from his past to find out the top 10 things that pissed him off about his ex, just nicely coax him into telling you. He'll be happy to let it rip about how she wasn't nurturing, was too this, that and the other. Keep a journal. Make notes. Then just create that new woman!

Of course, this has nothing to do with getting your soulmate and more to do with making a decision and going for it. (Unless you really are madly in love and he is your soulmate.) You're now stuck with that screwed-up, newly separated, headed-for-moving-in-and-marrying-you-within-six-months-because-I-Don't/won't/can't-be-alone guy!

BRING IN THE CLOWNS (I MEAN, KIDS)

If there are children involved and the ex is still in the picture, chances are you'll never measure up in the kid's eyes. You'll spend the entire relationship trying to buy the kid's affections. The more knowledge you have about what's in or trendy, the better. It's the only way you're going to win them over. They already have their mother for nurturing, what do they need you for other than nice gifts to lessen the blow as they talk behind your back? Chances are you get the wicked witch title any way you slice it. If the mother isn't in the picture, you get to be instant mommy. Hope you hadn't planned on any sort of life for yourself. You'll be dedicating at least the next 18 years to domesticity. I'd make sure that your new man is worth the trouble. You can say goodbye to those sexy weekend getaways you used to have with your uneducated, but responsibility-free ex. Or you can just hope that your new man is tight with his mother, lives close by and is willing to babysit.

You may be thinking, "A divorced guy just adds some more options to the mix of single girls". Divorced guys are great to date because they don't like being single. As quickly as they've come out of something, they're more than likely already starting up something else. (Chances are, the person they were fooling around with that ended the marriage in the first place, is long gone.) They may want to run to the altar as quickly as possible because they don't remember what it's like being single.

(Or they do, which may be why they are running to the altar).

Maybe they've suddenly found their player-side, and any girl they meet must not only exceed their expectations and memories of the first wife, but also be better than God. The 1st wife only had to be good in bed. Wife #2? She must fill every need that the first wife didn't. Maybe you were wrong about wanting to re-visit those never married guys? Divorced guys really think they have all the answers. First of all, every problem in the marriage was the wife's fault. Every woman that he dates after that must possess looks, charm and class, but the empathy that the first wife somehow lacked; even though she bent over backwards to make him happy. She just happened to have a job or extra curricular activities.

He didn't like that and he's going to make damn sure the second wife make sure that he's first—always. The best thing you can do to ensure that this marriage works out is to pay close attention to what went wrong (or what he *thinks* went wrong) in the first marriage. Then, do everything the opposite.

Actually, if you want to know the truth, you're better off being in the third marriage.

The 2nd marriage is bound to end because once your Prince Charming comes to-he'll realize that his expectations of wife #2 made her too robotic. He'll be complaining that you aren't being authentic and he misses that independent, fun girl you were when you dated. Never mind that once you married him, you became a trained seal, because of his demands. And, because you thought it was the only way to keep him. No, wife #3 (and beyond) is the lucky one. She's the young, hot chick, who doesn't put up with any of his crap. They are very happy and have a long, prosperous marriage with children, dogs and a nice house. So what if he's 70, she's 28 (and this will never be you?) It's exactly what he finally wants. It's okay. You're actually daydreaming about that young hunk down the street, but he's either married to a 22 year-old European model, or a cougar with tons of cash.

Don't worry. As long as you work out, he'll still find you hot and try to sex with you. Formerly married men are just as screwed up as single men. The formerly married man has already been out there in the playing field, thought he married the right one (or got the girlfriend pregnant and married her) and spends his separation and impending divorce screwing everything in sight (or trying out a new religion). He's a little too passionate…about everything. The way he feels about his ex. The way he feels about his new-found spirituality; his car, his new house, his stereo system. Even the fact that it doesn't take more than 2 shirts and a 1 pair of shoes to make him happy.

What good will this divorced man do for you, imposing all of his new-found beliefs on things that you haven't gotten to experience for yourself? You need to go through your own divorce (God forbid, considering how long it took you to get married in the first place) before you can share in his revelations and even appreciate his wisdom. This man will make a good friend. Maybe even a good sex partner, if he's not still having residual sex with his ex.

Even if he is, you can add him to your list because he won't get too emotionally involved with you. This doesn't help if you fall madly in love and want to marry him. But, you may not get him because he's otherwise unavailable. And in the end, you'll appreciate that it didn't work out. He'd have had too much baggage, anyway. If you happen to get a man just coming out of a marriage and he's feeling no bitterness (it was a mutual divorce and there are no kids or kids out of the house; and he doesn't have some weird sexual problem) marry the guy. He's a catch and really? Aren't you sick of looking around?

NEVER MARRIED

Isn't this you? Yes, we understand. It's different with you. You have excuses for living your life and not getting married…up to this point?

So what difference does it make if the guy hasn't gotten married yet either? Well, for one thing, you know the reasons you haven't been and you feel no need to explain them to anyone, let alone a perfect stranger (that you may or may not decide to date/sleep with/share a bed with for the rest of your life, or at least until one of you kicks the other one to the guest room)."No, marriage to another person set in their ways is just too difficult," you decide. Certainly, one of you would have to be willing to compromise and it sure ain't gonna be you. Hopefully that person you marry (that has never been married) will at least put you on a pedestal and let you do whatever, whenever you want (simply because they are so in love) so at least they will be doing the compromising. Oh, I'm sure you can figure something out, like 30/70, with the other party giving in and allowing whatever you want. I'm not even sure why we're bringing this up. Although you never married, you are still just as perfect as you always were; even better. That other person never married that you are considering? Forget about it. Chances are, he's only dating 20 year-olds and talking about himself the entire evening, anyway.

The tip off? The one date you went out on; he invited you to his house. Place is nice enough, you think, until you notice the pictures on the walls? Animals? Seaside? Family photos? No such luck. Every photo? Him. Him. And, yes...him. If this isn't a sure sign of what's most important to this human being, I'm not sure what you need to hit you over the head (besides another 8 by 10.)

Never married people are best left alone. (Or marry another youngest in a family).

Two...self-important...self-involved human being's interacting on a daily basis?

CHAPTER 13
BUYING PROPERTY
**If I'm going to invest my own money,
I might as well make all the decisions...or, I could
just blow it on clothing, trips and Chardonnay.**

CHAPTER 13
BUYING PROPERTY
(OR ANYTHING, FOR THAT MATTER)

At some point you may go through a stage of, "Should I buy some property?" This usually happens when you've made a substantial living, have the money saved (that you'd normally be splitting with your future spouse who doesn't exist at the moment). Who are you kidding? You were never going to split it with your spouse! All your married friends have owned property for years. You feel it's time to invest your money into a place of your own. You've been listening to their horror stories about septic tanks and ceiling leaks and find that you are actually jealous. You are looking forward to the cute air-conditioning guy coming over to fix things. You haven't yet thought about the money outweighing that vacation to Bali, Peru and/or Hong Kong for the summer. "Owning property", you tell yourself, "is the responsible thing to do". Why should you sit around and wait for a partner to spend your own hard earned money? Since it's yours and yours alone, you can decorate/fix up/re-do everything to your liking. (Except when you invite your parents, who will inevitably put in their two cents. Unless they give you lots more than 2 cents, in which case, you have a responsibility to let them do some of the decision making.) *PRO'S AND CON'S*...The decision to own property may come down to, "am I willing to forgo a large chunk of my social life, spend most of my hard earned cash to fix up this place instead of looking for guys, dating, having sex and going out to dinner? This recurring thought may keep you from owning property.

You come to find out (after re-snaking the leaking toilet for the 4th time) that you'd rather have new couture anything and Aspen on New Years than plop down (fill in the blank) on property you may not even live in when you marry. (But you will rent it out because it's a nice investment; if the market is good.) The thought of living in your place after you're married is not the point. Won't he have a much nicer place? You bought this for an investment for your future. You weren't planning on living in it with another human being. This place is for you. Although moving into to another person's property (especially if an ex lived there) can be tricky, at least you'll have your own place for back-up or quick getaways. You may decide that spending that hard earned cash on a place to call your own wasn't as romantic as you first thought it would be. That extra cash you used to have for your clothing budget; Botox, eating out 6 nights a week and your gym membership, may suddenly not be there at your disposal. On the other hand, you may realize that spending vast amounts of money on rent is throwing it away and at least you'll have something to show for it when you're old. Oh right, you may already be old.

Oh well. Hopefully the place you own is bigger than your old apartment. Although once you're in it, you're still living the same life you were before.

Same furniture, same couch, same TV. Since you may now be cash poor, this may leaves you unable to have a social life close to what you experienced before purchasing property. Yes, people laughed behind your back because you got to that age and never owned anything, but at least you're living a nice lifestyle. You're eating where you want, dressing how you like, you just don't have anything other than nice shoes, purses and a car to show for it. At this point, saving the money to use as a dowry to impress your future husband's parents won't matter (they might not even be alive, anymore).

Even though you may be unhappy with your apartment, you should revel in the joy that you have absolutely no responsibilities! If you own property and your shower breaks? You can no longer call your cute neighbor and use his. And unfortunately, the kind of house you'll most likely be able to afford? You won't want to be bothering your neighbors. (Ever.)

This doesn't hold true if you've bought the least expensive house on the block in which case, it will cost you a pretty fortune to fix up; although you will want to invite your neighbors over, especially to meet that "that cute single chick who just bought the cheapest house on the block". If you find that your investment was not worth it (I.E. the market crashed and you no longer have equity in it) you may decide you have to move back in with your parents. This may lead to something called desperation, which then immediately leads you to marry, well…anyone.

Having to marry someone just to save you (like you did when you were 20 and wanted out of the house) isn't the healthiest choice. If you feel you need to buy the condo/house so you can feel grown up, quickly remind yourself that you can always buy something when your money has doubled in the stock market. And for some reason, men think you don't need them when you own property. Or, the opposite happens. They jump to sleep with you and start fantasizing about moving in. This is not the kind of guy you want to marry, let alone spend the night. (This doesn't mean that he can't visit for an hour or two, a few times a month.)

Especially if he knows how to use a power saw and lay tile.

The reasons you want to own your own property besides a tax write off and throwing great dinner parties? You probably can't remember. You really thought all your married couple friends would come to dinner at your place and you'd have parties all the time.

But now you've found out that they don't like the guy you're dating, so they not only don't want to double, but they don't want to be part of your dinner parties. Your single friends? They don't want to hang out at your place either. They'd rather be out picking up guys. Something you may no longer be able to afford to do because you've spent all your dough on that fabulous shower/tub/bathroom remodel. Face it.

Buying that home may just be a waste of time and money. Once you move into your lush new pad, you may think, "The boys will be coming." (From where?)

Where in the world do you think all those boys making all that dough are? They're doing the same thing you're doing, fixing their cracked linoleum kitchen tile on Friday and Saturday night. So, you two are bound **never** to meet. And if you do eventually meet? Whose place do you move to? You've invested hundreds of thousands re-building your home, buying fine furnishings and neither one of you is willing to move. You can't. You have too much money tied up the place. You'll never get your money back. And what that tiger-print rug? Five thousand bucks! And guess what? He bought it 'cause he likes it! He spent damn good money on it and if you think he's willing to throw that ugly-ass furniture away just to move into your aqua-filled place, you must be living in Oz! Wait until after the marriage and then barrage him with insults about his taste. He'll be so shocked he married you, he'll be walking around asking his buddies, "and did you know there was a color called aqua?"

By purchasing your own home before you actually marry, do you see the havoc that you've wreaked? Old school theory states if you buy a big house, you'll never get a guy. It only makes sense because it's stating that a woman with power and money is intimidating to a man and he won't feel that she needs him for anything.

Yes, that's what 27 year-olds are for. They aren't intimidated, insecure and/or feel the need to impress.

They just want to please. A woman who has a lot of stuff either needs a guy with more stuff or someone with no stuff who may or may not want her stuff.

On the other hand, waiting around for anyone to buy you anything is just idiotic. (Not waiting around, but having things bought for you, withstanding.) If you have the cash, why not do with it what you want? Assuming you aren't going to end up dirt poor, you might as well spend your money on what you want and create the lifestyle you were previously waiting to have with someone else. This way, it's all up to you! Surroundings and/or $10,000 sub zero (it's nobody's business that it's empty) still being able to live the lifestyle you want and not interrupting your life from the way you want to live it, you should buy anything and everything your little heart desires. Waiting around to purchase something so that you own it with another person (who may or may not suck at math) may just end up ruining that perfect union that you both thought would work out so well. What's the worst case scenario if you both own property? You keep one and rent it out, move into the other, re-do a room/the yard/the closet/everything; or sell both and buy a new place.

*Disclaimer; You have a boatload of money and can do whatever you want, buy whatever you want, own as many pieces of property/houses/buildings/people...as you want.

Disclaimer is the ideal situation, FYI.

CHAPTER 14

THE GRASS IS ALWAYS GREENER...

Somewhere, on the other side of the hill −
The perfect family lives.
I've never seen them.

People say their grass is really, really green.

CHAPTER 14
THE GRASS IS ALWAYS GREENER

I've discovered Aliens on earth.

They're called happily married couples. You've actually passed them on the street, stood next to them at the ATM, behind them at the grocery store, next to them in a movie theatre; even stared straight at them, nodding your head in disbelief. They actually still like, love, have respect for each other, still having sex (and enjoying it) smile oddly at one another and still only want to be with each other; even though they've been together 5/10/15/20/35 plus years.

I know.

It's not only strange (and lovely at the same time) but also hard to believe.

Well, it's not to those married couples, just to single people who realize even if they got married tomorrow, they would not be celebrating their golden wedding anniversary.

At least, on earth.

I watched a couple making out at a restaurant the other night. I asked the guy who the gal was, as he was walking by. "My wife", he said, straight-faced. "Really?" I reply. "Yep, 20 years together".

And you still make out in public?" I say in disbelief. I walk up to his wife. "We met when we were 7". She states. Yes, now this is starting to make sense. Obviously you fall in love with the first person you play doctor with. That's a no brainer.

But, how about those other unusual species who are happily co-habituating after spending several years together? How does it happen?

And better yet, why? The ones who are still together because they want to be together, not because they share a mortgage, a Pre-nup (that would send them both to the funny farm) and/or a threat that holds them together till death does one part.

These happily married couples act like being together and enjoying it is so…simple. They're the first to throw out advice to let every single person know what they are doing wrong and how to fix it. Never mind they like to tell you how if they were single, they would be happy dating and having a ball. Even though they wouldn't trade places with us, because they're so happy. And this leads to them knowing exactly what will make us happy. This advice is never filled with concrete specifics, just general BS like "you're too picky", "you're too independent", "you like the wrong type of people", "you don't know what you're looking for" and "you don't give anyone a chance. All true, perhaps, but….shut-up.

Ah, give me a minute. I need some aspirin.

Bottom line? Some people are luckier than others. Remember how your mother used to say, "The grass is always greener on the other side?" Well, maybe she's right. On the other hand, you could find yourself leading a very exciting single life and never even want to peek into the neighbors yard. (Unless, it's to spy). If you are one of the preceding, feel free to skip over the entire book and jump to chapter 24. If you're still reading, there's nothing wrong with feeling sorry for yourself for still being single at 35, 40, 50, 92… There's also nothing wrong feeling like you're missing out on those romantic coupled up dinner parties you aren't invited to, because you aren't a couple. Chances are you're sick of going to that same bar, same party, same restaurant week after week, weekend after weekend, month after month.

You should be feeling sorry for yourself. This is pathetic. Even though it's fun going out all the time, drinking your favorite cocktail because you had such a tough/stressful/depressing/fun/crazy day (fill in the blank with the appropriate adjective, which is your excuse to have a few drinks and let loose. Or, spending hundreds on a new wardrobe every weekend, meeting new guys, then waking up the next day, and do it all over again.

(With a massive hangover that you'll get rid of at yoga class.) This can be…tiring after awhile, and may no longer feel…fun. Maybe your married friends are having more fun, even if they complain all the time. In fact, it could all be a conspiracy to look unhappy, to make you feel better about being single; which is very nice of them. If this is the case, you should thank them. Just don't be surprised if they're laughing behind your back. They may say they envy your life, no responsibility, traveling, freedom, your dating life; yet secretly adoring their newly found kinky sex life they share with their spouse. Remember those relationships you had when you were in your teens and had plans every weekend?

That's what they have. (Just with flabbier bodies and more sex toys.) Especially, the couple that played doctor at 7 and still making out in public. (Although, they could be secretly swinging.)

When you're single in your 30's, you may be invited with your significant other along on couples' weekend. If you're into the person and they're less than into you, it makes it uncomfortable to be around all those other couples (unless he's hot; the women are into him, and the husbands are into you). If you're not into him and he's into you, you are only bringing him there to cover your own ass because you're sick of them feeling sorry for you. They now know you are using the poor guy, think you're mean and not want to set you up anymore. This leads you right back into the arms of the guy you shouldn't be dating. A few more bad nights of Mr. wrong and the cycle begins again-you may even start to miss dinner-and-bowling; even though you make fun of your married friends for their lame nights.

THE FIFTH WHEEL

After hanging as the only single one with your group of coupled off friends, they may say something like, "you probably have so much more fun going to bars and hanging out with your single friends."

They act so fascinated by your tragic/funny/crazy stories, that they'll circle around you like pigeons. (Then, of course, they'll talk about you with their husbands in the comfort of their own beds, worried for your sanity). Married friends are not your enemies.

(They happen to just be the same boring old people you used to make fun of when you were 12). You have to be careful what you say in front of them.

Although they love the gossip and fun stories, they may secretly think you've gone off the deep end and wish you would just meet, "a nice guy and settle down". Don't make the mistake of thinking that you don't need your married friends. You may need them later when you finally do fall in love and want to hang out. Although by the time you're in love and married, they'll be hanging with people who have kids the same age as theirs.

Better face it now: since you didn't find a guy until you got your AARP card, you won't be hanging in that crowd. Chances of you ever being on the same page with these friends, is not a chance in hell.

You, on the other hand have taken years to settle down and are finally enjoying your first year of wedded bliss. All your friends, are either over-the-hill moms (according to everyone else) or 24 year-olds that think you're cool because you give them insight into the world of diaper rash and baby food that comes in jars.

You are envious that you didn't have kids sooner; that you aren't a part of that crowd your friends you've known forever are part of, and mostly you're envious you didn't marry the person they suggested so that you could be a part of their crowd, enjoy the country club, private school and tennis lunches you are now no longer a part of.

The times you don't want to be on the other person's lawn is when you realize most of your friends are in their 7-year itch and sleep in separate bedrooms. (Yes, they blame it on his snoring.)

If you're feeling depressed about your single life, simply keep a secret diary of marriages that didn't make it, to remind yourself you did the right thing by waiting. Remind yourself that if you had married Lazy Larry or Pathetic Peter, you either would be in the same boat as your divorced friends and/or still sharing space with that person you now can not get rid of because of all that shared space. Yes, you also could have been married to Amazing Allen, but he ran off with his Pilates instructor and you really didn't have a choice in the matter.

Okay, so there was Dapper Don.

Yes, he was pretty cool.

Yes, you dumped him. Why? No, you can't remember. Oh wait…you remember it may have had something to do with the way he parted his hair.

WHAT'S THE REAL GOAL?

The goal may change from wanting to be married, 2 dogs, 2.5 kids, a husband and a vacation once or twice a year. You may have decided that dating someone/anyone/everyone is great; but that the goal of getting married is no longer anything you care about accomplishing. Not because you're bitter/angry/sad/depressed/hormonal, but simply because you've decided, shocker, you love your life just the way it is. Although you love dating/being with someone/several-you don't need to walk down that aisle/live with someone/share a closet-which allows you to just enjoy being for the sake of being.

Odd.

(No, not that you're odd-just, hmm, odd…). Loving your life just the way it is takes…guts/courage/humility and appreciation for all the things you've got. It doesn't hurt to eavesdrop on some miserable couples to help you on your journey, but the goal is not to be happy in spite of other peoples' misery (you can if you want) but to have you realize just how lucky you are exactly where you are in spite of other people.

(Even if they're grass is really, really green). Whether someone else is happy or sad shouldn't matter. What matters is that you aren't trying to have something that you don't currently have.

Finding happiness is something that you should find within yourself, anyway. It shouldn't be found within another human being (although it would be nice if that would happen) you may find that being with that complete, happy person that you thought would make you happy-has just made you, ah, more miserable and realizing that what are they so happy about? You have to find what you want first before you find a partner to share it with. When you take marriage and kids out of the goal, are you still able to find love? The nice thing about just having love without trying to turn it into something else; an entire life, marriage, kids, mortgage, is that it takes the pressure off. It allows you to find someone that you just want to be with and enjoy living in the moment.

This includes great sex with someone you have absolutely nothing in common with, or want anything from-other than great sex.

MARRIAGE AND OTHER TYPES OF BONDAGE...Not that I'm implying that marriage is bondage, or that you have a marriage with bondage, or that bondage could be good for marriage...

When A Wife Loves A Husband More

Only a problem if the wife wants a little thing called respect. Unfortunately, when a wife loves a husband more, the husband takes advantage of this love. He may even begin to look around, wanting that challenge, again. Some narcissistic men will revel in their wife's adoration, even demanding bubble baths, pedicures and daily massages.

This could be a great relationship as long as the woman doesn't ask for anything in return; like attention for herself.

When A Husband Loves a Woman More

Only problem is when the wife decides she can suddenly do better. Then she'll start looking around, checking out her options. If a man obsesses over the wife, he's either a control freak or banging her sister behind her back.

If he's simply obsessive and so madly in love (still?) that he can't think straight, it may cause some problems for the wife if she wants a little thing called S-P-A-C-E.

Marriage Of Convenience

Technically, this marriage can work as long as both parties agree to the agreement. If the agreement is one-sided, there could be problems. Single women may do it for financial help with their kid(s) when the real baby daddy suddenly disappears and they realize they can't do it on their own. A woman may marry a man that she thinks is a good provider/nice to her dog/opens doors for her, even though something is missing and she was never madly in love to begin with. (Yet, stays in the marriage when she thinks back to how she used to behave when she was madly.) A man may marry a woman he thinks he's supposed to because she's good to him, even though he isn't in love thus leading him to cheat and her to a broken heart. The agreement works when the man (or both) is secretly gay, but doesn't want to tell his family. When two people decide they share the same business goals, which may include things other than love, commitment and sharing the same bed for the rest of their lives, but may include money, money and more money.

Till Death, I Do...and Other Miseries

You know the couple. They never stop yelling at each other, they're never affectionate with each other and you really have no idea what bonds them in the first place.

Every chance they get, they tell you everything they absolutely cannot stand about each other. Yet they stay together. Why? It probably comes down to money, or a shared love for the dog. (A mortgage could factor in, as well). They may actually be in love and this is the way that they show it. What should you do? Nothing. Leave the couple alone. Maybe they really just love chaos. And when they do have a moment of adoration? Ignore it.

It's just temporary insanity (or horniness). They really DO hate each other and will get back to the fighting soon enough.

Six Degrees Of Kyra Sedgwick And Kevin Bacon

They really are in love. They have fun together, work out together and play tennis once a week. They may even share a business together. They actually laugh at each other's jokes. (Even when no one else does.) They still get turned on when they see each other. This couple goes through the ups and down's of life. Through cycles, chapters, changes and yet they still manage to respect, love and cherish one another.

Yes, these are the aliens I was talking about.

A LITTLE TIP ABOUT RECEIVING CATALOGS

DON'T! Immediately send them all back. You know how they have that domestic section? The one where you can purchase the towels with the initials on them? It's just there to make you feel about yourself. Yes, you can order your own initials, but you already did that when you got your first apartment. These catalogs are for couples and if you're not a couple, you should not be looking. Why are you torturing yourself? Towels, plates, silverware, his and hers blankets? Come on, those catalogs are meant to lure you in and make you feel bad about being single.

It's also there to pressure you into marrying well, anyone; just so you can buy their stuff. Want to make yourself feel better?

Next time you're at your married friend's house, check out the hall closet. Here you will find several unused sets of towels, napkins, glasses with initials on them, even linens. Your married friends used them all of 6 months of wedded bliss, then immediately packed them up and shipped them to the closet.

Now that they've been married several years, anything with their initials-may just be annoying reminders that they're stuck together.

A FEW USELESS STATISTICS

1. It's not a figment of your imagination. There are more single women than single men. It's been going on since the 1940'. Yes, you can blame women's lib.

2. 56 million American Adults have never been married. (You may be one of them; or wish you were.)

3. More people live alone than with someone. Yes, people are messy to live with and mess with your stuff.

4. Less than half of the babies today are born into a married (mother/father) union. So go ahead, get knocked up with your lover. You can raise the baby on your own, or live with your mother. She raised *you,* didn't she?

5. Surprise, Surprise, most single people say they're happy that way. (Most of them may have been having sex at the time the statement was made.)

6. *49 % were only unhappy with their sex life, not the being single part).*

7. Half of all marriages end in divorce. 67 % of 2nd marriages end in divorce and 74 % of 3rd marriages end in divorce.

You have a 50 % chance of staying single and sleeping with great people (and holding onto your money) for the rest of your life.

8. Nearly 50 % of men admit to being unfaithful at some point in their lives. The other 50 percent are lying. (Or really unattractive.)

9.20 % of married couples are in a sexless marriage.

(But, not with other people.)

10. 40 % of single people today, aren't even sure they want to get married. The other 60 % are going to do it at some point and out of those? ½ will get divorced. The other half will stay married and remain unhappy because they've taken a look "out there" and deemed it "too much work".

11. If you want your marriage to last 50 years, wait until the last 50 years of your life to get married. How to figure out the last 50 years of your life? That's the tricky part.

12. Statistics show the answer to a happy marriage is the man saying yes and the woman not listening to the man when he says no.

Are people really meant to mate for life? Maybe. If they're really, really rich and have the money, space and time to be away from each other for long periods of time.

Then of course, when they decide they no longer want to be away from that person and desperately miss them again-fly immediately to their side, get a little and take off, again.

I suppose that's why married couples are so into their "boys night out" and "girls night out".

CHAPTER 15

LYING ABOUT YOUR AGE

I try not to lie about my age, unless, I have to. Reasons why I may have to...

1. Meeting a cute guy way too young for me.
2. Interviewing for a job when the interviewer has just graduated college.
3. When I'm honest about my age and no one compliments me.
4. At any wedding when everyone wants to know why I've never been married.
5. When younger people start to tell me that, "I'm cool, for my age".
6. I haven't said my age, yet some guy tells me they like me because they like older, experienced women.

Everything's Falling Down

(Sing to London Bridge is Falling Down)

All I have is falling down, falling down, falling down-
All I have is falling down, and I DON"T LIKE IT!!!

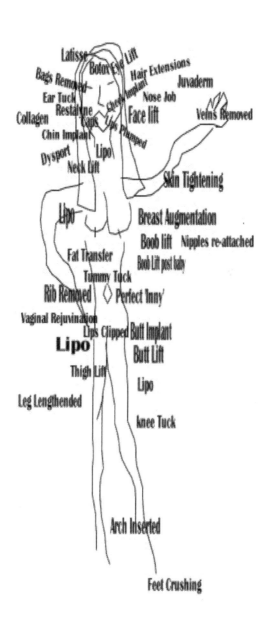

Latisse
Botox Eye Lift
Bags Removed
Hair Extensions
Ear Tuck
Juvaderm
Cheek Implant
Nose Job
Collagen
Restalyne
Caps
Face lift
Veins Removed
Chin Implant
Lips plumped
Dysport
Lipo
Neck Lift
Skin Tightening

Lipo
Breast Augmentation
Boob lift Nipples re-attached
Fat Transfer
Boob Lift post baby
Tummy Tuck
Rib Removed ◇ Perfect Inny
Vaginal Rejuvination
Lips Clipped Butt Implant
Lipo
Butt Lift
Thigh Lift
Lipo
Leg Lengthended
knee Tuck

Arch Inserted

Feet Crushing

CHAPTER 15
LYING ABOUT YOUR AGE

Women have to lie about their age because of younger women. If all women would decide to tell the truth, there wouldn't be a problem. When an older woman lies (who looks older) it ruins the scale of aging. When a woman who's had everything done (and lies about it) looks like she's had everything done, it makes the rest of women have to lie about their age. When someone lies about their age by 10 years, yet looks good for the real age they are (but not so great for the fake age) they're screwing it up for the rest of us. Ever meet a woman who easily looked 45, but would not back down from saying she was 36? She looks great for 45 and if she was honest about it, she would get lots of "wow, you look great!", instead of dead air.

The problem is that women have to lie about a lot of things because we live in an ageist society. When you date online, if you put your real age (no matter how good you look) you are knocked out of certain categories. Men your own age don't want to date you (even if you don't want to date them). Men lie about their age, as well. It's pretty obvious when they do, too.

If a younger guy dates you, it may be because you are older. (Which immediately makes you feel older.) They're into being taught things. They think you're much more sexually experienced and that turns them on. This may or may not be the case. And, in any case, just because you're older, doesn't mean you want to be told you're older and that turns them on.

A man your same age doesn't want to think he's dating someone his own age. In fact, a 70 year-old goes after a 30 year-old, Even though he's asking you out, you may try to set him up with your mother. But, he doesn't want your mother. He wants you. Why? Because he's, "young, viral and doesn't date old broads". It really has nothing to do with pairing up 2 people that would be good for each other or like each other's company. The man only wants the woman to 'look good' on his arm.

(Not hang onto his arm, because she cannot stand up straight.)

Plastic Surgery. My Body's going to Pot and I don't mean from smoking it

At some point, after you've decided the only reason you're not with your Prince Charming is because you don't have bigger boobs, better teeth or a perkier derriere, *you may* decide to go for plastic surgery. Never mind that once you're married, your husband tells you he would have loved you au natural. You've decided to go for it. You always hated your eyes, ears, nose, lips, butt, boob (fill in the blank) and have come to the conclusion that this is the thing(s) that's stopping you from being perfect, and from meeting Mr. Right. You deduce that none of the men you've been involved with up to this point have been up to par. They've all been 7's, when you know that if you were a 10, you could get a 10. Even if you hear a man say, "I like a natural beauty," you don't believe him. You've been a natural beauty for years and he never wanted you before. He must mean a natural beauty with double Ds and a smaller ass.

Before we get into a costly, expensive swim through all the wonderful things that can be done to a woman's body (who really cares about her mind?) let's rewind a bit to before we had these impure thoughts. When we're young, we're pretty confident and satisfied that everything on our body is where it's supposed to be. We don't worry about things sagging or shifting, and we definitely don't think it has anything to do with why we're single.

Then…

You get a bit older…

And…

You begin to question everything. Why not? You have to come up with a reason for not finding your significant other. When you're older and not married, your reasoning can get a little woozy and you don't think so straight. You begin to think about the real reason you're not married.

There are lots of women out there, and women are competitive. Women want to be beautiful. And if we can't be beautiful, we want to be rich.

So that we can buy our beauty.

I'm not saying beauty is the only thing that matters. Manners matter. But you can take a crash course in manners. Just because you have everything you want, and every part of your body has been reconstructed, doesn't mean you'll be happy. But am I talking about happiness? I'm talking about still being single and trying to land a man. Women need to look good. Women see other women who look better than they do and automatically hate them.

Most women have read The Art Of War...not for business, but to know their enemies. To a woman, an enemy is anyone prettier and younger. Ever hear the term keep your enemies closer? We need beautiful woman by our side. We don't want them stealing our man. Although being friends with beautiful women doesn't necessarily ensure your safety. Many women will use you to get to your man; any man. Many women simply hang out with you, because you know lots of men. It's okay. If you like a guy and your friends tries to steal him, you can always tell an itty-bitty white lie and say she has a herpes condition. Why wouldn't he believe you? She's one of your best friends. Hey, this book isn't about being fair. It's about being aware. So, once you hit the old 30's you start to play a little less...fair.

Then things start to...

Sag, deplete, get bigger, wider, less attractive...

Nose jobs, breast implants, collagen, eye tucks, tummy tucks, ass tucks and arm tucks are all fair in love and war. Women will spend any amount of money, to say nothing of time-to enhance anything and everything they can. A Woman will take every precaution to make sure her man doesn't leave her for someone younger.

When did you ever hear of a man leaving a woman for someone older? Yes, there's that one actress, but word is; he's gay. And she's had a ton of stuff done.

Woman To Woman

Women will stroke another woman's ego because they want that woman to compliment them. Women will tell the truth to gain sympathy.

Sometimes we'll tell our true age, if we have a momentary thought that it doesn't matter; which doesn't last long. Sooner, rather than later a prettier, younger version of us will pass before our eyes and we will realize that we need to lie. We have to lie. To tell the truth would be idiotic. Especially when that younger version of **you** is out there, ready to take the world by the balls (just like we were at that age). Even if you're someone who doesn't lie, you may omit the truth simply by saying nothing. It starts to happen around your late 30's; by mid 40's you're suddenly 41 for a few years. By late 40's, you're actually still 41. Which is great, except when you get the year wrong when someone asks you when you graduated high school. It's great when people take care of themselves, but isn't there a place where it's just okay to look like an older version of your younger self?

There's something very strange about a woman with a face tighter than a baby's ass with a neck that looks like it belongs on an elderly chicken. Why must we endure an endless succession of face-lifts, just to look like a plastic version of how we never looked in the first place?

You see someone with tons of plastic surgery and they say their age (waiting for you to give them a compliment) and your thought is, "they look older than their age, look like they've had everything done and actually, you didn't even recognize them when they yelled you're name, you just didn't want to be rude.

And then you see someone real, authentic, au-natural and it's…refreshing. Wow, a face that looks like a real face!

How odd, wrinkles and all. How, well, ah...normal? It's probably our fault for giving into everyone else's perception of what beauty is. And society says beauty is youth. Not that I'm against a little tummy tuck or brow-lift when the time is right. I'm just not going to tell you. Hopefully it will be tastefully done and only enhance what was already there, not change it entirely. I'll become one of those women you gossip about. "Did she have work done? "Nah, she never looked that great before, she must have had something done." Meantime, just smile your best $10K, capped-teeth smile, and walk awa. Let them get a look at your new, tight-as-a-babies...you-know-what!

Logan's Run, here we come!

I'M GETTING LAZY-JUST TELL ME WHO I'M SUPPOSED TO BE WITH ALREADY

The problem with getting older (besides the obvious body aches) is that you've been out there and not sure who to be with, anymore. You may date a lot; you may think you're with the one. You may be the kind of person who doesn't date, preferring to move forward with your life and miraculously hope the right person comes along.

On the other hand, you actually could be in a space in your life where you simply aren't interested. It does happen. Either out of lack of positive thinking, or being in the wrong headspace (or being in the right headspace and just being quite content with your life) and still feel you need to do something to enhance some part of your body to bring in the right person.

The majority of people want to find the person their supposed to be with already, and move on with their life. Not that finding the right person will suddenly put everything in order, but having that plastic surgery out of the way and being with the one? How perfect!

But past a certain age and not being coupled up becomes strange. You no longer feel welcome to your friend's dinner parties.

You suddenly don't feel cool anymore. The thought of going to a singles bar, or another event makes your head spin. In fact, most things you feel like you've been there, done that and so you just want to stop. It's okay, you probably should. Probably you should take a break, take a breather and maybe just take off.

Go somewhere where you won't feel like a mouse on a wheel doing the same thing over and over again. In fact, you may get to the point of not even wanting to be with any of those people you've in the past fantasized about, because they don't even look so good, anymore. So what are you supposed to do? You find yourself at a place in your life where you just want to chill out, relax and be with that person you are supposed to be with.

Perhaps you're supposed to be dating your surgeon? But you did that already and in fact, you realized that he uses you as a before and after in his book, which makes you feel even more pathetic.

In fact, you were trying to date him before you had anything done, because that would have been the ultimate compliment; that you can get your plastic surgeon and he isn't spending the entire night analyzing all the things he could do to you - to make you prettier. Then you (or he) stops dating and he invites you to dinner parties. "This is great", you think. There will be other guys there to date. Wrong! There are quite a bit of older guys (with plastic surgery, as well) and a bunch of versions of you. Same nose, same boobs, same cheekbones. This only freaks you out, worse. You wish you could have gone to one of these parties before you invested the 10 grand in all the work.

DOESN'T GETTING OLDER MAKE ME WISER?

According to the Internet, there is absolutely **nothing** to support this theory. This actually means that you may be making the same mistakes at 89 that you did at 15. The only difference is you didn't need plastic surgery at 15 (not including the nose job as a gift for your Bat mitzvah).

The kind of plastic surgery you may do to yourself as you age usually comes from the same shallow thoughts you've had your whole life, which is "I want to look hot". Wiser thinking should possibly produce moments of clarity such as, "I'm beautiful on the inside" or "I'm going to age gracefully". If you're having one of those moments now, by all means, cancel that Lipo and mini-facelift. But, on the other hand, that Lipo and mini-facelift may make other people attracted to you and want to be around you more, since statistics do say that attractive people are more social and have more friends. I didn't say people with plastic surgery...just attractive people. (The goal is for one and the same.)

...This is where mood lighting may come in handy.

CHAPTER 16

WHY DID I GO FOR DRINKS WITH HERMAN?
(Something Light and Fun)

When I went for drinks with Herman
And told him of my woe,
He sat and listened kindly,
Then offered to rub my toe.
As the evening wore on
And I got hammered from a drink,
It was clear to me that Herman was going to be
my shrink (and try to get in my pants).

CHAPTER 16

WHY DID I GO FOR DRINKS WITH HERMAN?

Sometimes, you'll have an experience that will change your life. It may not necessarily be a good thing-just the truth, in someone else's eyes. This was one of those times. Although I appreciate the thoughts and wisdom of older men, I often wish I didn't have access to their insights. Herman is an older, married, strictly platonic friend I met for drinks one evening. An evening, that by the end of it, I was wondering, "Why did I go for drinks with Herman."

INT. RESTAURANT/BAR

HERMAN

You seeing anyone?

ME

Yes, nothing serious. You work with all these great, cool 35 year-old investment guys. Have anyone to set me up with?

HERMAN

You're too old for a 35 year-old.

ME

But I'm 34.

HERMAN

Yes, but you're too much pressure for a 35 year-old guy. You need an older guy.

ME

Well, then I'll go for an 80 year-old that's about to keel over.

HERMAN

You can't get an 80 year old. An 80 year old wants 22 year-old. What you need is a nice 55 to 60 years old, who's been married before, willing to get married again and is possibly open to adopting, if you can't get pregnant.

I order another drink.

ME

What about what I'm looking for?

This isn't about you, it's about who wants you.

I switch my drink to a shot of Tequila.

FADE OUT

I'd have said Herman was crazy, except that he may have hit the pathetic nail on its pathetic little head. (Not that I'll ever have drinks with him again.) Okay, what are we to do with this information? Stay home and clean our apartment? Run out and start trying to date every guy our own age? I have a better idea. Get even and date every 26 year-old you can meet. Great sex—no bullshit!

Sexually, we're in the prime of our lives and so are 26 year olds. So forget meeting the right guy, the guy you think you're supposed to be with. Get laid, have fun, feel young. Younger men love older women.

Older women teach them things; Sexy things, erotic things; things that turn them on. And, when you get tired of the 26 year-old just like the 35 year old is going to do to you? Trade him in for a new one.

Just like a girl of 20 will always be impressed with an older man (especially if he's sporting a lot of cash). A younger guy will look up to an older, worldly woman to expose him to things he previously only read about on the Internet. Maybe Herman was right. Maybe 2 people the same age shouldn't date, anyway, regardless of whether he thinks the reason is because men don't want the pressure of a woman their own age. Perhaps it's the woman that doesn't need a guy her own age? Maybe a guy her own age is boring, dependable and thinks he's doing her a favor by finally settling down and choosing her. Perhaps he should re-think things. Maybe she doesn't want him to do her any favor. Maybe each sex is better off with a younger, sexier partner to make them feel better about themselves.

Maybe dating someone older, wiser and more established would enhance our self-esteem and make us feel like a million bucks.

What in the world do 2 people that are the same age have to offer one another, anyway? The same music? Big deal. The same cultural stories? Who cares. Being able to gossip about the same celebrities? Who needs it.

Moral Of The Story...

Maybe Herman knows what he's talking about. Regardless, you should only go to drinks with someone if you know, in advance, what they want to discuss. It takes a tough stomach to hear the words Herman shared with me that casual Wednesday evening. Did I believe him? Not really. Did I care? Not really. At the time I was dating Danny, a hot 29 year-old model. So, thanks Herman, no, I probably couldn't get the 35 year-old balding investment banker. But, I did manage to get the 29 year-old model. And guess what else? He knew how to change the breaks on my car, too!

CHAPTER 17
SEX
BOUNDARIES, ETHICS, MORALS AND ALL THAT CRAP

By a society of people, we are categorized by our boundaries, morals and ethics. Doesn't that suck? We search out friends that fit closely with our beliefs (unless, you've met in AA in which case you perhaps may only have drinking (too much) in common). Usually, as we go through life, we pick like-minded peeps to hang with. Because this way, we feel comfortable, have similar views in life and feel at ease knowing we may see the world in the same way. Searching for people outside our comfort zone is something we generally don't do, so why would we want to do it in relationships? Why in the most intimate area of our lives would we want to even consider someone that doesn't even have a clue what our beliefs systems are? Our morals? Our standards? In every area of our lives we make sure that we are going down the right road; following what we believe, how we want to live our life, what is good for us. What is going to make us closer to achieving our goals and what we want out of life.

And then we screw it all up…

With sex.

We meet someone. Someone very far removed from anyone we would ever imagine we'd be with; then something weird happens. We fall in love. (Or we think we do, which can resemble real love. The fake love, fakes us out.)

Usually, it's not love. It may just be called being horny; sometimes it's called blinders. And other times, well, we're just floating out of our comfort zone and trying something new. That's not to say that 2 completely opposite human beings won't meet, fall in love and live happily ever after. But I'm not talking strictly Republican and Democrat.

(They get in bed together all the time.) I'm talking about 2 completely different worlds colliding. Not just Mormon and Jew or Yale and MU, the differences can be vast. But somehow, love can take over and override any underlying sense of I shouldn't.

Which, it shouldn't, but it frequently does.

The, I shouldn't can come from your family, your friends and/or your local police force. But whoever is loudly interfering, will not stand a chance if your heart is telling you it's the right thing. You may or may not regret this love later, but by then it probably won't matter because you will have alienated everyone you were once close with anyway, so there will be no one left to talk to.

There's also the off-chance that you two will get along swimmingly and even though the differences are huge, your family/their family miraculously decided that they really all love each other, and you live the rest of your life in bliss.

But, I'm not betting on it. (Although, you have as much of a shot at love with someone that you have nothing in common with. (Not to be negative, or anything.)

When you see a weird couple together, you need to realize they're together because they-

1.   Like the same weird sex.
2.   Have fun hanging out with each other.
3.   Can't stand each other, but have threatened the other with some sort of voodoo if one leaves.
4. Sick of each other, but too lazy to find someone else.
5. Understand each other in some weird way that works.
6.Really are happy and yes, they really are weird.

If you're in your 30's, 40's or 50's (or more) and still having sex with someone you aren't planning to marry, you may be screwing yourself in more ways than one. What are you doing? You're not a teenager anymore, even if you feel like it. Yes, random great sex is, well, great!

But if you're trying to settle down, it's probably best to (at some point) forego the parties, clubs, one-night stands and daily hangovers. How many great looking people do you need to prove to yourself you can get, anyway? And at some point, what difference does it really make that you're screwing the hottest person in the room? Not to say that the sex isn't incredible, it's just that at some point, no one else cares who you're screwing.

The problem may be, you're afraid to grow up. Chances are your friends have been having sex with only their husbands for at least 5 years now. Why are you still going from guy to guy to guy? You still think sex is a game. When you're younger, you want it, but pretend you don't.

When your older, you may not get it as much as you want, or on the regular basis that you may or may not be used to. You may seek out someone just to have sex. Yes, women love sex just as much as men. And sometimes, they don't want to cuddle afterwards either. Don't believe me? Just sit around with a bunch of women at a table and listen to what they talk about. Sex. The men? Ex-girlfriends who dumped them, or games they play (with balls).

QUESTIONS YOU MAY BE ASKING YOURSELF

What's sex? When is the next time I'll have it?

Why don't I want to be seen in public with the person I'm having sex with? Will I have it once I'm married? Why do I continually want to have sex with all the wrong people? Why am I still having sex with this person and not marrying him/her/it? Sex - Those crazy 3 little letters that cause so much trouble. You're either doing it with the wrong guy, not doing it at all, or waiting to see where your new relationship will go before you screw it up with sex. (You also may be having lots of great sex with one to several great guys. If this is the case, skip this chapter.)

Here's the bottom line: sex is great. It's great with the right guy, the wrong guy and the in-between guy. Giving up sex should not be a prerequisite for finding love. Once in a blue moon, you may decide to give up the sex to see what you're life is really about. Which leads you to your vibrator. Sex is even great with your vibrator. Which if you are still single and in your 30's, you've gotten to know well.

You may even be on a first name basis with your vibrator. That's okay. Even married people, *ESPECIALLY* married people, use them. Since, apparently, they may not do it. (More on that later.)

WHAT'S SEX?

These are the women who have finally ended that last disastrous relationship. It may have been with the guy they thought they were going to marry, but everyone else told them they wouldn't. The one they fought tooth and nail to keep, even though everyone else said, "dump him." The one that ended up being so much easier to let go than keep? How hard it is to fight for someone, but how much easier it is, finally, to let go? So, this is where you ended up after much hemming, hawing and hysterical bawling— hours/days/weeks/months later; not having sex, not really dating, and blowing off any opportunity you've had to have sweaty, stranger or haven't we screwed, before? Sex. You are officially in the "what's sex?" phase of sex.

Right now you might be feeling too hurt and betrayed to think about letting another person in, again. You think, "I'll never get married. I'll never make out with anyone, ever again. No one else could possibly know me like he/she knew me."

You'll get over it.

You'll get over it faster when that gorgeous, single hunk from marketing struts in front of you at the office. You'll get over it when that hot guy from the gym starts jogging next to you on the treadmill.

You'll get over it, spinning next to that TV actor you

kind of always had a mini-crush on, but didn't know you could actually ever get.

See, already over it. It doesn't take long. But while you're in it, it feels like it lasts forever. All of a sudden, one day, you'll flip from what's that to when?

Most likely, this guy will not be the guy. Even if you want him to be, even if you light candles and pray. (Well, he might be. Candles and prayer can go a long way). It's usually only in the movies that you end up with love at first sight right after you were dumped, but it can happen.

And if it does happen? That's one less dude you have to lie about sleeping with. Perfect. Just as long as you know you can make out with another guy, even sleep, without calling your ex's cell and hanging up. You're ahead of the game.

Some weird things that may happen after you start having sex with that person...

He can't get it up/can't keep it hard/comes right away/needs that little blue pill/doesn't like sex/only likes sex/tells you how much he prefers anal/Asks you who you closed to/only gets off looking at a picture of male celebrities, yet insists he's straight.

SOME SEXUAL POSITIONS YOU MAY FIND YOURSELF in...

SEX ALONE

When you're young, you may never entertain the thought. "What's the point of sex if you aren't doing it with someone else?". This is, until you haven't done it in awhile and decide, "What am I waiting for?" Just wait. Wait until you're bored enough, or an ex introduces you to a toy; you'll see a whole new way to have sex.

You'll have a choice...abstinence or pleasing yourself. You may not find it as much fun as the real deal, but it is disease free and you don't have to dress up. (Unless, you want to.)

SEX WITH A STRANGER

This can be very evocative and exciting, but having to ask for a sexual history report, every time you have sex with someone new, becomes tedious and may ruin the moment. This is why sex with oneself seems to work out. You're not 23, anymore. Which means that picking up that stunning stranger may not feel the same. You may start thinking about stalkers, disease and someone seeing us naked. When we're 23, everyone sees everyone naked and has a much more laid back attitude, about, well...everything. Later, it may bother you to do it with the lights on, wondering, "What's the point? And really, unless you're sure that he's well endowed, knows exactly what to do and thinks you're an absolute 10, who needs to be looking at anything-by now, we certainly know where everything is and where everything goes. Sex with a stranger, although tempting (and induced by alcohol and/or drugs-most likely, unless you're just a nymph) may be just ...strange. It may just come down to, "Hey, thanks for using my body and letting me use yours, let's play again sometime." What's wrong with a little game playing amongst...strangers?

SEX WITH THE WRONG GUY

Chances are...

if you're not happily in love/engaged/about to rifle through that dowry of yours, you're having sex with the wrong guy. Otherwise, you'd be married to the right guy. (Or wrong guy and cheating with another wrong guy.)

Not that you started off having sex with him thinking he was the wrong one. Not that it mattered at the time, but at some point you woke up and you were still single. What are you supposed to do, stay celibate? Not a chance. It's the reason you're back in bed with Lazy Larry or Pathetic Peter. If you're having sex with the wrong guy, you should continue to do so. Not to would mean having to go out and purchase new batteries for your vibrator.

As long as you're getting it from someone you know, why stop? Just make sure that you continue looking for someone new. You'll want as little space between sex partners as possible.

SEX WITH THE RIGHT GUY

Once you've met the right guy, you should probably wait to have sex. (According to those books.) If you have it and then he dumps you, you'll be furious. Hold out. Play hard to get. You want him to ask you to marry you. In fact, if you can get married without dating, that would be ideal. With dating, there are so many obstacles that come out. You may decide (or the other party) that they don't want to marry/live with/date you any longer. Maybe dating, too long, is the problem.

Maybe waiting until you hate absolutely everything about that person (yet continue down the aisle) is not the smartest decision. If you know (before all the drama starts) that you both fit pretty perfectly and you agree on most things (some of the time) you should probably just head down that aisle and find out all the bad stuff later.

Remember the beginning of a relationship?

When you hid how you are (most of the time) so that other person will only see the best side of you? That's what you need to strive for, but unfortunately it's hard enough to keep your mouth shut when you've got something interesting to share (like your opinion). You may find that it's just too difficult not to be yourself. And although, your parents got married after 2 months, your dad **only** asked your mom because he was horny and she said no. And look how wonderful that union has turned out!

Hold out, anyway. What's 2 months?

SEX AFTER MARRIAGE

From what I hear, you'd better get it while you can. According to several married couples I know, they don't do it. Why not? They say the thrill is gone.

They say the relationship can turn into a brother/sister relationship, which only works if you find your sibling(s) attractive. Yes, there are those who are still doing it on a regular basis; getting it on between changing diapers and driving kids to school. They may even up the ante by adding quite the kink into the ole sex life, to keep things spicy. Having sex with your spouse takes work. Most of the women say they still want it and it's the guys who've slowed down. (With them, anyway.)

The man says it's the woman who doesn't want it anymore. (She's getting it ala-carte.)

Maybe they are both happily not doing it.

The ones still happily doing it should make a sex tape and take it viral, if only to prove to everyone else that some married couples are not only doing it, but it's still amazing!

FOUR! (Not the golf term)

This is a small group of individuals (à la celebrity A and much younger celebrity B—enough said) that 'invite' a 3rd party into the marriage or seek sexual gratification openly, outside of their marriage. These are called 'marriage contracts' and they do not include sacred vows of monogamy. Not that monogamy is so sacred. In fact, maybe open marriage is the way to go. I've seen several happy marriages with couples that swing, bring in a partner and/or fish outside, but still come home to each other and enjoy a nice dinner. Some people, on the other hand, tend to get, something called… jealous and prefer that their spouse be only ones to see them naked (sans the pool boy/cleaning lady lurking outside through the window).

Sometimes, they don't even want their spouse to see them naked, which may lead to the following…

Sex with the same gender

Same gender sex is probably pretty similar to straight sex, only with more tools. With female same gender sex, the male looking female is usually playing the male role.

This means that even when a female is gay, she is still expecting to catch her big fish (even if she's wearing a suit and tie). She's still looking for love, someone to save her, take care of her and be the dominant, so to speak. Gay male relationships seem to be the same way. No matter what, it's the yin and the yang, which means everyone's searching for the right yang to their yin. At the end of the day, people that are gay are still looking for the same thing straight people are looking for. *Yes, a nice walk-in closet, great sex and a doorman.*

NOTHING TURNS ME ON ANYMORE

At some point, you may find it difficult to fantasize over anyone. No actor will turn you on anymore. The thought of that hot guy you used to be into suddenly turns you off. Finding a picture in a magazine isn't even the same. (All those models look so young now).

So what to do? (Masturbating inside a walk in closet to your designer clothing is fun, but may get old.) On second thought, if it's the only thing that turns you on anymore, go for it. I get wet just thinking about my new suede loafers.

CONJURING UP THINGS THAT TURN YOU ON...

1. A nice car.
2. A hot model.
3. A great place you've never been.
4. Thinking about an ex.
5. Daydreaming about your future.
6. Daydreaming about your past.

WHAT NOW?

You may have to take a weekend sojourn and re-find yourself. You may have to call an old lover and ask for a copy of the homemade sex video you back. You may have to come up with some new, inventive things/people/porno that turn you on.

This can be difficult when you have become pickier as you've gotten older. When someone says, "You're too picky and it's the reason you're single", they really mean, "Why are you still going for people outside of your league." And, "Why do you continue to make (what we think) are unrealistic choices?"

Wanting a good looking/fit/sexy partner, at any age, doesn't change. No one is attracted to someone with a gut, and yet it can just suddenly appear after a certain age. No one is supposed to say anything, but it may secretly become a problem. Staying in shape really should be a pre-requisite for love.

Obviously love isn't all about the physical and there are thousands of people that are equally high in body fat and still have sex. And of course, love isn't all about the physical. You have to go deeper, peel away like an onion, to find the core of that person. This takes a lot of time, energy and strength of character. Especially as you watch your spouse grow increasingly lazy, fat and detached as they waste away in front of the TV, eating cheese puffs.

Of course, people don't always stay in the best shape of their life. My God, there's personal tragedy, accidents, financial loss, fire and health problems. Love should rise against every barrier one faces in life. Love should be about more than looks, body shape and etiquette.
It really should. Really. I don't know how these married people do it. God, we're all really, really shallow. YOU must be ashamed of yourself.

MEN WANTING TO BE WOMEN WANTING TO DATE MEN

I'm so confused, I don't even know what I'm saying as I write this. This basically means that as man they identify themselves as a woman (except they have male body parts, which may or may not be removed, per their own request) and they want the same thing straight women want; a good guy.

So basically, they're just like straight women. Screwed up and trying to meet a guy.

WOMEN WANTING TO BE MEN WANTING TO DATE WOMEN

Yea, let's just call it the same as the above only reversed. Women that feel like a guy, act like a guy, dress like a guy (enjoy peeing standing up?).

At any rate, they are also not gay. Even after being in the female body for (however long they have) they still have an interest in being with another woman, because they never really identified themselves as women; even though they had all the required body parts that would fit them in that category-according to signs on the bathroom doors.

MEN WANTING TO BE WOMEN WANTING TO DATE WOMEN/WOMEN WANTING TO BE MEN WANTING TO DATE MEN

Now, I really need a nap! Do I even go here?

If this is you, just call your local support group or take a long look in the mirror and chant three times, "Face it, I'm straight".

BORN WITH BOTH GENETALIA

This should automatically entitle you to be anything and everything you want.

God has given you a free pass.

You are the only person (People) on the face of the earth to know what it feels like to have sex as male and as female. (No, dildos are still plastic.)

HAVING NO SEX DRIVE

It's called anti-depressants and/or a bad partner. Those anti-depressants may be keeping you sane (most of the time) but probably making you not want to screw. That partner? Yes, he/she is doing the same thing. You do have a choice. You can start taking tranquilizers or fantasize about what gets you horny (like a really nice pair of shoes or the tennis instructor from your club).

GETTING YOUR EMOTIONAL NEEDS MET

This doesn't even belong in this chapter.

(I'm going to speak with the author about it; if I can find her.) Your emotional needs should have absolutely nothing to do with sex. Oh God, you're crying already? This is exactly why sex and emotions should be kept separately. Come on, crybaby, what are you doing getting emotionally involved, anyway? Where did that ever get you?

It got you on those anti-depressants to begin with.

Now knock it off.

GETTING YOUR ROMANTIC NEEDS MET?

Oh sure, this one is fine! Your romantic needs are just the 'frilly, silly, made up, fantasy, fun stuff' that make sex really good. You should cater to the demands of your significant other (within boundaries, of course) to make the other person happy. If you've met at sex anonymous, then possibly you should just go bowling, instead.

Other than that, I guess it's whatever floats either of your boat, or bed.

I JUST WANNA GET LAID

If you're just looking for sex, you can find it, well…everywhere. In fact, according to my brother, women (before even giving they're name) send naked body parts via text.

I know. I've seen them.

And sometimes I don't even know what they're so close-up; you can't even tell what it is.

If those women aren't giving it up, then not sure who is. There are quite a few sex addicts out there. People that just want to do it, all the time, with lots of people, for free. Which sucks for prostitutes, but I'm sure there are still plenty of people that pay for it, too. If you can get if for free, how good is it, anyway? (Some people have to pay for it, if they want to get it at all. And some, depending on what they look like, may have to pay a little bit more than others and/or beg.

When a woman just wants to get laid, it becomes about wanting a hot guy that she may never see again.
…And again.
If they only do it once, it's all right, as well. (As long as she does the moving on). If he dumps her after she sleeps with him (even if she only wanted him for sex) her ego may be bruised. That is, until she meets another hot guy. Preferably, people who want to just have sex, want to have sex with that same hot person, no strings attached with both on the same page emotionally, physically and sexually; so they can hook up and still live their lives.

This is called no guilt-no shame, no STD sex.

Men who just want sex from a woman can be confusing to the woman if she's actually trying to date him. There becomes a breakdown in communication when she actually thinks he's asking her out, but instead, he's really asking her in.

This can lead to disillusionment on the woman's part. While she finds herself to be pretty amazing, smart, sexy and worth dating-and the guy she fancies just wants in her pantsies. (I couldn't resist.) This happens when the guy finds her hot (thank-you, we say) and then proceeds to tell her, "I just want to have sex with you".

Although we may say, 'I'll add you to the list', secretly we are thinking, if he wants to screw me, why doesn't he want to date me? Which leads women to start thinking what they need to do to become well, dateable, in the mind of that guy. Girls do the same thing to guys when they just want sex, but usually we don't come out and tell you. We just do it, and then blow you off.

Oh, come to think of it, guys do the same thing.
SEXTING/PICS/SKYPE/VIDEO
Everyone is hooking up via electronics. People are sending, not only nude body parts; but also sex acts, as well. Apparently, if you have not sent a naked body part before you're even date, you may run the risk of losing the person to someone who will.

There are so many naked body angles you didn't even know existed! You have to be creative to date and sext. Everything is done online before you've even met. Getting to third base online is the norm before even meeting for a cup of coffee. People are not above giving virtual blowjobs. (You're in trouble when the person on the virtual receiving end says, "that was fantastic.") On the other hand, giving a virtual blowjob that doesn't lead to a compliment, which then leads to being blown off (without ever even going on the date) can be even more depressing. The good news is, you can have entire relationships and never have to meet in person. You don't have to shower, brush your teeth or even change your underwear. (If this sounds appealing to you, you probably shouldn't date anyone because sooner or later, you will have to do the above.) Dating has some interesting challenges in these modern times. It seems that men and women cut straight from "hi" to "what are you wearing". Dinner and a movie is immediately thrown out the window in favor of, "wanna come over?".

The movie.... becomes.... you! I'm not even sure how to answer the question 'What are you wearing?' let alone "send me a picture of your p...". The fact, that strangers are sending body parts of themselves to other strangers? It's just, ah...strange? (Although, there is something to be said for seeing the size of a penis ahead of time.)

Just saying.

OLDER WOMEN - YOUNGER MEN = YUMMY *

Although it's a turn on that a younger, hot guy is interested in an older woman (who still looks pretty hot) the whispers of, "what's he doing with his mother's friend?" may start getting to you. The fact that younger women (who know you're older) may try their best to knock you out of the way and get to him, it can be annoying.

While your friends respect the fact that you are still getting it on with a hot, younger guy, at some point-you may look in the mirror and decide that you will never let him see you, naked-again, in the light of day. Okay, you're body may still be amazing (for someone half your age) and your face nicely stretched, tucked and pulled, but at some point you may get sick of watching him play video games and text you for sex dates (from the living room). And then again, you may be happily ensconced in your love relationship with your much younger boy-toy, having the time of your life. Waiting for the problem with this? Can't come up with one right now.

Give me some time.

Nah, pretty much can't come up with one. Carry on with your bad self.

Oh, wait, I've come up with one. You may have to give him an allowance. This means that you may just be taking the allowance that older ex gives you replenishing it to your young thing. It's called tithing. And, you don't even have to be religious to do it. Your money to begin with? Well, that's just called giving it away for something in return. And sometimes it's called prostitution.

OLDER MEN - YOUNGER WOMEN = HOW'D HE GET HER?

While a man envies another mans score with the perfect, young hot thing on his arm. (Which he may or may not have bought. In one-way or another) he secretly wonders how he got her. No, it's probably not love. Yes, he probably got her because he has money. (Or spends whatever he does have, on her). While other women may envy the woman who is hitting it with that hot, young thing (for a week or so) The younger man ogles and aahs at the man's ability to score such a hot prime example of the female species. "How do I get one of those?", "how did he get her" and "how rich do I need to be (or well endowed) to get her" are just a few thoughts that pass through a jealous male mind.

Getting a hot chick (and young) is the ego booster a guy looks for when perusing the female species, during a night on the town. Thinking they can get that hot, young thing (without a clue to what they look like in the mirror) is irrelevant to the search for youth-In a body (with a little cash allowance to keep that cheerleader happy). Although, he may be able to hold onto her with sheer personality, force and power, chances are once that gut comes out, the hair on the back starts protruding and that bad hair rejuvenation starts to come in; he may re-think things and want to…running back to that annoying wife. Getting her is one thing, but keeping her? That's another all together. No, just because you've got her on your arm, it does not make other women think you're hot.

It does make women wonder how you got her to begin with and how much it's taking to keep her happy.

If you really want to know the answer, look for the smile on her face when he's walked away to get their drinks.

CHAPTER 18

BABIES

Ode to My (Yet unborn) Baby
Oh, my love, I've been waiting for you, for so long.
The hours I spent wanting you, needing you
Wishing you're in my arms to cuddle and hold.
Oh, my love, what I wouldn't give for just a few hours of laughter and baby burps to brighten my day.
If only. Yes if only, for a moment.

(Ew! Is that baby poop on my dress? What the hell was I thinking?)

CHAPTER 18
BABIES

Ah! The stork. What to do, what to do! Once you've reached a certain age and do not have a potential mate, you may decide to have a child on your own. Here's a possible exchange between your eggs:

EGG 1

What's that smell?

EGG 2

(Sniffing around your uterus)
        I don't smell anything.

EGG 1

(Annoyed)
        How can you tell me you don't smell that?

EGG 2

My nose is bad.

EGG 1

Smell is the first to go.

Usually, one egg will taunt another until you're left with overripe insides. At this point they will send a sticky note to your brain. It may read something like this -

STICKY NOTE

What should we do?

At this point, you need to come to a decision. It starts out simply enough.

Here are some common stages:

Stage 1 Your period -- Ooh, what is that?

Stage 2 A month later --This sucks.

Stage 3 A year of dating -- How'd I get pregnant?

Stage 4 A year later --I'm glad I didn't keep the kid.

Stage 5 Five years later –I just wasted five years with you and you don't want to get married and have kids?

Stage 6 A year later -- When should I have a kid?

Stage 7 Much later -- Oops! I forgot to have a kid.

Stage 8 Might as well go ahead and have the kid.

Stage 9 You think you can still have a kid-who you kidding?

Although I've narrowed down this chapter to 7 reasonable and imaginative options to popping out a kid (or several at once) hold onto your vaginal lips because there are (drum roll, please) officially over 18 ways to make a baby!

On a side note, if you're thinking of starting a new business? Well, if you're under 30, you should consider selling those eggs. At $8 grand an egg, you'll be living in that house you were trying to move into with that guy-**and** you won't even have to have him living **WITH YOU.**

Missed the boat to sell your eggs? How about working on the inside of the fertility industry? It's ...you ready?

4 BILLION DOLLAR INDUSTRY

Why share this useless, yet fascinating information? So you know that you-the one having trouble having a baby-will make you feel less alone.

Perhaps not any wealthier from this information, but still not alone.

Just because-Here are the 23 ways to make a baby-

1. Old fashioned, good ole penis in the vagina.
2. Artificial insemination-Mother with father's sperm.
3. Artificial insemination-Mother with donor sperm
4. Artificial insemination-Egg and sperm donors, surrogate mother.
5. In-vitro: Using the eggs and sperm of parents.
6. Adopting/Claiming a frozen embryo-A woman carries someone else's embryo that she didn't genetically produce. It's inserted into her, thus making her still able to carry a baby inside her belly.

(*Fun baby shower game-Go around the room, whoever gets closest to 19, wins a prize).

7.   Sperm Banks.

8.   Sperm washing-yep, once infected sperm can be washed-thus creating healthy sperm.

9.   Zygote Intrafallopian Transfer-Putting the woman's' eggs into the fallopian tubes, still allowing her to carry to term.

...NEED A NAP YET?

10. IVF with Intra-Cytoplasmic Sperm Injection-To help male infertility-Doctors get a single live sperm and inject directly into mother's egg.

11. IVF-with Frozen embryos: freezing woman's embryos for later use. Can also freeze donor eggs to have ready for surrogate mother's uterus.

12. IVF-with Pre-implantation Genetic Diagnosis, screening embryos before implantation to check for abnormalities.

(No, not like if his side of the family has premature hair loss and/or flunked skipping in kindergarten)

13. IVF-with Egg Donor (Your husband may try to talk you into sleeping with her and that he will "Collect her sperm and bring it home". This isn't what this means.

14. IVF-with Sperm Donor (You can either sleep with someone or take their sperm and have it injected into you).

15. IVF-with egg and sperm donor (By now, you're probably so sick of each other, you not only don't sleep together, but could care less if the baby looks like either one of you.

(Cont.) In fact, after birth, you may be considering letting the other party take full adoption.

16. IVF-with surrogate using parents' egg and sperm-This is very lazy of you (unless you *really* can't carry your baby) what's nine months? You took nine months to arrange your living room and you still don't like where everything is.

17. IVF-with surrogate and egg donor.

18. IVF-with surrogate and sperm donor.

19. IVF-with surrogate using her eggs, sperm from baby's father.

20. IVF-with surrogate using egg and sperm donors (Several-it's a party-having an orgy and letting all the men come inside you is not what this means).

21. Cytoplasmic Transfer –Taking something from the donors egg, drawn into something which takes a single sperm from male partner-then those are injected into the patients egg.

...Confused yet?

22. Nuclear Transfer- taking an egg that's not fully ripe yet (From the mother to be) and put it into the egg donated by the younger (Fertile) woman.

This means older women may be able to have babies using the younger person's eggs and still have a baby with your egg cells.

23. Cloning-Using cells (Other than sperm and egg) from an adult male or female and introducing them into an unfertilized egg that's had it's genetic material removed-Encouraging embryo development.

7 choices to scrambling that egg and making a baby

1. Freezing your eggs.

2. Artificial insemination.

3. Having a baby with your best gay male friend.

4. Having a baby with a one-night stand.

5. Having a baby with your boyfriend (You don't care if he marries you because you're old enough and can do it on your own, but once you tell him you're pregnant, he'd better marry you or else).

6. The Old Fashioned Way (getting married).

7. What baby? You're too damn old to have a baby!

FREEZING YOUR EGGS

This becomes a real option once a woman reaches a certain age without a prospective spouse, or even with a spouse. Women are even doing it well into there forties because they still aren't ready or want to have a baby.

Just because your inner clock is forcing you to have one, you may simply to be too busy living that thing…we call…life. (Some doctors say that after the age of 42, you shouldn't freeze your eggs. (Yes, and wearing hair extensions year after year isn't good for your hair. FYI-people still do it.)

If you haven't decided by 45, maybe you should forget it. Remember how hard it was to lose that extra four lbs. from that over-indulgent weekend in Cabo? How about **not** drinking for the 8 days you did that stupid cleanse?

How are you going to walk around pregnant for 9 months when you've just organized your closet the way you like it?

You finally have it color coordinated and everything *JUST* fits.

By the time a woman gets to be 40's and 50's, she finally has her groove.

By that age, we've primped, prodded and forced every kind of tool somewhere either inside or around our bodies; so, to carry around a child, (unless you're doing it for a cousin who can't get pregnant) may simply be too much hard work.

You may want to freeze your eggs so that it's an option down the road.

You may just be dating someone, not ready for a kid at the moment, but know you're running out of time; and it comforts you to know you've got some eggs safe and on-hold. This way, when you decide to adopt a child at 70, with your 23 year-old old boyfriend, he can care for it. (If he doesn't try to trade it for an amplifier system at a garage sale.)

By 70, hopefully you'll have saved enough to have round the clock nannies so you'll be able to nap. (You won't be able to pump milk out, anyway.) If you want to see what the kid(s) will look like, you can use that computer software that shows you, blending your two photos together. (This only works if you know who the guy is and have stolen/taken/asked for his sperm.)

Or, try this on your own: take one of the pictures of your eggs and superimpose it on a baby photo of **him.** Now, this very well may look like a photo of a baby boy holding an egg.

We really just want to be able to save our eggs, so that we can have babies right up to the day we die. (If we wanted to!) Just in case.

ARTIFICIAL INSEMINATION (Doing it with the guy)

It's difficult to be a romantic and decide this is the way to have a baby.

Even if we have a one-night stand, we like to think we're in love. Or, we lie and tell ourselves we're in love- even if just for an hour. (Disregard women, who act like men, have sex just for sex; and have absolutely zero interest in anything more-except perhaps more sex.)

When it comes to artificial insemination, may the best sperm-win. You look through the bios of the men you're considering choosing to have your baby with. The first thing that may come to mind is, "Where the hell are these guys in real life?"

You may find that you're falling in love with a bio and picture. In fact, they're everything you're looking for - on paper.

You're looking through magazines at people you've never met in your life to anonymously give you their sperm, and they're not even jacking off thinking about you? Or, you can go on some dates and place a sperm cup in the bathroom.

(Although right after sex, having him ejaculate into a random cup, may be an odd moment. But guys are kind of dumb. He may not even notice.) You may even try to find out where the guy lives and date him for real (since you have officially procreated a child from a list of things that you always wanted for yourself and a relationship).

It's okay; you'll have more control over this than that guy you were trying to find, anyway.

You've now ensured your child a place in line next to that aristocratic family you've secretly harbored the fantasy of being a part of. (Never mind the fact that most are alcoholics, in rehab of some sort and/or in an insane asylum.)

Chances are if you're going for artificial insemination, you have passed on the gas station attendant who stands at 5'4" and scratches his ass while he pumps the gas. You are allowed to be picky. This is also a mechanical process. (This means your inner thighs will **not** be sore from sex.) Ah, remember those days? At any rate you'll be assured of a baby in a nice neat little package (sperm ejaculated to some Bunny of the Month). Even though this method is a sure path to pregnancy. It certainly doesn't do much for the ego. Ego? What ego? Your not married and decided you want a kid.

There is no room for romance or ego in this scenario. Let it go, move on and get real.

ARTIFICIAL INSEMINATION WITH A BASTER

You've used one for Thanksgiving-I'm pretty sure it's the same thing.

You call up a friend/ex lover and ask him to fill it up for you-or you go to a 'lab' where they have 'ready made' sperm just waiting for you.

You don't even have to meet the guy as long as you have between $7,000 to $20,000 dollars for every shot. (Which usually doesn't take the first time.)

No, you don't get an orgasm with it! Ah, look at the bright side. Your ex didn't give you one, either. Realizing you would have had to deal with that a-hole the rest of your life makes this choice a no-brainer.

HAVING A BABY WITH YOUR BEST GAY MALE FRIEND

You'd better be prepared to raise the baby on your own, or with him, and his other lover(s). You think women are horny? He'll be out the door for the first piece of ass that comes along. (Although, he may be willing to bring the baby along!) The nice thing about this arrangement is that your child will learn how to dress (well) and sing show tunes.

(Yes, I'm stereotyping.)

Your best gay friend won't cheat on you - at least with your boyfriend of the moment. (Unless your boyfriend of the moment is bi; and secretly harbors a crush.

Do not give up on love. Once you give it up to live with your best gay friend (where does that leave you...Gay Taco Mondays?)

Excessive Halloween fun (way past the age of 35?) Have that baby with your gay best friend, just make sure you don't give up looking for love, sex and having your own apartment/house/dwelling.

HAVING A BABY WITH A ONE-NIGHT STAND

Let's just cut to the chase. This is artificial insemination with the actual body. What's the point? When he dumps you, you get to spend the entire nine months fantasizing about your last incredible sexual encounter with a stranger. You will memorize everything from his toes to his face. Chances are you professed your undying love for him-at which point he ejaculated early, anyway. You will waste a lot of valuable time, pining over a bad lay, simply because he became the father of your child.

You will remind yourself over and over again (as well as every one of your friends) that he was The One—the most brilliant, sexy, funniest guy that got away. In your mind, he's the perfect guy who took a cab and got away. And because he didn't want you, you've decided that you have to have him. If you try to have a baby with a one-night stand, you're liable to take a perfectly lousy experience and mess it up.

At some point during the pregnancy, when your hormones have hit the moon, you'll track this down this stranger in the middle of the night or you may call him, tell him you're pregnant and beg him to tell you why you two didn't make it past the one-night stand. He may answer with, "Who is this? Beth, Pam, Cindy, Cheryl, Tiffany?"

This isn't the brightest idea, you realize, as you hang up the phone. You may ruin your future baby's life by making up all sort of romantic stories about how the baby's father ran off to Paris before he was indicted on fraud charges. (You'll do your best to make it sound adventurous.) If you're going to have a baby with a one-night stand, you're probably better off getting him to jerk off in a cup (while looking at you, of course). This will save you from possible disease (you can have his semen checked) as well as the five grand you were going to spend on the insemination.

(If you're feeling kinky.)

HAVING A BABY WITH YOUR BOYFRIEND

You've probably gone through several relationships and are now officially a serial monogamist dater as well as decided that your current boyfriend is; the one/fine for the situation/would make a good baby-daddy/is my only option left.

You could do this the rest of your life, which is kind of what you already have been doing up to this point, no? Just as you start getting comfy in your relationship-you blow it.

(No, by bringing up marriage or that Geisha/hooker outfit you plan to surprise him with Friday night.) You blow it by bringing up having a baby. You tell him, "We don't have to get married, but my eggs are expiring, and I think I may need to pop one out fairly quick…what do you think?". When you're dating, you're supposed to concentrate on just dating.

Unfortunately, after a certain age women change their mindset. Yeah, yeah, yeah, she may bullshit you all she wants that she isn't in a hurry to have a baby, but all those trips to the baby department (in every store) should have given it away. Or, every time you pass a baby it's "Oh, look honey, look how cute the baby is! "This generally begins around 30..

Some women much earlier. (Some, never.) Not that the younger women don't want babies. It's not a good idea to have a baby with your boyfriend unless you're prepared to have a baby on your own in case the relationship doesn't work out. The tactic, "I'll just have him knock me up. Then, after I've told him I accidently got pregnant **and** he realizes how madly in love with me his is, he'll never leave me". You think you'll guilt him into loving you? Maybe you will. Maybe he'll even marry you. But he may leave you ten years down the road. Maybe it was the only way you could get him, but was he worth getting?

I've had friends who got pregnant by their current husband (boyfriend at the time). They didn't pre-plan the big nine-month bang. It just happened. (Or so the story goes.) At any rate, pre-planning your pregnancy with your man when he isn't even sure he wants to continue dating you is probably not a good idea.

Are you doing it just to control that you'll have Good lineage? His nose? His trust fund?

If your boyfriend dumps you and your plan backfires, you'll have to see him all over town with his new girlfriend (who is 22) and in no hurry to get pregnant.

Or, you may not even care and have the baby on your own. No problem. Just be sure the gay male friend you turned down earlier is there for you change diapers and color coordinate linens.

You could just make sure your boyfriend's ready to marry you. You could just keep that little 9-month secret until after the wedding, couldn't you? But that would be trapping him, wouldn't it? Now, now, we don't want to go to that extreme. Or, do we?

THE OLD-FASHIONED WAY

If you make a baby the old-fashioned way, you have fresh eggs, got lucky and/or you may have had several false starts/a few near misses and finally got pregnant. The old fashioned way may mean…waiting. It can depend less on age and more on your private stock; which your gynecologist will probably share, "your eggs are fine", or "We have a bit of a problem here". While you didn't pre-plan the whole baby thing, you didn't really think it would ever be an issue. You may have been a bit busy searching everywhere (including outside the planet since apparently you can't find your soulmate/baby-daddy/sugardaddy/sperm-supplier-on earth).

Once you do find him, you'll need to do everything you can to seduce your future soulmate so that you can immediately procreate. The old-fashioned way of dating and courtship, no longer applies. Once you're older and become in a hurry to have the kid(s) is that you'll probably be preparing baby rooms while your husband's looking at retirement packages. Here lies the problem.

If your husband is looking at retirement packages, you may not want his sperm. It's nothing personal (just like a man's desire to date that 22 years old, because she's less pressure and has more time). The likelihood of your older husband giving you a healthy baby may not be a reality, either. I know, harsh. Even if your eggs are perfectly ripe/a little shady/turning shades of green…his sperm is no longer swimming with a full tank.

According to research, older male sperm isn't so ripe and babies are more prone to be born with birth defects. Yes, eating walnuts are supposed to help.

Besides those nuts? You may just be better off skipping the little bundle of joy altogether. Spend enough time with your husband and you may realize that he's all the kid you'll ever need. It's also important to remember those (dare we bring it up) abortion(s) you had in your reckless youth when the thought of having a kid didn't sound so appetizing. And a 180-degree turn of...

WHAT BABY?

Is this where we finally end up?

Did we decide that we really don't even want a kid(s)? Is it our age? Did life get in the way? Did I forget? Did I kind of remember, but really never found the right person? Did I decide I was just too independent/career driven/selfish/tired/lazy/financially strapped-to do it on my own, no matter how much my mother begged for grandchildren? (Blame your siblings; it's not all up to you.)

You decided you didn't/never/changed your mind/missed the boat-and ended up childless, but fulfilled. It may have taken you a few years to get there, but you made it. It may not have been a conscious choice; it's just the way things happened. And guess what? You realized that you finally found the pure joy in romancing that twenty-eight year-old bartender. You love your two-seater convertible, you love your nieces and nephews and you love your space. (As long as Ernie, the carpenter is always on call to change your light bulb, you're happy.) You may even convince yourself that Ernie, the carpenter, is the perfect man for you. You might even start to pursue Ernie, in which case he will probably have sex with you then run back to his dowdy 300-pound wife. (Whom he's been with since sixth grade.)

You are much too powerful for Ernie, the carpenter.

And, if you're not careful, you'll give him heartache considering you're the first person Ernie has had sex with in seventeen years besides his wife. You may even start to fantasize about having a kid with Ernie.

Its okay, this thought will pass.

Just like summer…nicely moves into fall.

Once you've reached (dare I say it) 40ish and let go of all desire to have a baby, you're free to live.

Go crazy!

Unfortunately, going crazy with the condom isn't as much fun as in the old days before disease and that thing called accountability. Just making the decision to forego having that baby will open up a whole new ball game for you.

You'll already have gone through those painful 1st and 2nd birthday parties for every one of your friends' kids and act interested.

You may not even have ever wanted kids. If this is the case, you're most likely just selfish and self-centered; which is fine. Your friends already knew this about you, anyway. You're off the hook! They'll never ask you to babysit.

By the time you hit 40ish, most of your friends' kids are at least 10 to 15 years old. Once you see how they've turned into obnoxious teenagers wreaking havoc on their parent's lives, you may have a meditative moment validating your choice to not have kids. Especially when you notice how much older your friends with children…look.

On the other hand, your clock, still viably ticking, may take you down the path of, "crap, I better hurry, I don't think I've got much time left", which now leads you on a desperate search for that thing called chemistry/love/partnership/getting laid- so that you can procreate and pop out a baby before you hit menopause- which is always a sexy conversation to have with a future husband/partner/sex plaything.

On the bright side, having decided **not** to have a baby now leads you on to more important things...like planning your new year's vacation...in June.

HAVING A BABY WITH YOUR HUSBAND

(I didn't pick him, you did.)

Having a baby with your husband is still presently done in society.

Okay, it's not so much the norm anymore, but some people really do still date for a while. They fall in love, get married then get pregnant. The getting pregnant part doesn't always work out the way the couple has planned.

Sure, maybe her eggs were fine (maybe his sperm) blah-blah-blah years earlier (Before chasing careers, mortgages and outside affairs). But now they decide no matter what (come hell or high water) they are going to have a baby together. So, they try and try and try. They're so tired of trying, they even get sick of sex. Thus begins the road of different routes to baby making-dome.

They may go from freezing eggs, in-vitro, baby basting, surrogacy, another woman's egg or another guy's sperm. They may give it all up and go the celebrity route, adopting a baby from a different Country/race/state. It really doesn't matter, there are lots of needy babies out there that are just waiting to be loved and nurtured –just like you were planning to do with the one you were going to birth... (And you'll still have a tight vagina afterwards!)

(If all else fails, stick with pets. Their overall easier and you can take them on a flight for $50 each way.)

Just a thought...

The three later stages of baby-making years

35 to 40...You've been trying or deciding sometime before the age of 40 you better have a baby. Not that you're so desperate, you've just heard so much drama surrounding having to have one within a certain time frame-

259

That it's almost mandatory that you start to freak out. Why? Because every gynecologist (and specialist) tells you that you have less of a chance of having a baby the older you are. And as women age (I'm told) there eggs are no longer supple and ripe to give you a kid. You may be better off knowing you cannot have children well in advance. This way, you know you have time on your hands. Simply start the adoption process or head to Mexico and take one selling bubble gum off the street. *(I can hear it now "Author encourages Americans to steal Mexican children),*

At 35, you should still have plenty of time to meet your man (unless you've already met him) and have a kid. At 39, when you're not married or with the guy, you will probably have a mini-breakdown and/or panic until you do meet the guy. Once you've hit 40, become pregnant and gotten the guy, you'll have that huge sigh of relief. You'll then look over your shoulder at the 43-year-old's still trying and secretly feel sorry for her.

40-45... You think you're in trouble, but you may not be at all. In fact, as long as you have eggs (okay, so maybe it's true there's a 5% percent chance to get pregnant at this point) and get your period regularly, you can actually still have a kid. It may not happen as quickly or easily as it would have when you were in your 20's or 30's (you may have not had an easier time just because you were younger). There are plenty of women getting pregnant in there 40's without the help of any outside sources. A woman in her 40's possibly will decide to make an active decision to get pregnant. This Is different than an oops when one is younger and runs off to the abortion clinic, gives the baby up for adoption or takes a morning after pill. This is a definitive attempt to get pregnant/knocked-up/with child/with or without a hubby (or significant other) to go along with it. After several false starts you may decide to see a specialist and begin to figure out other options.

(Mexico will probably not be listed as an option).
45-50…Oh yes. I hear them laughing now! "What baby? Are you kidding me?" You can't have a baby at this age". "Your eggs! You don't have any eggs left!"

But you can…if you believe…kind of like in children's fairytales. If your eggs are ripe and you aren't in menopause, still getting your period regularly (and your cycle hasn't changed) you actually may be able to get knocked up.

(You must have sex to do this.)

Or, you can hire someone to carry the baby for you. (Just like a nanny does after your friends have their babies, so they can resume their pre-baby busy life). Many women at this age (and beyond) that aren't able to have children, will go to great lengths via surrogacy, in-vitro or adoption until their dreams have finally been realized.

The importance of, "I hope he/she has my husband/my eyes/nose/ears", suddenly disappears and may be replaced by "I just want a healthy baby". The only problem with having a kid at 50 is that you will most likely have menopause and potty training at the same time. Add marriage to an older man, and you'll most likely be dealing with menopause, AARP family discounts and two different types of diapers). Chasing after a kid (and your husband) is a great way to stay in shape. (Unless of course, you're rich/lazy/suddenly not interested and/or depressed and hire someone to do all the work for you, just like all your friends! You don't want to feel left out, do you?) Having a kid later in life, you realize, may be a blessing because you really didn't have much to do for the rest of it (your life) anyway.

And, watching all your friends revert to being a teenager (while their grown kids are now in college) gives you a sense of responsibility and calmness you either never had/forgot you had/decided you wanted-because watching your grown-up friends-

(Who always acted so responsible and berated you for your independence/no responsibility) suddenly act like idiots, which, oddly enough, Suddenly makes you grow-up. Those silly texts once a month that invites you to girl's night out? (Sure, you should probably be flattered that as the only single one, you're still invited.)

But, really?

Don't you have single night out every night?

When did simply going out for a few hours become such an event?

Oh right, after 3 kids have straddled you, a husband you've been schtupping whenever you want for (fill in the blank) years…and you miss what we have.

Ha. Relax. Go back to your baby poop and throw up, I have another stupid art opening to go to.

Then there's always this comforting thought…you probably would have made a lousy Mother/Father anyway, but you're a heck of an Aunt/Cousin/Stranger that gives little kids candy, buys them great toys and knows fun games (for about ten minutes before you happily hand them back to their stressed out parents.

Some reasons you'd make a lousy Mother… You're selfish, self-involved, self-absorbed, egomaniacal, have lousy morals/ethics/standards/hide things out in the open, have ADD, OCD (and any other initials you can think of) are narcissistic and have no patience.

(Yes, we know, your mother was, too. But that was before that doctor on daytime television informed us it was because of pre-Menopause…yes, we know, your Mother went through menopause for what seemed like 18 years-at least she acted like it.)

CHAPTER 19

THE PURCHASING OF PETS

I talk to her like she's my sister.
Or dog.
She is.
I talk to her about my dating life, like she
understands what I'm saying. I think she does.
Sometimes, I wish she could converse with me.
But if she really could...she'd tell all my deepest
secrets. And believe me...they are better left
Unsaid.

CHAPTER 19
THE PURCHASING OF PETS

I used to ask my boyfriend(s) if my they mind the dog sleeping in the bed...now I ask my Dog.

You may ask your potential partner, "Will you let my dog, Elvis, sleep in bed?" This is a trick question that may be answered one of two ways:

1. *Yes.*
2. *Yes.*

Any answer other than the above may require a full jolt out the door. (If you're feeling hard up, you may want to have sex with him first before asking him to leave.) Or... have sex with him first; then let the dog slip in under the covers for a little lick research to see how your date responds. Chances are pretty good that you've gone from, "Are you okay with the dog sleeping in bed?" to "Hope you don't mind the dog sleeping in bed" and finally to, "we can have sex in my bed, but maybe you could just go back to your place afterwards?"

It's probably best at this point if he sleeps in his own bed...in his own home. Izabella and I need a good night's sleep. And, being a Dachshund, she needs space. She sleeps across the bed and there's barely room for me. (No, I don't feel comfortable asking her to move. This is the position she chose, who am I to tell her she has to scoot over?) "Once you've acquired a pet, your dating life is over", my brother tells me one particularly slow Sunday. Of course, if the person you're dating loves pets just as much as you do, you just might find yourself sharing your bed with not only that partner-

But several four legged creatures, as well.

Both of you will adopt the more the merrier attitude; and in this case, will live happily-ever-after in hair-all-over-my-stuff-heaven. There may be a secret dating handbook that states, "Now that you're a pet owner, you've relinquished all rights in the dating world."

(I don't think it's this one.)

Once you've acquired several pets, you may as well just go ahead and have a baby with a stranger because you've pretty much altered your dating life for good. (Much like suddenly deciding to become a Vegan, thus simultaneously deciding you will not date anyone who isn't a Vegan, thus alienating all non-dateable-Non-Vegans.) Or something like that.

You want a dog for companionship—someone to give your love to that loves you back. You probably didn't realize that this would hinder your chances for a relationship. What are you supposed to do, wait until you're 80 to get a pet? What if you never find a husband? You purchased the pet to give yourself the love you've been missing. You just might want to chill on letting people see you smothering the animal with French kisses while talking baby talk.

DATING A GUY FOR HIS PET(S)

Just like dating a guy with kids and then realizing that you actually like the kids more than the guy, dating a guy for his pet(s) can be difficult when you decide that you want to break up. If you purchased the pet(s) together and you do the breaking up, you're screwed. He will never give you back your animal(s).

You better make sure you're in it for the long haul before you invest in that third party pet for your relationship.

Otherwise, you better let him be the one to end it (even if you secretly want to) so that you get to play the victim and end up with the pet. You may even have to go to court over visitation rights. You would never be as malicious as he would be over visitation, even if he were the one ripping your heart out. Besides, seeing him after he's broken up with you gives you the excuse to look cute and run into him at the park, to exchange the pet.

Showing up with a fake (or real) boyfriend can't hurt either. Especially if you're trying to get him back.

You weren't counting on him showing up with his new squeeze of the moment. Seeing her at the dog park with her micro-mini shorts, 21 year-old legs and fresh face (sans makeup) isn't going to do much for your ego. Perhaps you should re-think those going easy on him visitation rights? Dating a guy for his pet(s) is great only if you stay together as a couple.

Seeing a psychic to determine if you will be staying together, before purchasing the animal(s), is probably best.

BACK TO THE DOGS...

You've stopped hoping you'll meet someone to marry and now entered into the, "all I need is my cat to make me happy" phase. This may come about after your, "I'm never getting married, am I?" phase. Although you may think animal-lovers are stranger than other people, they require love just like everyone else.

Animal lovers feel in love with their pets and find that unconditional thing they thought they were searching for with a human. And, it's actually *better* than with a human, except the sex part. (Hopefully, this goes without saying.)

DOES A PET GET IN THE WAY?

In order to date, you need to be available. (Not emotionally mind you, just physically.)

Owning a pet is a responsibility and hinders your ability to jet off to France (or Boise, Idaho) at a moments notice. Men don't like entanglements; they like to be the entanglement, which they will remind you of day and night. I have a friend, who has a friend (she doesn't really like her and talks behind her back all the time, but that's not the point) She's a ready-made pain in the ass package. 2 black labs over 90 lb. and 3 cats; one deaf (or, blind).

I can't remember which. (No, it has nothing to do with the story.) Not only is she high maintenance, she's got a handicap on top of the handicap. This takes a lot of points off her dating card.

She claims not to care. I high-five her independence, but fear for the tidal wave of love against her.

Update: she recently got married. He has four German Shepherds. They all sleep in a queen size bed. (Sometimes, when it gets too crowded, they move to the guest-room. The humans...not the dogs and cats.)

WHEN YOUR PET DIES

It's very important to grieve for your pet.

If you are single, do not immediately run out and get another one. You may tell yourself, "I should really find a boyfriend/girlfriend/sex partner, first, this time around; before I purchase another cat/dog/hamster/horse. If you find yourself running out to purchase a replacement pet, you may find yourself in the same position, as you were the first time around and suddenly not want a relationship. No, they can't provide human love/shelter (very large dogs excluded- because they are great spooners) or pay for things, but pretty much everything else is covered to fill that small vessel that sits nicely inside the left cavity of your chest. It's hard to explain, but with your pet around, you simply feel filled with love and filled is usually all you need to feel. If you feel the immediate need to continue acquiring pets, you may want to ask yourself this question. How much do I miss sex?

If your answer is not much then run out and begin that potty training all over again!

(No, not the boyfriend. The dog.) On the other hand, if you are trying to meet someone (and have stay the night) perhaps it's better if you tell yourself to hold off on the pet. Try needing a person instead.

Get out there and actively try to have a relationship.

Yep, sounds like a lot of work.

Off to dachshund rescue tomorrow, Izabella needs a boyfriend.

PETS IN THE SACK...MY BREED OR YOURS...

Liking the breed of pet(s) will depend on the disposition of the human you're dating.

That's right, I said guy or gal you're dating. Most people pick the pet(s) that they either grew up with or are attracted to, just like dating in real life. Finding out (in advance) what breed of dog he/she owns, will help you understand how to communicate with him/her.

You may even notice (more often then not) people and their pets look alike. If you see a cute dog on the street, look up...it just might be attached to a cute human.

Getting to know the personality of the dog while dating your human might save you some unnecessary investment and questions that you deem too embarrassing later on. Spend an afternoon around your man and the dog and chances are you'll learn everything you need to know; how strict the guy is, how loving he is, how affectionate.

In fact, you probably don't even need the guy for the first date...just the dog. Weird to ask the guy to spend the day with his dog? You can always double (your dog and his. If they get along, maybe it's a sign. Just make sure they don't fall in love, in case you have zero interest in seeing the human again).

I was going to list breeds and temperaments, but then I realized it would be too much work; and this isn't a pet-dating book.

(But you can find the information on the Internet...if you want to).

DOG VS. MAN

Owning pets requires you to prioritize. Men do not like anything to be a priority (except themselves and even if they don't put you first).

Having a pet may leave you a little less time to be attentive to your man. He may not want to sleep with you after he sees the way you are around your precious pet. You've probably reverted from sex talk in the bedroom to baby talk with your dog. This does not turn him on. The fact that he's dating you is enough pressure for him without the animal.

But, adding that baby talk and the way you cuddle the damn thing? (Word to the wise; never leaving your mate alone with your pet. You never know what could happen.) He may even ask you to choose. If he does, choose Arnold. The guy isn't worth it if he makes you choose and Arnold's a better at cuddling, anyway.

If you have decided to continue dating him (Or he, you) you may find things out about your boyfriend that you never knew; like, how he doesn't like to clean up dog poop and this isn't the threesome he was referring to. It will just zoom the relationship right along. But you'll get a good glimpse of his real personality. The way he treats your dog, Arnold, will give you an idea of the way he'll treat your children (wisdom courtesy of Mom). Although, when you start purchasing lots of pets together, you may be subconsciously acquiring them instead of children.

(Or, you simply will have an extremely busy household with lots of kids, dirty diapers and pee pads).

*My cousin has 4 dogs, 3 cats, a bird and a bunny rabbit. (They also recently acquired a bear after moving to Alaska. (No, it doesn't live in the house. It sleeps on the porch...and pretty much everywhere else he/she wants). Not only are they happily still together, but they have an animal radio show...

An animal magazine and started an annual bark-out (Yes, like a cookout but with dogs). They have several thousand mutual animal lovers who date/shack-up/get betrothed.

A mutual love of pets can bring people together.

It helps when both are okay with animals licking their owners on the mouth. (Other areas excluded.)

"In fact", I tell my brother, "there's an entire planet of people betrothed/shacked-up/happily dating that own pets. I see couples all the time with pets! Everyone has a dog! Most people have pets. Don't you see them with the dogs with their heads out the window of almost every car?

"Yes, but *you're* still single."

Hmm.

CHAPTER 20

MEN MAY BE FROM MARS, BUT WE STILL NEED THEIR PENIS

When I was a little girl, I used to play with the garden hose.
It was long and green and...slimy, ('cause it would get dirty from lying in the mud.)
I didn't have to play with the hose, but it was fun.

MEN MAY BE FROM MARS BUT WE NEED THEIR PENIS

A FEW USELESS STATS

Yes, it's not just a figment of your imagination. There are more single women than single men. It's been going on since the 1940's. Yes, can blame it on women's lib.

56,000,000 (yes, that's million) American Adults have never been married. (Does this include people that lie and tell you they've never been married?)

More people live alone than ever before. Yes, people are messy to live with and mess with your stuff.

Less than half of babies today are born into a married Mother/father union), so go ahead, get knocked up with your lover! You can raise the baby on your own, or live with your mother (She raised you, didn't she?)

Most single people say they're happy living on their own. (Some may have been having good sex at the time they made the statement.)

49% were only unhappy with their sex life. They were still happy being single.

50% of all marriages end in divorce (which means you may end up marrying one of them).

67% of second marriages end in divorce, 74 % of third marriages end in divorce. This means, you have a 50% chance of staying single and sleeping with great people for the rest of your life.

Nearly 50% of men admit to being unfaithful at some point in their lives. The other 50% lie.

30% of married women admit they secretly fantasize about their tennis coach, pool boy and/or best friends' football jock son.

20% of married couples are in a sexless marriage. (Inside, not outside, necessarily.)

This leaves the assumption that the other 80% are extremely happy and drool sweat over each other's bodies on a regular basis.

40% of single people today aren't even sure they want to get married. The other 60% will do it at some point; out of those, half with get divorced. (That's okay, the other half will stay married and either be a part of the happily married group, or the I'm not so happy, but it doesn't look so great there on the other side' group.)

Yes, your grandparents stayed married for 65 years because they married within two months of dating and there was that thing called the depression, which bonded people. There were also things like family core values, morals, ethics and responsibility.

If you want your marriage to last 50 years, wait until the last 50 years of your life. How to figure out the last 50 years? Therein lies the tricky part.

Most couples say the answer to happy marriage is the man saying yes and the woman not listening to the man when he says no.

What Now?

Men want to feel needed. Women want to feel needed. Two needy people are a pain in the ass.

One of you must be less needy than the other and it's not up to me, but I suggest you better figure this crap out before you walk down the aisle. Since women today are out slaying the dragon as much (and sometimes more) than men, the societal roles have changed.

Most single women today are too busy to stroke a guy's ego. We're too busy buying homes, running companies and trading stocks. We lost our mommy-and-me card a long time ago. Somewhere between 30 and 50, we may have forgotten that we were supposed to be wined and dined, date, fall in love and get married. We may have decided the point was no longer to…get there…marriage, and it was not really a goal to begin with.

Perhaps, it once was and in the busy times of life, we decided it wasn't really as important to us. We also may have realized somewhere along the line, men became more...dare I say it...feminine. Yes, it could be because women became more no-nonsense, more driven or more powerful. It could be because men think that's what women want when we say we want a man to share his feelings.

This may be true to some extent, but telling me on a first date that you'd like to, "connect the dots on my face, using your tongue", is not what we mean by sharing our feelings."

I must admit-I really don't want a man to tell me how he feels. I have female (and gay male) friends for that. My man? I want him to be strong, confident and have absolutely no issues, (He still solve all of mine.) I know, I know, a bit unrealistic.

Men used to be strong, assertive, take control and lead the way. Women used to allow the man to take control and lead the way.

Now, it seems, women are leading the way and having to hold the guys hand telling him what she wants and needs. We don't want to have to do that.

Men are taking a back seat because they aren't sure how they're supposed to act with a woman. Men don't want to have to try to figure women out.

No, sexting doesn't help.

Result: No one knows what to do.

Whose fault is this? No one is really sure.

Men forgot how to be chivalrous, chase and pursue (without stalking). Women have become aggressive and try to control situations. Men blame women and women blame men. Gay women blame other gay women and gay men blame other gay men. Is everyone just going around blaming the other person? Sometimes, we blame ourselves for things that are out of our control. Sometimes we sabotage a perfectly good situation.

Sometimes, we don't really want anything to begin with (even though we may lie to ourselves and pretend that we do).

Nobody has the time or patience anymore to let a relationship develop. We've been on our own for so long, we forgot the dance of the species.

Some women put all of their energy into being a hellcat and embracing our independence; we let the good men go, thus pushing the men into the arms of waifs who can't tie their shoes. We'd be much better off if we could just fake needing someone. (And, mellowing out when we do like someone wouldn't hurt either.) Having to meet someone new, get to know all their quirks and baggage becomes too much to handle (especially when people tell you everything from the beginning).

I suppose it saves time in the long wrong. What used to take 3 months of falling in and out of love can now be achieved in one disastrous long night. Remember back in the day when no one was weird? Or, there were just a few weird people, but you knew who they were?

Now, everyone you date is so freaking weird, and not in a good, sexy way.

They're just…well, strange.

Yes, when you first met, you may have thought that quirk was unique and added character, until you realized OCD as a character flaw is not fun.

There is that thing called partnership, companionship, mutual admiration, blah blah bla, but I think it's mostly reserved for people that never had sex before marriage, met at 7 and grew up across the street from each other.

(When women are younger they have a list, which *may go something like this:*

Smart, Funny, Blue eyes, 6'2", Adventurous-

Captivating, Good family, Nice, loves kids and animals, Educated, Passionate, Ambitious, Hard Working, Loyal, Easygoing, Confident, Social, Athletic. (Feel free to add your own.)

Then, it starts to look more like this: Over 5'7", Full head of hair, Funny, Has a job-To Finally:

Just send anyone with genitalia-born male, preferred (but not mandatory?)

The older we get and the longer we're single, the less we think we can ask for?

Screw that, what do you think all those divorced and widowed peeps are for?

You figure asking for so much when you were younger may have gotten you into trouble in the first place. Maybe you slept with too many guys. Maybe you didn't sleep with enough.

Maybe you should have married Dan, Dave, Steve, Chris or Jeff. Now's a good time to remind yourself, "At the time, for whatever reason(s) you didn't want him/she/it."

So now what? Oh, I don't know. Run to your nearest gym and get in shape? Call all your friends and make them set you up? Give up dating and join a new world religious order? Run off to Bali and sleep with some locals in a band?

Who cares? Exactly.

The bottom line is, women need men and men need women. We need men to laugh with, have sex with, to compliment us and share secrets about our friends. We need men because their bodies are larger (hopefully) than ours and they can make us feel safe from the boogieman. We need a man to make us feel feminine, to make us feel loved and nurtured. We need a man to make us feel like a woman, a lover and a friend. We even need men to do dumb things so we can feel smart.

Women need to feel needed, just not as much as men. We take more crap and dish out less. God forbid we should pick on men the way they pick on us. Ever see those love handles and saggy balls after 40? The shape of the face that no longer stayed as sharp? The extra few lbs.?

We still love men. And yes, we still think we will have the happily ever after (however it shows up) which leads to companionship, admiration, trust and a damn good time. (Just like we currently experience with our pet.)

HOW TO DO I FIND THE LOVE OF MY LIFE WHEN I THINK I MISSED THE BOAT

You may have a slight problem.

It's called *you're too independent.*

This independence is great for you, and you do the best you can…with the ones that are left.

You may be also one of the following; Scared of commitment/Can't make up your mind/Don't know what you want/Are too picky/Too complicated/Out of control/Need to grow up.

After You Figure Out What Your Problem Is (and decide it's everyone else) you try to figure out where to go to experience/fine/mate with someone new.

This may be dependent on where you live (and how far you're willing to go). If you're lazy, you will want to find someone that lives/works/sleeps/relatively close to where you live, at this very moment.

Once you've realized that you were, indeed, wrong about that person who lives next door to you/works with you/is your roommate, you're going to have a bit of a problem getting away, unless it's a mutual break-up. Best to watch someone from afar, scope their habits, the way they interact with animals and old people; follow them to work, see if you really do want to date them (based on other things besides if they're cute or not).

Oh, right. That's what dating is for. (Perhaps it's best to let a friend date them first and report back to you. Can save quite a bit of time. Let them go through the heartache and chaos, haven't you had enough in your life?)

Which currently would still leave you…single.

And since being single has take up quite a bit of time your time in the past and you're still single-here-now, we have to figure out what to do from-here.

What led you down the path of missing the boat to begin with? It wasn't like you're alone, really. You're still one of (although now dwindling) friends that are all still single and think they missed the boat, too. Wow, maybe you're group is the only group that has missed the boat.

Look around. Make sure you're not the only ones left. All right, all right, calm down, quit freaking out. There are lots of you/us out there. No, not every one of them is desperate/horny/out of luck. Some are just busy/into their careers, pets, property, life-and lost sight of that thing called time. Time then came in and reminded us that we better get a move on things, we've let a lot of the good one's go (and equally bad ones) and now it's time to step up, do some soul searching and find the person we're meant to be with. (Or at least have a sex partner until we do find the one we're meant to be with.)

Observation: There very well may be no one left.

This statement can't be true, considering thousands of people fall in love/get married/have babies every day. Thousands of people walking down the street randomly meet, get introduced by friends, taking a yoga class together, sitting in a hospital waiting room, scanning the Internet and/or picking bananas at the grocery store. It happens. Sometimes, you may not even be in the mood to meet someone. This is okay, too. You're entitled to not have to want to be in a relationship all the time. In fact, some people like to be alone, at least some of the time. When you're alone and thinking about what you want, it may actually be the best time to figure out what you really do want. And, maybe writing a list of all your past relationships with the positives that each one brought to the table, can help you figure out what you're looking for. (Or remind you of bad stuff and put you in a bad mood for a few hours.)

A PLAN

From today forward, you can beat yourself up for thinking you screwed up the ones that walked away, the ones you walked away from, or the ones your friends tell you, "you wouldn't have ended up with him, anyway". But you're not going to do yourself any favors. You're better off letting it all go and starting to put everything in perspective now. (Yea, it's not going to hurt to make you happy first, get healthy, strong and pick better people.)

No, this isn't a self-help book.

Yes, once in a while, there may be a slice of wisdom (or two) thrown in, just to spice things up.

A Few Reasons You May Be Single...not in any particular order...

You date assholes.
You date nice guys that you aren't into.
You don't date.
You're too easy.
You're not easy enough.
You don't know what you want.
You're too picky, you're too lazy, you don't like people and/or people don't like you (which generally has nothing to do with one's ability to get a date).
You like being free (and by free I don't mean that you give it away. But you might).
You may be/have/suffer from one of the following...
    Scared of commitment.
    Can't make up your mind.
    Don't know what you want.
    Are too picky.
    Too complicated.
    Out of control.
    Need to grow up.
    Are perfect, and it's everyone else.

CHAPTER 21

I'LL FLY ANYWHERE TO MEET ANYONE

If you lived in Zimbabwe, I would fly there.
If you lived in Alaska, I would fly there.
I will fly to any destination you ask me to.
Just tell me what the weather is, so I can pack accordingly.
Two questions:
Are you paying for the ticket or do I need to use my frequent flyer miles-
Cause...
I may need to visit someone else, after you.

CHAPTER 20
I'LL FLY ANYWHERE TO MEET ANYONE

This isn't the kind of baggage our mother is referring to. For this kind of baggage, you'll need to fly somewhere (else…other than where you currently are) to meet someone that you haven't yet met (for whatever reason). Yes, we know happily married people will re-enforce how easy it is to meet available people, well…everywhere. "If I was single"…the conversation usually begins. It's best to quietly walk out of the room (or have earplugs handy).

Something unfair. Why do you have to travel to him? You not only have to physically cart your luggage, but also bring emotional luggage. (He's only bringing the emotional part). Let's at least hope he's a gentleman and carries the luggage (and you) when you arrive by train/boat/plane/jet/. (Yes, he could come to you, but do you really want to take the chance that it doesn't work out and you now can't get rid of **him**?) It probably **is** best that you do the traveling…so that you're able to get away if need be. When a woman is in her early 20's, she thinks she has the world at her fingertips. (If her breasts are supple, she most likely does.) But, as things sag (like they do) so do options. Walking across the street just to attract a man's attention, let alone flying to another state, is no longer the first thing on your mind.

By the time you've reached that ripe old age of 35 and still single, many people may begin to ponder…why. "It's none of your business", you can say. Or, "I haven't met the right one, yet". Even though they may respond with, "still?" you really need to just shake it off and move on. 35 is not old, and especially if you live in a metropolis chasing your career, you've had other things on your plate besides good old-fashioned love.

If you've been single, living in a small town; dating/slept with/stalked everyone in your vicinity, still go to bars every night and drink with the locals (you are one of them, you know), perhaps it's the reason you resonate so well with this chapter).

Even though 35 is not old in life (unless you die at 36, then yes, it is old…for you), according to statistics, at 35 you have a better chance at being struck by lightning than finding a husband.

(*Except for me. I don't think they're talking about me, in particular.)

(**You may find being struck by lightning more entertaining than marriage.)

Just saying.

When a married woman tells you 35's young, there's a good chance she's lying. Although she highly enjoys tales about your single, fun life (while breast-feeding twins) she's secretly thanking God she's not out there going through what you're going through). You may find yourself dateless in a town in which everyone is paired off except for you. You run into old boyfriends (now dating exact clones of your younger self; only cuter or homelier-depending on your confidence level at the time), respectively. You've done this dating/non-dating/I hate men/I love men/I need a man thing…for quite awhile now. After you've exhausted every possible resource (or people tell you that you have) it's possibly time to look elsewhere…on the planet…for other single species you haven't yet encountered. Then it hits you, (or someone calls to set you up), "Hey, what about another City/State/Country?

A not so hypothetical phone call may go something like this…

YOUR MOTHER

Why don't you come to town'?

I met the nicest butcher to set you up with…

> YOU
>
> (Ready to lose your lunch)
> How tall is he?

> YOUR MOTHER
>
> You're never going to meet a man if you're so picky!
> And he was sitting down, so I have no idea.

> YOU
>
> Butcher wasn't my first choice, mom. (Pause) Why
> was he sitting down? Butchers stand up to chop
> things, don't they? Is he lazy?

> YOUR MOTHER
>
> Just fly in. He's *willing* to meet you.

This exchange of dialogue does not require your mother. It can be cousin Ethel, as far as I'm concerned.

> COUSIN ETHEL
>
> Why don't you come visit your uncle Mort and
> me? We know a nice proctologist. He's never
> been married.

> YOU
>
> How old is he?

> COUSIN ETHEL
>
> 57. You're never going to meet anyone if you're
> going to be so picky.

> YOU
>
> But do I have to date a 57 year old who spends
> all day with his finger up people's bums?

> COUSIN ETHEL
>
> I know a nice butcher…

And why do you agree to go? Because you don't have any other options. This may be your fault. For the past 10 years of your dating life, you've ignored everyone else's idea of who would be perfect for you and who you should be dating. Now you've run out of guys, which leads you to the proctologist and the butcher.

I didn't say they looked good, but they sound good.

I take that back. At this point they're options. So, you fly to meet them. Now, once you've committed to getting on that plane (after days of shopping for the perfect outfit, quite possibly because you've convinced yourself that the reason you are single has everything to do with your clothing choices and not your brain/personality/body type/halitosis) you're ready to meet the (probably not) man of your dreams.

I'll fly anywhere to meet anyone has officially begun. Just because you're going to meet the 57 year old proctologist, however, doesn't mean you shouldn't be looking elsewhere from the time you're dropped off at the airport. You must always have freshly applied lipstick, a smile on your face and the look of a lost puppy. (I do not encourage you to purposely lose a puppy, thus watching its behavior just so you can see how it's done. Instead refer to Dumb Girls chapter.)

Feigning an accent and acting lost in front of a cute guy is perfect. (Have I ever done this to tell you that it works? No, I'm afraid of meeting weirdows, but I'm pretty sure it would.)

Okay, don't do it then. Just get on the damn plane, be yourself and get ready to meet the proctologist.

Once you've committed to I'll fly anywhere to meet anyone plan, it helps to be open and ready for anything. It also helps to sit in first class, if you can afford it (or worm your way there). You'll want to be sitting where the upper echelon sit and you'll have a better chance of par oozing the goods in first class if you are among them. Even though you're traveling to St. Louis to have dinner with the proctologist, you just might find yourself sitting next to a hot, single, 36 year-old investment banker, who's headed home to see his parents.

In this case, you will say, "Thank you, Aunt Ethel". (But not for the Proctologist.)

A Few Problems (Or not) Falling In Love Out Of State

Although you may love the idea of your relationship with that human in another state; and actually prefer it because you have time to yourself, revel in your independence, yet look forward to the time you do spend with your lover/boyfriend/muse-you may at some point decide that it's a bit too much work. Traveling back and forth every other weekend is becoming like a long distance booty call. Although booty calls can be fun, leaving your suitcase packed and ready because you spend more time away from your home instead of in it, becomes unnerving.

You like having everything in its place and although you love him/her in their place, you also are getting sick of going back and forth. This leaves you with an option. Yes, it's called making a physical commitment for one of you to move and which one is it going to be? Yes, it should be him because you have an established career and he can't just expect you to pick up and move your entire life (that you worked so hard to build) and move into his open loft bachelor duplex, can he? I mean, going there for a weekend is great, and you never felt the need to make fun of his bear skin rug because it was his, not yours. But now that you're considering a move, everything (yes, everything) has got to go. And what about your stuff? You put it all in storage? For what? In case things don't work out and you have to fly all the way back, pull everything out of storage and start all over again. So he moves to you? How fair is that? Making him permanently sleep in your flowered filled room with the tuberose candle burning at all hours of the night. And where does he think he's going to put all of his clothes, your closet doesn't have enough room for your stuff, as it is.

Great, so now you both have to give up your places (or rent them out) and move in together. This now changes the entire dynamic of the relationship. Sure, you're great as a couple when you spend more time apart than you do together, but now you are going to be...well, together? Really? Is this what you want? Wasn't the whole idea working because you were apart? Aren't your lives perfectly meshed because...well, they aren't?

Thank Aunt Ethel, not me. I didn't make you fall in love with the guy.

CHAPTER 22

I WOKE UP ALONE AGAIN... Cuddling the dog doesn't count

Sometimes, late at night, I'll be lying in bed with 2 dogs.
(One's not mine. Dog sitting for a friend. My dog's husband; if you will)...

And it still feels on a pretty regular basis, that this is possibly all the love I really need.

Dogs understand love. It's their thing.
Maybe I just need a bigger bed.

CHAPTER 21
I WOKE UP ALONE AGAIN
(CUDDLING THE DOG DOESN'T COUNT)

AM I GOING INSANE?

Yes, you may very well be going insane.

It's okay. It will pass. (It may take some time.)

You hit 40 and realize you're more likely to die in a meteor strike than get married. (Don't blame me; I didn't make up the stupid statistic.) When you begin to have those dreaded heart palpitations and panic attacks (no, not from menopause) you know you're starting your descent into, "I'm 35, my eggs are rotting, how's your sperm?" Just ride the wave. I have no idea where it ends up. I've met 35-year olds/40 year olds/45 year olds, who've gone from single to married (and with child) within the blink of an eye. I've met plenty still single/still searching as well as I'm over it/I'm fine the way I am; moved onto hot sex, emotionally unavailable, please live in a different state (depending probably more on how amazing or crappy their last relationship was. Although I am suitcase ready for prince charming, Business suits now outweigh the teddies.

So back to the heart palpitations and panic attacks. What are we supposed to do when we wake up at 3 A.M. panicking about our lives? I suggest Melatonin, but you probably already take a few sleeping enhancements and still awaken in a panic. Masturbating to nice jazz music may put you back to sleep quickly and help you forget any silly thoughts you may have had about where you're supposed to be in your life. Even though this may include wealthy women recently widowed, separated or divorced; yet still feigning poverty, depression and/or anxiety over finding the love of their life, feeling empathy for them takes on a bit of a different spin.

$20 mil. Can turn any…I wanna be in love to bring me the hot, young…

And Now Back To The Panic Attacks…

Late night is the best time for these attacks. It doesn't pay to have them at work where people may give you funny looks. And please! Don't pull any of this depression/anxiety/panic attack crap in front of your friends. If all your friends are freaking out just like you? Dump them and get a new set of friends. Misery only breeds more misery. There are only so many anxiety-ridden stories to go around. And, your happy friends? They won't want to hang with you if all you do is freak out and ask them to analyze…everything…again.

They like you just the way you are. But, only when you're happy.

The trick? Act happy. This isn't to say that you aren't happy and haven't been happy. You just have something missing. (Kind of how you'd feel if you lost your winter wardrobe.) Oh, don't worry. The pang goes away. I guess when all your eggs have gone, when your friends begin to lose their teeth, their husbands start to die off and you all once again single together, just like the old days.

The only difference? They'll most likely have their kids to wheel them around. You'll have to hire a stranger (or try really hard to not end up in a wheelchair, at all). Long-term health insurance helps. Well, that's the price you pay for being single. Look at the bright side. Most of your friends' kids are selfish little punks and they'll probably stick their sickly parent(s) into a nursing home at the first sign of physical deterioration. So the fact that you never had a kid(s) to treat you poorly? All the better! So, you may not get to 50 years of wedded bliss! So what! (Most of your friends want to off their husbands, anyway.)

And, your parents? If they stayed married, didn't your Dad sleep in the study most nights for the last 15 years?

Yes, they still hold hands, but it's because he hasn't had cataract surgery and can't see 2 feet in front of him. And that guy, the 1, 2, 3, and 47 that got away? One's in jail for embezzlement for the past 20 years and you could have visited him any time you wanted. White-collar prisoners can get married in jail, you know. (Unless he's already married. She's sticking by him while spending the money he sent to Switzerland, with her yoga instructor of course.)

Smart gal! Do we really need to condemn and berate others lives just to make us feel better about our own? Maybe. In fact...why not? Married people do it to single people behind their backs all the time. Sure, in public it's, "You have so many options." "You can do whatever you want". "You don't have to answer to anyone! What a great life."

Behind your back it's a different story. "It's so sad Susie never met anyone. What's wrong with her?" "Don't we know anyone to set her up with? How about Uncle Todd? Isn't he, like, 60? Oh, that's right, I forget. She's 47. Too old for him." You know what I say? Stuff it and stuff Todd! You try living the single life. Date everyone in town, and then tell me how great it is. Obviously, we all start out single. Then somewhere along the way, people begin to couple off. That thing called love happens, which is great when it works out and sometimes it's even better when it doesn't.

Sometimes you marry the person and sometimes that person steps on your heart and mushes it into a flat object. We all go through it.

And then sometimes we do it again.

And, again and again.

All to find that thing called a soulmate.

Does it exist? Will we ever find him/her/it? Who knows! How many times do I do it until I get it right?

And...

Regardless, I've had a great time. (Good, bad and indifferent).

SOME MORE funny things WE TELL OURSELVES WHEN WE'RE STILL SINGLE...

* If I get to sleep anywhere I want to in bed, why haven't I moved from that ¼ quarter corner since he/she/it…left?
* I can now fall asleep to the wave machine. (On second thought, it always annoyed me too, but just because it annoyed him, I liked to run it, anyway.)
*I can eat food in the bed and no one will care. (That's kind of sad if you think about it; are you a slob?)
*I can make plans with a different guy every night. You go slutty girl! (Finding them may be another.)

What the hell have you been panicking about? This single stuff is fun!

CHAPTER 23
MY CAREER IS ENOUGH

(And other funny things we tell ourselves to get through the day)

I work 70 hours a week.
Plus overtime.
I'm exhausted.   But content.
The main thing I miss is TV...
Maybe I should fill that night with a date.

WORKING ON YOUR CAREER/LIFE/BODY/MIND...AND THAT THING CALLED LETTING GO

I did...

There's nothing-here...hello?

We are raised to believe in ourselves and go after our dreams. Achievement in society is regarded as an accomplishment. We go to school, work hard (some of us) go after what we want (based on a desire, or our parents making us) and sometimes we even get what we want (or, thought we wanted).

In life, there are stages that we, supposedly, goes through; graduate school, go to college, maybe meet a few (or hundreds) of suitors, get a job, find a career (or get married) have children (or not) grow old together (or divorce/become a widow/marry again) and eventually die.

Just because many people get married, does not mean it's the only option. There are thousands of people perfectly happy shacking up, going from suitor to suitor to suitor, or happy alone and doing whatever they want.

We may all start out with the same goal(s) in mind, but depending on where your life takes you (or, you take your life) sometimes it just works out different than you may have planned. (Or not planned.) It really depends on what floats your boat. And wanting to fall in love does not

292

always mean it's going to automatically happen.

Just because you want to be in love, or wish you were in love doesn't necessarily send the love fairies down to bring you the light of your life.

Sometimes, wanting something is not enough. In which case, you decide it's not important anymore

Perhaps you were going about it the wrong way? Perhaps you really didn't want it as bad as you thought? Perhaps it's just like riding a bike, you just have to get back on and try again? Sometimes in life, you wake up and wonder, "What happened?" or "How did things turn out this way?" Everything cannot be blamed on booze and poor memory. Sometimes one must re-evaluate their life, what's important and may find they asking, "What do I do from here?" (That's why it's called getting a good night's sleep.) Many people find themselves starting over no matter what stage they are in life.

People get divorced everyday, people leave relationships, start fresh, eat crow, lose a spouse to a disease (or drop them at a bus stop and continue driving). At some point in life, you have to re-invent yourself, take a chance, try something new and head down a different road. Perhaps there's another answer somewhere out there, which may mean lots of places to look (that you haven't before) for what you want, what you need, how you need to live to feel fulfilled. Love can't just be in a box, all wrapped up in a neat little package. Sometimes love is complicated. Love starts, love ends, love changes. We change. Our wants. Our needs. Our desires.

We can't expect to always stay the same, nor can we expect to find one great love and that will sustain us through life forever. (In a perfect world, that perfect person shows up and we do fall in love forever, so we can then be neurotic about other things in our life.) Some people fall in love, create their own family, stick together through thick and thin, weather the storm, pass through the hurricane, temper the highs and lows together, Til death do us part.

There's something to be said for sticking it out and seeing what's on the other side, even if it's 40 lbs, flabbier boobs and dentures. At least you'll have someone to share the gum paste with.

I know, I know, there are thousands of couples out there in awesome shape, still madly in love after 65 years and play tennis, go on cruises (mandatory in some states after the age of 55) and have the time of their lives. Unfortunately, every time I try to ask them any questions about the relationship, they're running off to some event and can't talk.

THINKING SMALL

Is it important to think small in terms of your life in order find love? Can you have big thoughts, big dreams, want an adventure and find love at the same time?

The answer to that question it seems is some people can. Others cannot. I didn't make up the guidelines, it just seems some people are luckier than others, plain and simple. (Also depends on how you perceive luck.) Some people go through life getting everything they want; make a list, and somehow they actually get everything on that list.

For other people, it becomes a blessing when they don't get what's on the list. Others still, spend their life trying to fill that list (come hell or high water!).

Sometimes, the complete opposite of what you think you're attracted to; want, need, desire, require, shows up and surprises you. Someone you want who doesn't want you. Someone that wants you, you don't want. Certain stages in your life, you feel confident. Other times, you simply want to 'throw in the towel'. The term, 'you're too picky' is usually only stated after a certain age or a certain number of relationships. Not being with anyone after a certain age becomes about one's own ability to not compromise, according to other people. Perhaps those people just 'compromised' sooner.

I've seen some of the couples that ended up married, and believe me, someone compromised. Both (or neither) were picky enough.

And yet, for whatever reason(s), they made the commitment to each other to have, to hold and forever…(fill in the blank). That's not to say that some people are not perfectly suited for each other, really do love and adore one another and have a pretty easy time of making it work.

(Usually they look alike, too.)

Us singles go under the premise that's relationship we're looking for, thus the reason we hold out. We still believe we will find the perfect partner. The ability to think 'big' just like we did when (other people) thought we really had a chance at getting what we wanted still exists.

Just because one becomes older, the perception of wanting someone to 'fill in the gaps' doesn't go away. Sure, you learn to fill in your own and sometimes, you really like being on your own. The idea of sharing space can become less appealing; the idea of your own space becomes more appealing, but that little thing called love somehow creeps up on you, no matter where you are in life. Depending on how you grew up, what your beliefs about love were (courtesy of your parents, relatives and neighbors) you build your life according to those beliefs. Since we no longer live in the 1950's (It was outdated then), The idea that a woman (anyone, really) has to 'think small' in order to fulfill your life with the ideal partner, sounds really crazy. Although, the opposite (chasing your dream, going after your career, getting what you want) can in it's own right, be tiring and sometimes make you feel like a mouse on a wheel.

All of it can be exhausting.

Unless of course, you have that remarkable ability to treat everything in life as a sport, which means you let everything run off your back.

You move confidently in the direction of your dreams, as well as allowing any love (the right love) to enter into your life and be your perfect match. (What are you, enlightened?).

Other people may see your life a lot differently than you do. This is called perception and it's a terrific thing to have, if you can find it. Other people's perception of your life may look a lot larger than it feels to you.

They may comment on how wonderful your life seems to them. You went after your dreams, achieved a bunch of them, don't have a lot of responsibility, get to do what you want, when you want it, didn't have to have your vagina re-stitched (not all cases) and actually, you may find some even envy you.

They may even say, "I live vicariously through you", which in laymen's terms, means "Your life kind of freaks me out and sometimes you scare me, but it seems like you're having fun most of the time, although I wouldn't want to live it". Wow, the fact that you've snowed all these people should make you feel like a million bucks. You actually have gone after everything other people wished they'd done themselves. You didn't take the safe route, the sure bet and yet, you've managed to set your life up to be pretty much how you'd like it to be. If you have the belief system that you (now that your older) aren't allowed to wish for the same things you did when you were younger, then your belief system is telling you that you cannot think big and allow yourself the same kind of love some other people have, then you are creating that belief system. You are allowed to think big, dream big, and still have love in your life.

Even, if you're over 35.

Even, if you're eggs are rotting…

Even, if you want an 18 year-old guys sperm.

(Yes, 18 **is** legal in several states)

I cannot list for you all the states it's legal in,

but I'm sure you can Google it.

Is this the part where your mother and everyone else tells you what a rich, fulfilling life you lead and you should be grateful for all you have and not dwell on what you don't?

***This does not disregard the fact that my brother tells me, "All women are nuts. (Pause) all of them".

How about the part where everyone tells you what a wonderful job/business/career you've put your energy into all these years, which is the reason you don't have a rich, rewarding relationship? Here's what I have to say to them? *SHUT UP!* How about Susie the plastic surgeon, Becky the Dentist, Sally who's owns a Catering Business and Donna the lawyer...all happily betrothed to wonderful men. Okay, Donnas' guy is super hot, but dumb. Everyone else? Equal partners; successful, cool, business-driven guys. Yes it's true, they rarely see their spouses, but they make up for it with great sex a few times a month.

JUST BECAUSE...

Some of us are busy with our careers. This does **not** mean we're not also trying to date/get married/have sex/live with and/or procreate. Just because it's not the entire focal point of our life, does not mean we aren't open to the possibility of...

What were we talking about?

Oh, yea, love...

I was going through my call log for tomorrow's business meeting, sorry...

In spite of everything you envisioned for yourself, you know; marriage, several children, 2 cars, 5 dogs and a nanny, you got the exact opposite of what you thought you'd have.

You are running a company (or sleeping with someone who has one) you have 2 cars of your own, 20 ex-boyfriends and 1 abortion behind you. You have a huge office with a window, but no husband. You make more money than most of the guys you know (or at least the ones you still want to sleep with). What are you supposed to do now?

Continue working…that's what!

Even if you make less than what you used to, spend most of it on clothes, shoes and eating out, getting burned out on your career and yes, still single.

**This theory still applies even if you never made a ton of money, still never found the one and still trying to make a living.*

***This theory does not apply if you are a stripper, call girl or work at a law firm answering phones just to sleep with one of the partners (although, good for you, what the hell do you need this book for?)*

TICK TOCK, TICK TOCK!

After women have been single for a while and watched far too many of their friends get married, they throw themselves into work. (Much like a man does after he's married.) Women will tell themselves that this is fulfilling enough: "No, I don't need love, "Marriage isn't important to me."

Sometimes, we decide all we really need is hot sex with someone we don't know very well, who doesn't say much, but looks good. (Kind of what men like.) Or you may start to do the opposite. You may decide you better get on the fast track to finding love and get this all accomplished in 30 days, just like you closed your last sale.

Needing A Man VS. Wanting A Man

The difference between needing a man and wanting someone still consist of the same component; his genitalia. No matter if you simply want him for fun and frivolous good times, horrid screaming matches, or coming to the conclusion (perhaps in your own mind) that he is going to save you from anything and everything that you have been running from your entire life (or trying to catch/have/achieve) the goal is still the same. To have and to hold (or, until you/he/both move on to another). Needing a man makes them feel special as in, "Hey, she needs me to tie her shoelaces, open her door, pay her bills, I must be an amazing guy". Crying in front of your guy and having him solve all sorts of problems will also make him feel needed. This can be faked or you may actually be a needy, bumbling mess.

Wanting a man can make a man feel special in the "Wow, she doesn't need, but she actually wants me for me. I must be pretty special".

You can need material, emotional, psychological or sexual things. All of these still add up to needing. Once you need something from someone, there's that little word called expectation. It can screw with you pretty badly.

It goes something like this...

RIGHT BRAIN

I was doing just fine before I met him/her.

LEFT BRAIN

Who you kidding? The minute you met him/her, your heart has been banging against our chest and it's really making me have a panic attack.

RIGHT BRAIN

I was like that before.

LEFT BRAIN

Look, right, here's the deal. You need to get okay with yourself. Take a walk, go on a hike or join some sort of anonymous meeting, (even if you don't need it).

RIGHT BRAIN

That's a good idea. Maybe I'll meet someone who can take our mind off him/her.

LEFT BRAIN

Think you're missing the point.

Telling yourself that you don't need someone when your heart/head/mind tells you otherwise isn't great for the psyche. It's pretty tough to tell yourself you absolutely need no one when you still fantasize about that perfect partner. Everyone has an idea of what perfect means.

And perfect can change. When you're younger. You may need someone that completes everything that you need and feel you lack in your life. "Oh, I found my other half", "We fit like a puzzle", "We're too peas in a pod". Rarely does this saying last 60, 70, 80 years later. Even when people are happily married that long, they have (at some time or another) considered divorce, cheating, putting a hit on the other, pushing one out of bed/the car/an airplane.

It's normal human behavior, that the person you so desperately need suddenly becomes someone that you then question, "What did I think I needed him/her for?" Wanting someone fits into a category that we make up. Successful women talk themselves out of the fact that they need a man for anything. Anything, that is, other than sex and possible companionship.

The minute you miss the person, want to see them again, enjoy something from them that you did not expect-**y**our want now becomes a need and you turn into someone who needs someone from someone, but didn't want to. This actually makes you worse than the person that admitted they needed the person in the first place.

At this point, the best thing probably to do is to just get a dog and call it a day.

I'M OVER MY JOB/CAREER/AMBITION

Yes, then this happens.

You work your ass off because you're ambitious, driven and want to accomplish things. You could care less that your friends are married and playing happy home life. (Or desperately seeking divorce life.)

You've slayed your own dragon, (or dragon(s) building several careers for yourself; not just one, that's so yesterday) built a great life, travel, do what you want and then (at some point) It hits you. You're sick of your life. All of it1 you want 'out' and by out, you mean, anywhere but where you actually are. You're sick of your job, you're fed up with your lifestyle, tired of doing the same thing over and over and over again, seeing the same people, listening to the same stories, chasing – anything and everything. Which brought us to this chapter in the first place. We should take pride in our jobs or careers, whether or not it's of any interest to a man. What if we didn't have our jobs? What would we have? We have to put our energies somewhere. Thank goodness we were successful in one area. Remember that. And remember this: The same qualities that made you successful in your job or career can make you successful in anything you really want to accomplish badly enough. Anything! It's up to you. Oh, and you may want to remind yourself (like you often do) those amazing friends, all the stuff you've acquired, the ability to eat out 5 nights a week, the expensive gym you're a member of, all the great parties/events/social outings you are invited to.

Oh, right. We kind of got sick of all that and want something…else.

*If you really want some answers, go back to that psychic you've been visiting since you were 27.

**For Gods' sake, don't do what I did and put everything in storage without knowing where

CHAPTER 24

LETTING GO
To Tell You The Truth...

I'm rather happy alone.
I can sleep in...I can drink all the coffee
From...the pot.   Or, all the pot.   And
have my coffee, too.

Or...

"I wish you well". (I.E. "Go to ...")

CHAPTER 23
Letting Go

(Are you crazy? What if he runs?)

Let go.
Right now.
Really.
Let go of that chair you're holding onto.
Just for a minute.
Drop the phone you're talking on (oh, who care's if it breaks, you can always buy a new one.)
There.
Detach.
Doesn't that feel….
Well, weird?
   Sure, that's what letting go feels like-
It feels weird for a while, then you get used to it.
   Like breaking up-someone, dying, being in transition.
   Sure, your whole life feels like its **in** transition.
   In fact, you're not even sure when transition really starts, is it during relationships? After they're over? While you're looking for a new person to date? After a certain stage of your life?
   What do you do when you're entire adult life feels like you're just waiting in…transition? I've got news for you. You may feel that way. But life is still moving forward, whether you like it or not, which is probably why you take that A.D.D. medication to begin with. Without it, you find yourself masturbating the day away instead of spending your days moving forward. You may focus on that task in your brain, which tells you how you're constantly screwing everything up. Yes, letting go literally means to just let everything go. No reeling in the guilt of what ifs. No trying to understand what went wrong with certain relationships; how you let certain

people get away while you were chasing other options.

No more pondering hours upon hours all the reasons why you didn't just **commit** to blah and blah and blah. Because if you had, you're life would undoubtedly be absolutely amazing. You'd be completely happy and your life would be filled with so much joy, you would blind yourself from the light.

Or not.

Letting go is supposed to free you.

Freeing you is supposed to allow you to tell yourself that where you are right now (yes, you-standing; not holding the chair with the phone in a million pieces on the floor) where you are supposed to be.

I know.

It's a hard pill to swallow (probably a little harder than the little happiness in a pill you've been swallowing, and other meds you currently take to get through your day) but nevertheless, the only pill you probably should be swallowing.

And this one doesn't require a prescription.

(Although my brother has given several ex-girlfriends anxiety meds from his own stash.)

GIVING UP MANTRA:

I GIVE UP! DAMN IT! (Damn it optional.)

GIVING UP

This giving up/letting go business usually happens after you're fed up. You've had enough dating, enough being single, enough of the wrong guy and even enough of the right guy, enough of bad timing, and you've pretty much decided to go it alone. "Maybe you're not meant to meet someone", you tell yourself. You know, just because your mother always say's, "There's a cover for every pot," doesn't mean that your pot has one. These sayings are stupid, anyway. Your mother just got them from her mother; it's a family tradition to pass them on from one generation to the next. You may have previously lived your life revolved around the thought that everything you do, may lead you to the one.

Otherwise, what's your excuse for attending the Radical baby boomers diet guru seminar 3 times? Going to all those being single is fun groups, that you dragged yourself to after being set up with yet another matchmaker who had the one!

Hasn't every matchmaker you've ever met been single?

How about adding 10,000 miles to your frequent flyers program? Did you really need another call from Aunt Sadie about that Proctologist you never called back? Admit it, you did everything you could to find a guy (or run from certain ones) and guess what? You still haven't found the one. Well, you may have, many times. Sometimes the wrong times-sometimes all at once.

SEVERAL MEN IN MANY STATES

Having several men in many states will allow you to live your life exactly how you want without any expectation that **any** one person will complete you. Having   an understanding that several men will complete you can open your life up in numerous ways. If you are the type of eater that likes lots of sides this dating lifestyle is for you. It's so hard to find one person who magically fills everything you're looking for anyway, and why bother? Having several in several states (or, one state if you can't find and juggle them) will allow you to put less pressure on yourself by knowing that what one doesn't fulfill, and perhaps even the other doesn't fulfill...one of them will! How fun to know that you will have several different partners to go through life with.

You fun slut!

THE FUTURE IS OPEN

This means that I have to take full responsibility and own my own future. Crap. Now I have to make adult decisions based on that. This means that, theoretically,

I'm supposed to let the past go.

If I let the past go, that means that Rick, Dave, Tom, Steve, John (shall I go on?) must go with it. It means that all those relationships/dates/ experiences/soggy tissues/mean things I've said and done…have got to go, as well. It means making peace with the past, so that you can create the future that you want. My God, it's all so…Well, hippy dippy.

It all seems so, well…obvious.

What's the point in sitting around beating yourself up about the past? What's the point in resurrecting one more relationship that didn't work out?

What's the point in trying to still unravel that mystery that was named…fill in the blank…

The point is, if you were supposed to be there you would be. If you were meant to be married/living with/screwing/fighting with (fill in the blank) you would be. In fact, you still could be at this very moment.

If the sex is good, by all means, don't walk away from it. Letting good sex go might just be…stupid.

We aren't looking to take pleasure-away, we're looking to add pleasure to our life. That's the point. (Unless that pleasure is more pain than it's worth. And not in an S and M way.) In that case, you may want to give yourself a lobotomy, so that you don't beat yourself up over where you think it should go and where it actually is. (Asking the other person if they ever have any intention of having the relationship leave the bedroom might not hurt, either.) Understanding where people fit into your life is an act of maturity. Being happy, being fulfilled, no matter where we are in our life so that we can move forward through life and create how we wish for it to be, without lowering our expectations or other people lowering it for us, is the goal.

What great advice.

If only I could follow it.

The point is, you (you, not me) should probably take inventory of your life up to this point and move on.

Having a healthy attitude about your past, thus creating a healthy attitude for your future is probably the wise choice.

Understanding and taking responsibility only for your own shitty behavior is also smart. Beating up yourself for things you had/have no control over probably isn't the smartest thing to do.

When you don't have balance in your life, you tend to be drawn every which way and loose. Yes, I meant Loose, which can lead to losing. That's not to say that being loose always leads to losing, but you can choose to be loose and still be winning in your life. In fact, sometimes being loose is a great way to let off steam, explore a good time with someone and can even lead to love (if you have the right attitude going in, it's called confidence and independence).

Usually women (and sometimes men) too quickly become attached, thus freaking the other party out and causing something called running. It's no use trying to figure out every situation that you did wrong. What you want to try to do is move forward from here and take advantage of all those people still out there on the planet doing the same thing you're doing, trying to figure it all out. FYI…51% of the population is single right now. If you can't find someone out of all those percentages, you better re-think what you're looking for.

I just was at a friends wedding last night and ran into 5 couples that are engaged, so this figure may no longer be valid (although 2 of the couples were fighting, so who knows if they'll make it down the aisle).

By the way, the odds are better if you date more than one person. This way you get to, hopefully, choose. Kind of your own version of that show on TV that pits 17 chicks against 1 guy (and visa versa).

Having options and choices will build your confidence and let you move forward from one situation to the next.

Once you realistically look at who you are and what you're looking for, everything else should fall into place. Yea, that's why I said should. This book is not a how to. It's more of a *TRY NOT TO SCREW UP THE NEXT OPPORTUNITY THAT COMES INTO YOUR LIFE*.

HOW TO GET UN-SCREWED UP

The same way you talked yourself into being screwed up, which means you can talk yourself out of being screwed up. Letting go is telling yourself that you are happy in your life.

Even, if you…surprise…really are!

Yes, I know, I said really are.

Because it's not like you have to be miserable just because you haven't found that special someone to drive you crazy for the rest of your life.

Really, think back about all the exes you've had in your life that did drive you crazy-all kinds, many of them throughout your life. So, at least you know they exist. (Which means you can always find more.) Hopefully, you get to a point in your life where emotional turmoil is simply no longer fun. (Even if the sex is rocking hot.)

Letting go should allow you the luxury of living in the moment, and living in the moment should allow you the luxury of letting go of any negative crap that you feed yourself in your brain, everyday.

Negative crap is not necessary for your survival. Trust me.

It's like the devil on one shoulder and the angel on the other, fighting for your sanity. You shouldn't let the devil win, even if he's stronger, hotter and has more money than the angel. Just remember, the angel gets you into heaven. The devil? Been to Vegas in July? Not fun.

Letting go means saying, "I'm not going to beat myself up anymore. Seeing that particular one that got away not looking so hot anymore certainly helps.

Getting your life where you want it to be, be focusing on your career, making money, organizing your closet, enjoying your friends, lover(s), certain people from afar (Aren't they so much better…over there? And aren't you a lot calmer when they're…over there?).

Staying focused on being happy (yes, that may include schtuping Rodrigo, your personal trainer). You actually may come to realize that letting go allows you to focus on what you really want. Which may, or may not include a relationship at all.

Hell, it's not like you haven't had a few in your lifetime. By the way, 'I attract suck ass guys' is simply code for 'My taste sucks'.

So, letting go may actually be a good thing. It not only will allow you to re-evaluate your choices, but also may actually free you into thinking there's a certain type you've always had or, that you actually have to make a choice at all. This puts you back into the driver's seat, which hopefully helps you make smarter choices for your future because you've decided to let go of everything from your past. Get rid of that shrink too, while you're at it.

All he/she's doing is taking your money and helping you re-hash that stupid story 500 times or unsuccessfully give you insight into deciphering the, "what up?" (via text) means. Buy your friend a drink and complain to him/her. They're better at giving advice and it's cheaper.

You're probably getting pretty dizzy just standing there. You can sit back down now. (If you want to, I'm not forcing you.) When we aren't happy with ourselves, we tend to bring in the wrong type of person. Don't beat yourself up. Even when we are happy with ourselves we sometimes bring in the wrong person. The problem is, with the wrong person **and** not being happy with ourselves-

We then really turn life into a tizzy and create things to be much worse.

If we are in a good place in our life, living the way we want to live…being happy where we are, our surroundings… even if we bring in a bad seed, we probably will be at a much smarter place to just let it go and move on, breathe. Find someone new.

A nice Chardonnay never hurt anyone, either…

WHERE DOES LOVE FIT IN WITH MY LIFE?
HOPELESS ROMANTIC

Ah, the hopeless romantic. Although still moving about life in the same categorical fashion they always have, they manage to fit love in whenever and wherever it happens to come from. Problem is, it can mess with the game plan. Once you've opened up to letting love in (after you've worked hard at making your life work) suddenly you've messed with the formula. Now it's going to take days/weeks/months to get back on that horse and get your life back. Probably the best idea is to separate your life into a pie chart, where love (no matter what) is entitled to say, 15% and that's it. That leaves 85% percent for the rest of your life. I know, I know, hopeless romantics (and most men) will want more of you than this, but if you've waited around a long time for love, and suddenly give everything up, where you gonna be when it's over? That being said, I'm optimistic so perhaps it won't ever be over and that lead was worth it. Hold your breathe, it's gonna be a bumpy ride.

Especially, if you've moved your entire life to NYC/China/Chicago/Kansas/Cambodia/Near…a prison. Best to have fallen in love before they went to jail. Waiting for someone in prison, *might be considered* hopelessly romantic. Falling in love with someone currently incarcerated (that you met par oozing through Men behind bars sexy month club) is desperate and should probably be avoided no matter how much of a romantic you think you really are.

If you're living a full, happy life complete with your career, friends, events/parties/dating, hobbies and sports, you really may not have any room for love in your life. A lover may be perfect, as long as they don't infringe on what you already have set up and planned for your week.

Waiting around for anyone to ask you out (or, *IN*) becomes monotonous, almost boringly obvious and you probably won't have any time (2 weeks from Sunday 2 to 5...*maybe*).

Anyway, you're life is so jam packed with everything you spent years trying to create that you don't even know how or where you'd fit the guy in.

This is where the young hot 28 year-old is great as your plus 1. He's easy, great to look at, smart (for his age) and makes everyone around you jealous, which is just fine. You have zero interest in trying to have anything serious with the guy. You just want everything to fit into a nice, neat little package so that everything in your life keeps moving forward. Falling in love...I mean really falling in love (hook, line, sinker) gets messy. It rarely works out the way you planned and often times, those tears begin to fall. (And sometimes you can't get them to stop.) Unless, of course, you've been doing the above so long that your tear ducks have completely dried out and you cannot get them to work. No matter how hard you try. "Cried? Are you kidding me, I can't remember the last time someone was worth it", your heart may say to your brain.

You're so cautious about falling in love and trusting someone that you have categorically fixed your life so that even if you did fall in love, it has no place to go. Well, it can enter your life, but you vow that you will never allow another person to dominate your emotions *that* way ever again... hopefully.

FINDING HAPPY

Where the hell is happiness?

I used to think it was in Chardonnay. (And it was for quite a long time.) Then I thought it was in Mexican food. I'm absolutely sure it was in my dog, Izabella. I wanted to believe it was in Dave, Mike, Steve, Scott, Don and Bob and what's his name. (Relax Dave, Mike, Steve, Scott, Don and Bob. I'm being hypothetical.)

I know it was in my Ms. Beasley doll, my doll with the interchangeable heads and definitely my walk-In closet (which I find myself masturbating to more frequently than any date I've had in the past few months), which leads me to here… now.
The new normal.

This is…you. This is…me. This is…*US.*

This is the way it is. We're generally happy (Sometimes more than others) pretty successful (sometimes more than others) driven, sharp, attractive (with or without a little help) and we find we are pretty content with our lives. Except for that small thing called LOVE (which we may or may not give a crap about anymore or talk ourselves into not giving a crap anymore) the same way we used to talk ourselves out of not giving a crap about love…we're doing pretty well.

Love. That kicker of a feeling that takes that organ to the left of your chest, making it thump loud, burst and sometimes makes you feel like your heart is broken into millions of tiny pieces. You don't even mean to cry. It just happens. Then you move beyond that crap. Beyond love.

Beyond wanting, desiring, needing and having to have. You decide that the life you thought you were going to build with someone else, you will now build on your own. That purse you were waiting on Mr. wonderful to buy you who wouldn't even pay for your valet parking?

You've realized not only are you better off buying the damn thing yourself, but he was lousy in bed.

Perhaps your perspective was off because of alcohol and/or pot? You're open to meeting Mr. wonderful (or several) but you've decided you're not going to stop your life to find him/her. Happiness, you decide, may simply be organizing your underwear drawer in a nice color scheme. (Or, cuddling your dog on a rainy afternoon.) It may be challenging yourself to a 20 mile run, trying new cuisine, taking a sewing class, flying to Hong Kong and deciding to stay for 6 months...just because. Happiness doesn't necessarily stand 6'2'', 185, blue eyes and dark hair (but I sure hope *HE* does.)

One is supposed to be happy...before they commit to another human being.

Pause, pause, pause....that's why I said *supposed to.* Once we find happiness (which I've found, by the way; Upper East Side. Best Chili ever!). Happiness may include, but not limited to; being alone, getting to know you...once again).

Most people that are alone acquired many pets/friends/enemies/cash/parking tickets, so either way, you're life is sure to be filled with things. *Things* generally do not equate to happiness and in our society. Most people are on the track to couple up in one way or another, which means dating/getting married/shacking up/or recurring slumber parties with different and (hopefully exotic) mates. Thus where the happy part comes in.

Although, every doctor and/or relative (and happy person who are madly in love) will tell you that in order to find happiness, you must be happy with yourself...

I was happy several different times in my life. And yes, I suppose I was dating several different guys at any given time, but it certainly didn't help me settle down and choose one or allowing someone to choose me.

(But that's because my picker is off and I may go after the not-so-nice-guys.)

Now you, I'm not so sure. If you're reasonably attractive (matter of taste) chances are, you can get someone guy and live an exotic life. (Matter of perspective.)

Chances are, no matter how beautiful/tall/short/funny/weird...you are...there are still several people out there in that big, bad world for you to choose from. Being busy with work/career/business, takes your mind off of making it mandatory that you find a mate. Life doesn't always stay the same. Re-inventing yourself is mandatory. This requires that you do something called...living in moment, taking charge and making life work the way you want it to. (I have no idea how you're supposed to do it. I'm tired just thinking about it.)

Whether you are happy or not, you must fulfill your life with all things meaningful, I have heard this include, but is not limited to...

1.   Fine dining.
2.   Nice Music.
3.   Chandeliers.
4.   Expensive wine, perfumes and cashmere.
5.   Walking through a 5 star hotel.
6.   Being kind to others...if it gets you somewhere, natch.
7.   Okay, be kind to others...just because.
8.   Take time to focus on what you want. (This is for the people who **can** make a decision...and stick with it.)
9.   Appreciate what you've got (even if you feel like you have nothing. Make a list-a few things should come to mind).
10.   Try to find who made up ridiculous #8 and have a nice sit down. Find out how to be more *like that*.
11.   Be kind to strangers.

12. Yes, even be kind to family members, especially ones who wonder what's wrong with you.
13. Gratitude. (I had to look it up in the dictionary. It's right next to Grating. Interesting.)

Becoming happy with yourself is supposed to enhance bringing out the best **you** (according to some hocus pocus theories), which brings in the correct mate. I think that's terrific. If you can lie to yourself, that may work, as well.

I suppose, finding what truly makes you happy is a great way to decide (when the right mate comes a calling) that they indeed do make you happy, and really are what you are looking for.

(Crap, I really need a nap!)
On The Other Hand...

Not everyone wants to walk down the aisle, stay married to the same guy for 55 years...although it is cute to watch those 90 year-olds that still talk about when they first met. (But most are high as a kite on dementia meds). Some people just don't feel like it's reasonable, rational or logical to make those kinds of decisions, choices and commitments. You worked so hard to find peace. It comforts you just knowing you won't have someone picking on you for the next 50 years.

Life happens in stages, and like it or not, we change at different times in our lives. What we want and need at 22 isn't necessarily what we want, need, require/desire/die over when we're 40. So, when people fall in love when they're older and walk down the aisle to begin their life anew, they know this may later include; diapers, dentures and facelifts. Fortunately it's legal to fall in love at any age, within any tax bracket and any city/state/region/country we want.

That's a comforting thought because it certainly opens up our options.

Unfortunately, when you've been single past a certain age and you have nothing except options; the world just looks too big, too intimidating and it can make it seem impossible…to find *the one. E*specially when your expectations include both of you to be happy, healthy and relatively sane at the same time.

(I know, I know, I had to throw a real wrench in the whole thing, didn't I?)

You see, if are both happy then there's a much
Better chance you will still like each other after you've woken up from the vodka filled wedding. Just because you're happy doesn't mean you'll like each other. But being happy and having a positive attitude are small things that can only enhance a relationship. (I've heard.)

It may be important to like one another (I suppose) because you will be sharing space and space is hard to come by…(unless one of you is super rich. If one of you is super rich and cheap? I suggest marriage with someone poor, but generous)… happy people need space. Not just physical space (which is an absolute must) but emotional space, as well. People get set in their ways. People get more anal as they get older; how we like things, our furniture, arrangement, our toothbrushes, clothing, plates, bowls, nick-knacks, pens, papers, everything! When sharing your abode, you'll want to make sure you each have me space, which is going to have to be determined by either a coin toss (or a blow job.)

Yes, you may feel happily giddy in the first year, so you don't even feel a need to decide all that now, but come a few weeks/months/years down the road and you'll be happy as a clam that you have your own mini-meditation corner, your own office, closet, chaise to call your own;

Even that apartment you never gave up (even though you lied and said you did).

SOME THINGS YOU'RE SUPPOSED TO GIVE UP TO BE HAPPY...

1. The need to control. (If I can't even control my own life).
2. Giving up your need to blame others. Are you kidding me, all this is my fault?)
3. Giving up on limiting beliefs. (You mean my ass isn't still as tight as it was at 25?)
4. Give up needing to impress others. (Not a problem, I don't even impress myself, anymore.)
5. Give up the past. (Damn, what will I think about?)
6. Give up attachment. (Doesn't that defeat the whole purpose of looking for a partner? *Or does the author mean that baby blanket I'm still sleeping with at night?)*

TAKE INVENTORY AND MOVE ON. WHAT DOES THIS ALL MEAN?

Absolutely nothing.

Nada.

It still isn't going to change you being single...now. But that's fine. We may be perfectly happy this way. Anyway, *happy* is a state of mind; an attitude; a reflection of ones self, an agreement with oneself that no matter what, no matter where I am at any given place in my life, I will choose to be happy. Damn it.

Now send the right guy in, already this is really pissing me off.

All those vapid self-help books and crappy seminars, that tells you, *"BE HAPPY WITH YOURSELF FIRST. LOVE YOURSELF AND ALL ELSE WILL FOLLOW"*.

Is it just me, or were you under the impression that you weren't happy before? Isn't it possible you've always been happy, but just didn't meet the right person? And if you were so incredibly unhappy and unfulfilled, then how come every other area of your life is so great?

You have 5,000,000 (still counting zeros) friends (some aren't really your friends, FYI) a great job and a wonderful family.

So, if you were so unhappy and screwed up, wouldn't someone have told you? Better yet, how come some of your most screwed up, unfulfilled friends are married?

If what those seminars say is true, shouldn't those friends be alone? Maybe you should be with their husbands? No, that's not the point. The point is those seminars are stupid. How about, "You just haven't met the right person yet

How about, "you have a right to be picky, even though you're getting older?" Now, that would be more realistic!

So, now that we've straightened that up, there's one point that hasn't changed: *YOU ARE STILL ALONE. Me too, and so on and so on* and so on...In the meantime, I'll be running errands, working, traveling, hanging with friends, going to parties, flirting and living my life.

Look around. So are a lot of really great, single people. So, what's my point? Ever hear the expression PUNT?

I had four great-aunts who never got married, shared the same apartment for 50 years. (Three were virgins and kept Kosher.)

Was this not the place to bring that up?

Oh, well. Maybe they never wanted to get married.

(Actually, they weren't that attractive. And, one actually did get married, but he had a heart attack on the honeymoon. Yea, sad story.)

Even ugly people get married, so that can't be it.

And as for Aunt Lilly who's husband died on the honeymoon? She had 10 great days before it was over, went back to her single life fairly easily, always had a smile on her face and seemed pretty content with her life.

You may just have to face it. Some people never get married. I know what you're thinking. You'll try the giving up/letting go thing because of that saying, "Once you let go, it comes to you."

How's **that** going?

No, really! It's worth a try. Maybe when you loosen up, things change. You never know. Here's the only thing we do know: It ain't over till it's over.

Anything happen yet?
****

EPILOGUE
Something Light and Fun

Some days I wear makeup.
And some days I don't.
On the days I don't   I feel a fright.

Inevitably, it's on one of those days that SUPERMAN
walks into the grocery store, stands right next to me,
picks up some Rocky Road ice cream and moves on.
Out of my life.

That's the day I should have worn the makeup.

EPILOGUE

Everywhere we look, there are single people. In restaurants, beauty parlors, bars, you name it; talking about their lives, working, playing, running errands, sitting in parks and working out.

Sure, sure. You've heard it for years, "You're smart, funny, successful, independent, attractive, How come you're still single?"

I actually have no idea how to answer that question, considering that I've never met you nor know your particular predicament. But here's a few silly, perhaps tried, maybe true (or not) bullet points to make you feel better, worse and/or indifferent…just like you've always been-

TRUTH Never be available. And if you are, Act like you aren't.
…Given the amount of time you actually put into your job and/or career, there will always be the workload to explain your elusiveness. (All those late nights you're forced to put in with a roomful of wealthy corporate executives will always leave you back-up just in case the aloofness you're using to get your guy backfires and he really does…leave.)

TRUTH Never call (a guy) back after he calls you.
If you call him back, you'll have to wait for him to call you back.
This is too nerve-racking. You should be happy with the simple fact that he called you and let it go. He may eventually dump you, anyway. This way, you've beat him too the punch.
(Obviously, if you want to marry him at some point, you'll have to call him back, or let him know where to chase you).

TRUTH 2 needy, desperate people should be kept apart.

>   *GUY*
>   Hi. I'm desperate.
>   *GIRL*
>   Hi. Me Too.
>   *GUY*
>   I like you and it's making me feel sick to my
> stomach.
>   *GIRL*
>   Me too…call me.

TRUTH - 2 independent, self-reliant people don't have anything to offer anyone because they're too into themselves, their own feelings and have no time to fit anyone else in to their world. Which makes them the perfect candidate for…LOVE.

The ideal situation…two people who aren't looking.

It all comes down to love – the only thing really worth fighting for. So, go ahead and get married…or don't. In the end, it's your name on the Headstone. (Do you really want to share it with someone else?)

Who really cares if your eggs are rotting?

There's an old saying that goes, "One day you won't have any eggs at all - you should live so long".

Circa 1692

You've got family and friends.

People you love that love you (no matter what they say behind your back).

You'd rather be on your own than with the wrong person.

And, in fact-tomorrow is already today, so the future is happening right now.

And now.

And now.

The past is already gone. Did you feel it?

Alrighty then.

How about this theory...

Maybe the life you're living now is actually better than the one you've made up in your mind? Perhaps, what you are searching for is actually what you are already doing...and, if you'd just stop long enough to accept (I know, big word) that everything you've been working on in your entire life that got you to exactly the point you are now, is exactly the right place (and probably better than where you would have been if God had actually given you all of those things you're pissed off about at him/her for not giving to you) you'll realize all of this is for a reason. Meant to be. Or, maybe not. Just a thought-

Just Breathe.

Life is good.

And there's always tomorrow.

Unless, of course, you get struck by lightning.

*(Which statistically, at **your** age, is more likely to happen than getting married... FYI)*

The End

ABOUT THE AUTHOR

Terri Apple is one of the top voiceover actresses in the country. She resides in Los Angeles.

Terri Apple VOICEOVERS (Michael Weise Productions 2012) is currently in stores and online across the country. (2 other voiceover books-Lone Eagle and Random House 1997-2011.)

Walking In Heels (HELL) Through Madison Avenue (A Humorous Novel and Jewbelish (A satire) in stores Fall/Winter 2013 and 2014, respectively.

She is the writer of Undefeated; The True Life Story Of Rocky Marciano (2010) Bomb Squad (An optioned TV pilot) Dysfunction, My Family (An animated pilot) as well as other optioned TV. She freelances as an online writer and magazines.

Made in the USA
Charleston, SC
30 June 2013